The

BLACKIE
SHERROD

Collection

ALSO BY BLACKIE SHERROD
Scattershooting
Darrell Royal Talks Football
I Play To Win

Series Editor, Carlton Stowers

The
BLACKIE
SHERROD
Collection

Introduction by
DAN JENKINS

TAYLOR PUBLISHING COMPANY
Dallas, Texas

Published by Taylor Publishing Company
1550 West Mockingbird Lane
Dallas, Texas 75235

The columns included in this collection
dated before 1985 originally appeared in
The Dallas Times Herald; all later columns
originally appeared in *The Dallas Morning News.*
Reprinted by permission. All rights reserved.

Library of Congress Cataloging-in-Publication Data

Sherrod, Blackie.
   [Essays. Selections]
   The Blackie Sherrod collection / foreword by Dan Jenkins.
   . p.   cm. — (Contemporary American sportswriters)
   Includes index.
   ISBN 0-87833-606-0
      1. Sports.   2. Newspapers—Sections, columns, etc.—Sports.
   I. Title.   II. Series.
   GV707.S488   1988
   070.4'49796—dc19   87-35106
                                      CIP

Printed in the United States of America

0 9 8 7 6 5 4 3 2 1

With a glass for the old Fort Worth Press
rapscallions—Bud Shrake, Spanky (The Child Star) Todd,
Dan Jenkins, Darwin B. Anderson, Jap Cartwright,
Puss Irvin, Sick Charlie Modesette—who came to work
laughing every day, even though readership
was limited to immediate families and payday was
under a dim bulb so the ones would look like tens.

Introduction

A myth exists in Texas newspaper circles that working for, or alongside, Blackie Sherrod at some early station in your life was the equivalent of a journalism degree.

I wish to correct this myth.

It was better than a doctorate.

Blackie hired me in the first two jobs I ever had, first, right out of high school, at the *Fort Worth Press* ("We mail our copy"), and then a few years later as his lieutenant general at the *Dallas Times Herald* ("My God, they furnish pencils!").

I calculate that I spent a total of something like 13 years under Blackie learning how to put my soul in a pickle jar if I ever missed a story, got beat on one, or lapsed into a Fitzgerald-Hemingway coma and got too pretentious in a lead.

"Late in the summer of that year, Arlington Heights started thinking about Paschal's defense."

"So we beat on, boats against the current, borne back ceaselessly into the Southwest Conference track meet."

"He was an old man who finished alone with Guy (Sonny) Gibbs.

Blackie invented the dreaded bulletin board at the old *Fort Worth Press.*

Rotten stories, lazy efforts, failed scoops, precious prose, dopey similes, they all wound up on the bulletin board for Blackie and other staff members to ridicule with whoops, cackling, and falling about.

It was the best training ground in the world.

One wrong word, one bad sentence, and death—which was a better fate than Blackie not going to breakfast with you because you had let him down.

He denies this, of course. He's probably also forgotten how he used to make the bulletin board himself occasionally. Like every time he used "Himalayas" in a metaphor.

When all of us were younger and learning, Blackie told us what and who to read. Thurber, Perelman, Lardner. Stuff like that. I don't think this is where Blackie learned everything, but it was where he got his fine-tuning—and he wanted us to have it, too.

I often think back on the best single journalism lesson I ever got from Blackie. One day during my first year on the *Press,* he said, "You want to learn how to write sports, go read Henry McLemore."

I went to the files and opened one of those big old binders to a day in 1936. Henry McLemore, then a columnist for United Press, was covering the Berlin Olympics.

I read a McLemore lead, which went like this:

"BERLIN—It is now Thursday. The Olympic Marathon was run on Tuesday and I'm still waiting for the Americans to finish."

Yeah, I thought. That's how I want to try to do it.

I have Blackie to thank for many other things, one of which was putting my story on the bulletin board when I wrote:

"It is now Monday. Birdville played Handley on Friday night and I'm still waiting for Bubba Dean Stanley to complete a pass."

William Forrest (Blackie) Sherrod led by example, and this collection of columns offers proof that he was—and still is— the best sports columnist in the history of Texas newspapers as well as one of the greatest in the history of earth.

But I always thought he was as great an all-around newspaperman as he was a columnist.

Led by example?

One night this guy named Bob Austin pitched a no-hitter for the Fort Worth Cats at LaGrave Field. The next morning it took Blackie about five seconds to write the headline:

"WHY DON'T WE NAME THE STATE CAPITOL AFTER HIM?"

I'm delighted to see this collection achieve the permanence of hardcover. Vintage Sherrod deserves hardcover. Vintage Sherrod deserved to be fondled and slept with and studied by all who aspire to sportswriting.

I'm only sorry about the title. I would have called it "How to Stay Off the Bulletin Board."

Dan Jenkins

Contents

Stadium Noise / 51

Malice In Wonderland / 85

Teed Off / 103

Ring-A-Dings / 181

Personal Diary / 219

CONTENTS

Index / 265

Preface

A few years back, some lady called from the Left Coast and wished to know my productivity. The first inclination was to suggest the lady caller mind her own business but then she explained she was conducting a newspaper columnist survey for the editor of the *Los Angeles Examiner* and my name had been mentioned to her as one who had been around since The Teapot Dome Scandal or very near.

Given dates and average output, her trusty computer figured that I had written just about 7.5 million words over the last three decades and change.

This realization was enough to send me to the couch with a cold compress. It struck home with a depressing thud that this amount of words could easily have taken care of maybe 40 novels; there were probably several Tolstoys in there, perhaps even Harold Robbins. I was staggered by the financial projections, although it does not take much to stagger me these days, especially after 5 p.m. Instead of living on pinto beans and washing my own socks, I could easily be relaxing on a poop deck in the sunny Mediterranean, discussing theory with Mrs. Carlo Ponti.

I josh, of course. The great majority of those words are gone forever and justly so. One sweatshop in which I toiled 10 years did not even keep files. God knows how many Tolstoys went down *that* drain! Most other compositions entered immediate service to line shelves or be stuffed into drinking glasses at moving time. A few thousand, however, have been swept together as one gathers wood shavings from an untidy whittler and bound in this volume to live forever, or at least until the next fuel shortage.

Honesty compels me to admit it is not the first such collection. Sometime during the Golden Seventies, a publisher undertook a similar project and several copies were sold in my immediate precinct, prompting said publisher to disappear from the face of the earth, taking his ledger and checkbook with him. The essays included between these covers are from the last dozen calendars, spent partly with the *Dallas Times Herald* and now with the *Dallas Morning News.* I left the former after a quarter-century to join the latter.

("I think everybody should change jobs every 25 years," I said to Dallas Cowboy coach Tom Landry, and after a hearty laugh, although not very, we went out for pizza and beer.)

The process of selecting these pieces demanded many hours. Most were spent in a glum trance with occasional outbursts of "My God, did I write that?" However, I know few sportswriters who consider their work any semblance of literature, other than in the sense that shank's mare be categorized as a mode of transportation. And mostly the compositions are done rather quickly with a deadline perched on one's shoulder like a malevolent roc and are just as quickly forgotten. The newspaper reading public, if it indeed gives thought beyond the daily horoscope, envisions a sports columnist ripping off a half-dozen pieces at a single sitting and retiring to a hammock with something cool. But most of us work in arrears, rather than in advance. Most are great procrastinators who need, even *welcome* the deadline as a masochistic goad. It was Poor Old John Mooney (as he calls himself) who once forwarded a thought from his Salt Lake City typewriter:

"I live my life in mortal dread
Some day I'll die, one column ahead."

A longtime compadre named Bud Shrake, a writer of considerable stature, once challenged me to write a "behind the scenes" sports book of untold stores. What did Darrell Royal *really* think about Barry Switzer and why? How did Bear Bryant *actually* spend his off-hours? Was there truly a pro quarterback secretly suspected of fixing games? What is Gary Player *really* like? You can just imagine the libel lawyers shedding their warmups and dashing for the starting blocks.

Frankly and perhaps a bit selfishly, I've always considered the pressboxers themselves equally complex and infinitely more entertaining than the subjects they write about. Present company excepted, of course. (I am frequently mistaken for a footstool and am getting damn tired of it.) So to lead off this book, I had rather spend the allotment of words on the press-box business itself. The jocks are covered, in all their unique glory, on subsequent pages.

Several years ago, a Seattle sportswriter named Phil Taylor, no longer with us, packed his notebook and typewriter and stopped by a pal's space in the Masters press hut.

"Through already?" said the surprised colleague.

"It's surprising how little time it takes," said Taylor, "when you have no pride." Phil was joking, of course, but his remark has forever circulated in press coops. There rarely has been a writer worth his keep who, down deep, did not have a certain pride in his work, although you could drive every bamboo shoot in the Orient under his fingernails before he would admit it. He scoffs at his product, never losing the premise that it will wrap tomorrow's carp. And that, on journalistic scales, he may rank somewhere above the obit writer but far below Dear Abby.

There are recognized exceptions, to be sure. The late Red Smith and the late John Lardner and the current Jim Murray, for a few examples, are not pressboxers in the accepted sense, but excellent writers who just happen to choose sports for a vehicle. They represent a certain attitude, or attack if you will, that is somewhat rare in the grim broadax approach of current journalism in this country. Above all, they refuse to consider their topics on the solemn level as nuclear disarmament. They remain constantly cognizant, as Smith said, that there is a world beyond the outfield fence and that there are many, many readers who couldn't care less about the screen pass or the sacrifice fly. None charges the Pillars of Injustice with a machete. None presents himself as The One And Only Truth. None takes his subject nor himself seriously, only his craft. "The natural habitat of the tongue," as Smith once said, "is in the left cheek."

However, theirs is but one approach. It just happens to be a favorite of mine but that does not make it gospel. There are blunter, more authoritative styles and techniques, hipshooting as it were, that readers may find more—a favorite journalistic word of the day—*provocative* and modern. We live, I suppose, in an angrier world.

Be that as it may, the gentle satirists seem to stand the test of time rather well. Don January, the well-known miner of mature gold, once said a golfer's longevity on the PGA tour is in direct proportion to the length of his backswing. It may follow that a sports columnist's stay in the saddle is in direct proportion to his sense of humor. Goodness, look at the tenure of Shirley

Povich of Washington and Freddie Russell, the Nashville land-
mark forever in search of the impish side, and the late Si Burick
of Dayton, who spent almost 60 years at a mischievous typewriter.

For whatever attitude or style or degree of patience, the re-
wards may be considered limited by those in the dodge, other
than a few more laughs than the plumber or the candlestick
maker gets at his bench and, oh, maybe an occasional plaque.
During the Olympics in Los Angeles, a group gathered at Murray's home one evening for a swipe at the wassail bowl before
bowing to beefsteak gluttony. Bill Millsaps was there and Bob
Collins, two delightful story tellers, and Irv Brodsky, the network flack who serves as everybody's favorite audience. As we
left for dinner, we passed through Murray's den where one
huge wall was covered, floor to ceiling, with countless plaques
and awards and certificates and symbols befitting Jim's recognition within the trade. Dan Foster, a constant quipster from
South Carolina, gave the display a shrug in passing acknowl-
edgment.

"Aw, I was going to do the same thing in my den," he said
airily, "but my wall wasn't small enough."

There are those of us who vow, perhaps defensively, that
ours is not the easiest task, that the output is regular and demanding and the deadlines, impossible. Once in Miami, the
celebrated satirist Dan Jenkins and I were sharing a cab with
Roy Blount, a younger freelance author of respected talent.
Roy was reviewing his brief experience as a sports columnist in
Pittsburgh.

"I loved those days. It was a helluva lot of fun," said Blount,
"and it was so easy." Jenkins and I traded quick glances and
said nothing. For some, perhaps, it is easy. Most of us have
never found it so. But then again, for most of us, the assignment finishes ahead of whatever else we are equipped to do. As
in the case of Ace Reid, the old West Texas cartoonist who
faced a career choice as a youth. He could continue raising
sheep for a living, or he could draw pictures. He picked the one
he could do in the shade.

The Human Factor

SNAKE OILED

What with the flutter of the Superbowl and coaches playing musical chairs and goodness knows what all, it had slipped this typewriter that Mr. Dan Jenkins, the book author, has gone to Bophuthatswana to research black mambas. This, believe me, is not exactly what he had in mind.

Sahib Jenkins and his missus, referred to always as The Lovely June, ostensibly went to Africa to witness the world's richest and, I suspect, silliest golf tournament. A few big-shot golfers like Lee Trevino and Johnny Miller and Gary Player and Seve Ballesteros were carted over to a new resort promotion to play for one million berries. The last-place man supposedly got $50,000 plus expenses and this generous display of gelt, even if a gimmick, aroused the curiosity of Jenkins' editors at *Sports Elevated*. This is a publication easily impressed by expensive projects, such as diving for the elusive ermine in far-off Bonwit Tellers and egret watching from Princess Grace's balcony.

This particular assignment took some soul-searching on Jenkins' part, for he usually has no use for the great outdoors beyond the sixth hole. Bophuthatswana, he soon discovered, was considerably beyond. And he *didn't* know about the *dendroaspis polylepis*.

"They got black mambas over here!" he shouted at daughter Sally over the trans-Atlantic wire. Sally is a senior at Stanford and sports editor of the paper there, although several family friends are trying desperately to get her into something more respectable, like rum-running or operating a fixed faro game at Boystown.

"They completely paralyze you in six seconds!" Jenkins said, panic in his voice. "You don't even have time to holler for help!"

"How is the golf tournament?" asked daughter Sally.

"How the hell should I know? I haven't been out of the room

and I don't intend to," said the intrepid father. "Black mambas all over the place. Big as gaww-dam fire hoses. Here's your mother."

The Lovely June got on the horn and said that sahib had indeed left his suite on two occasions, both times because room service was closed and he was in dire need of J&B and cigarettes. He ran both ways.

And that they had gone overnight into the bush on one occasion to inspect the flora and fauna. Jenkins agreed, only after he was promised that the Land Rover had a passing gear and he could sleep under the iron cooking pot instead of mosquito net. He kept his eyes squeezed shut the entire trip while The Lovely June crooned soothing arias about St. Patrick chasing the mambas out of Ireland.

To understand the trauma of the touring author, you must first know that he has championship fear of reptiles. The world record-holder. Doesn't have to be black mambas, the six-second wonder. A garter snake renders him speechless and very swift. It has always been so.

As a youth in Fort Worth, Jenkins was terrified of snakes. In movie scenes when a snake would appear, he would cry out, jerk his head to one side and cover his eyes, sobbing, "Tell me when it's gone!" There was one memorable scene in a Walter Brennan swamp movie, when old Walt awoke during the night with a thirst, went to a stream, knelt and leaned over and a thick cottonmouth, irate at interrupted dreams, made direct contact with Walt's left cheekbone. The sound was like Walt Dropo hitting a triple.

It caught Jenkins by surprise. "EEEEwaukeeee!" he screamed, bounding to his feet, fighting his way over knees and coats and tangled lovers to the aisle where he began a magnificent 15,000-meter sprint home to his grandmother. He was 23 at the time.

At a Fort Worth newspaper where we both toiled, the word got around.

Andy Anderson, now a local naturalist, brought a small jar to the office, containing some sort of a slimy fish bait. Jenkins was sitting by a window madly composing an essay on why Jim Swink deserved sainthood. Idly, Andy removed the hideous plastic thing with his fingers and tossed it on Jenkins' desk. It flopped moistly. "Hiyeeeeeee!" cried our hero, and proceeded to stage an admirable imitation of a grown man climbing a Venetian blind.

Pranksters around the office would painstakingly color pictures of snakes from nature magazines and slip them inside Jenkins' mail. He would open a press release on the glories of Texas Western basketball, unfold the pages and out would fall a replica of a Rocky Mountain copperhead. Eeeeeowinggggggiii!

Sometimes the tormentors would take a trimmed snake picture, place it in Jenkins' typewriter and turn the roller until it disappeared from sight. Dan would rush in like Front Page Farrell, place copy paper in the old Smith-Corona, turn the roller and the snake would slowly emerge. "Whahhhhhooo!" he would moan distinctly and disappear down the stairwell. During this brief period, his hair turned completely white, where it is to this very day, despite several mighty onslaughts by Grecian Formula. He also developed two stomach ulcers, which he failed to appreciate until his draft physical came along.

The horror complex, ophidiophobia we call it over at the reptile place, became so acute that Jenkins could not bring himself even to pronounce the word *snake*. He called them "esssses."

We once went on a fishing expedition to a forsaken lake in Johnson County, not a scrap of underbrush, with the temperature near freezing and all the esses gone to China or thereabouts, and ole blood-and-guts spent the entire afternoon on the hood of his car, chain-smoking. In fact, this horrible experience became a passage in Jenkins' latest book, something called *Baja Tough* or *Semi-Oklahoma*, or one of those things he whips up on his lunch hour and sells for a million dollars or so, so he can buy an esss-free island in the Hawaiian group and two pair of custom boots.

Oh yes, the golf tournament was won by Johnny Miller routinely enough and surely the white hunter and The Lovely June are back in their Park Avenue apartment and he may even be able to sit up and take nourishment and speak above a whisper. It's been three weeks and Jenkins could have run back from Bophuthatswana by now, and probably did.

CHANGING TASTES

NOVEMBER 30, 1978

It was with considerable curiosity and not a little squeamishness that us traditional codgers read about Grant Teaff and His Amazing Worm Act. You know, about how the Baylor football coach inspired his charges into upsetting the Texas Longhorns by dropping a real live earthworm in his mouth during his pre-game sermon. Correction: real dead earthworm. Big ole rascal, Teaff said with a certain pride.

The coach's act was a demonstration, don't you see, of some Aggie joke about how a successful fisherman kept his bait warm in the winter. If you haven't heard it, stop me for goodness sakes. None of us wish to go through *that* again.

Teaff, if you didn't know, has gained a reputation around the country for his inspirational messages, both to religious bodies as a stimulant to their faith fervor, and to business groups as a motivating force toward success. Some of his motivation talks are recorded as albums and sold. So you're not dealing just with a carnival geek, eating live pullets for a pint of wine, but a professional motivator.

Besides, it was just an act.

"I didn't swallow it," said Teaff. "Honest, I didn't."

There are those naturalists who will probably hold that a nice clean earthworm is a lot better for the system than a wad of chewing tobacco in your trough or a pinch between cheek and gum or, for that matter, a ladle of four-alarm chili. I can remember the immortal words of the late Benny Bickers, a midnite philosopher hereabouts, who once said, "Dammit, it's *my* mouth. I can haul coal in it if I want to!"

There are those who claim Teaff's Amazing Worm Act was designed not only to whip his Bears into a glorious froth, but to attract heavy newspaper ink that would aid his recruiting program, just now swinging into earnest action. After all, the coach of a 2–8 team normally doesn't make the headlines all that much unless he wrestles an alligator at halftime or rents a hotel room and smokes in bed.

("If that's what it takes to coach," said A&M's Tom Wilson, "then I'm in the wrong business.")

Frankly, some of us fail to recognize how The Amazing Worm Act can help Baylor recruiting. Oh, Grant might attract an early bird or two, but he could also find the modern jock will opt for Barry Switzer doing The Hustle on the parlor carpet or Lou Holtz springing a nice clean card trick at the dining room table. The Amazing Worm Act demands a specialized audience, preferably one that hasn't just eaten. You must hand it to Teaff for taking a calculated risk. He could have hiccupped.

Still, The Amazing Worm Act is a noteworthy milestone, I suppose, because it marks a definite stage of progress in motivation talks. There was a time when a little frog-voiced coach could pull out his handkerchief and ask the boys to win one for the Gipper, and let it go at that.

Gosh, once Abe Lemons' Oklahoma City basketball team got 20 points behind at halftime and Abe, of all people, was stricken mute for a motivating talk in the lockerroom.

"I had a speech for 10 points behind, or 11 or 15," said Abe, "but I never figured on 20." So Abe silently motioned his cowering lads back to the court and held a scrimmage until the other team showed up to start the second half.

Tom Landry, once trying to goad his laggard Cowboys into furious shame, made a show of removing his championship ring at halftime. It made the squad mad alrighty, but not at the other side. At *him.*

Darrell Royal was never one for halftime oratory but at one Cotton Bowl intermission, he suggested to the Texas squad: "There's a helluva fight going on out there on the field. Why don't you fellows join it?"

Once the Fighting Irish were stirred to fanatical delivery when after a long wait, Knute Rockne stuck his bald head in the door and removed his hat. "Pardon me, ladies, I thought this was the Notre Dame dressing room," he said and left.

But now motivation is big league. It was only a few years ago that Al Conover, trying to spur his Rice Owls to wilder efforts against Arkansas, grabbed a chair and threw it through a lockerroom window. Then you may have read last year about the high school coach somewhere who brought a live chicken to the practice field and ordered his players to kick it to death to demonstrate their determination.

And just last season, a Florida high school coach bit the head off a live frog to illustrate what *could* be done if a person set his mind to it.

Doubtless all these audiences were stimulated to superior performance. Certainly it seemed to work at Baylor. According to witnesses, when Teaff finished his act, the Bears almost tore the walls down in their rush to get on the field and whomp the Longhorns. Personally I don't much blame them. If a man is standing there biting on a live frog or dropping worms in his mouth, I wouldn't be too eager to stay in the same room with him, either.

ROLE PLAYER

JULY 3, 1985

It would be somewhat of an egotistical exaggeration to say I know Charlton Heston. But it is a fact I have *met* Charlton Heston.

Or Chuck.

This was at a WCT dinner, formal and fancy at the Fairmont Hotel, and happenstance placed your social butterfly here at the same table as one of the featured contestants. Mr. Bjorn Borg was still in his teens and not well versed in Dallas dialect, so he sat there in a white dinner coat several sizes too large and applied himself to some special Scandinavian beer with shy but sincere gusto.

There was an empty plate opposite, and as the shrimp arrived, a trim, middle-aged man with sharp features pulled back the chair and started to sit. But he stopped in a half-crouch and introduced himself to everyone at the table. "Chuck Heston," he said distinctly to each. We respectively shook hands and gave our identification, except young Borg, who smiled and grunted in Swedish. Chuck engaged the lad in earnest conversation, the gist of which I remember as assurance that Bjorn would grow into that coat.

A half-hour later, between courses, I was visiting people at another table and a familiar voice and handshake appeared, all around. "Chuck Heston," he said. We shook again.

Even later, I returned to our original table, the actor was halfway through his soup. As I sat, he stretched a hand across the breadsticks.

"Chuck Heston," he said distinctly. That was the night I met Chuck Heston. Constantly. He seemed friendly enough, although not much for faces.

But the other day I learned that our old chum can be rather unfriendly, too, especially when it comes to the case of John McEnroe. Chuck is a tennis nut, but he refused an invitation to the Royal Box at Wimbledon because he did not wish to witness

8

the tantrums of his fellow American, Mr. McEnroe. Further, he made public a note he had written to Arthur Ashe, imploring him to leave McEnroe the heck off the Davis Cup team.

"He is an insufferable bore," wrote Chuck. "He demeans the sport that made him a millionaire."

Right about then, the thought struck. What if the insufferable bore McEnroe is playing us all like a Stradivarius fiddle?

What if all this is a Hulk Hogan act? Remember, this is a civilization that made a rich man out of Mr. T. What if the McEnroe personality came from the same factory as that Jackson person who wears brilliantine and one glove.

Would McEnroe be in the newsprints so much, on the telly, in the gossip magazines, if he were young Mr. Straightarrow, with Harvard manners and a spokesman for the Peace Corps and Baskin-Robbins sundaes?

Would McEnroe be in such great demand for exhibitions and tournaments, could he ask and receive such appearance millions, if he played every match in an Eton collar and a Gideon under his arm?

The English tabloids profess to abhor McBrat or whatever they call him. Balderdash. They *love* him.

They hoard their choice insults all year, awaiting the Insufferable Bore's arrival at Wimbledon. Should McBoor spend a tournament with impeccable manners, the British press would leap out of the highest window on Fleet Street. He is an ideal target.

The gossip columnists leap on every juicy tidbit. Would the photographic jackals dog his heels so constantly if he didn't spit at them?

"For many of us, he has ruined tennis as a spectator sport," wrote Chuck Heston. "The contemptuous arrogance with which he mocks his fellow player, the officials and the principles of sportsmanship, is unspeakable."

We assume he still is speaking of John McEnroe. On the other hand, the subject sounds as though it *could* be Muhammad Ali, another Insufferable Bore who did pretty fair at the box office.

BLOOD LINED

The item was brief and ordinarily it would have floated away from attention in the usual jetsam of weekend sports results: *Kyle Petty, 18, winner ARCA 200, stock cars, Daytona.*

The name caught a snag, of course. This would be the tall, curly, grinning spawn of Richard Petty, the once and forever stock car king. And it proved once more how prevalent are bloodlines in the business of driving race cars. Race driving travels in the genes perhaps more than any human sports endeavor.

Football players' sons play golf or soccer; baseball players' sons turn to tennis. Boxers' sons are actors and wrestlers' sons throw the javelin. But race car drivers' sons drive race cars, by gum. Soon as they can fieldstrip a carburetor blindfolded and save enough money for a helmet, they jump in one of the old man's discards and fly away.

Look at the Indy 500 entry list. Billy Vukovich is there, just as his daddy was, winning Indy in 1953–54 and leading the 1960 run over the brickyard when he was killed. Tony Bettenhausen, national driving champ twice in the 50s, is represented by son Gary. Johnny Parsons won at Indy in 1950, and young Johnny Parsons is after it today. Duane Carter drove the 500 seven times before he handed the wheel to son Pancho. Jim McElreath drives at Indianapolis about as consistently as anybody ever. Son James was headed for the big time, too, when a tragic accident erased him.

Bobby and Al Unser learned driving from dad, Jerry, and two toughnut uncles, Joe and Louie, the latter a nine-time winner of the Pike's Peak race, the last coming at age 58! Buddy Baker is a larger and younger edition of Buck Baker, the former Greyhound bus driver who transferred to stocks. A.J. Foyt's father pushed engines around dirt tracks before he opened a garage in Houston.

Richard Petty, stock car racing's first millionaire, got his heritage from pop Lee Petty, one of the saltiest old flinteyes who ever set his own fingers or pulled his own teeth. And now it's come to the third Petty generation. Kyle Petty, at 18, is not yet ready to line up alongside his daddy at Daytona. The ARCA 200 he won the other day was sort of a minor league affair, but it was Kyle's *first* race. He won it in a Dodge that his dad discarded last year. It's a start.

Just a couple years back, Richard was considering the prospect of Kyle following in the family ruts. The father doesn't pamper, as you may surmise, even as he wasn't pampered himself.

"I know he don't want to work, so he may *have* to race," Petty said with grim humor. "He won't work on the car. He won't work around the house. He won't work, period. But if he wants to drive for Richard Petty, he's gonna have to work for Richard Petty. He's gonna have to work on race cars and learn cars before I'll give him one to drive."

Some of us were sprawled in a North Carolina motel room, chewing the racing fat with Petty and experiencing the miracle cure of malt on parched tonsils. Naturally, the question got around to Petty's first racing ride.

"Wal, it wasn't by choice," said Petty, who seemed to be laughing most of the time. "I was about 13 and I was helping out in daddy's pit at a track in High Point. It was bad muddy and Daddy's windshield was coated over so he couldn't see.

"He pulled into the pits and I grabbed a rag and hopped on the hood and started wiping the glass."

Lee Petty had his head turned back watching to see an opening in the track traffic. When one presented itself, he gunned forward, slamming the gears and spinning onto the track before he ever realized his young son was still on the hood, hanging on desperately.

"He never let up," said Richard. "He just whipped around that track full out one more time and then pulled back through the pits so I could hop off. I was scared to death, but less about riding the hood than what my daddy might do to me later. But he just hollered at me."

When Richard was 18, after he had slid jalopys through all those turns on the Carolina backroads, he asked Lee for a race ride. "Wait until you're 21," said the old man. "You'll be three years older and I hope three years smarter."

Three years later, Richard again approached his dad, who had his head in a car engine.

"Pa, I'd *really* like to go racing."

Lee turned his head, looked at his son for a moment, and then motioned to an Olds convertible in the corner of the workshop. "All right, we'll fix that one up for you. Now hand me that wrench."

Richard raced against his father on the Grand National stock car circuit that year, 1960.

"I'm serious when I say Lee Petty was the smartest race driver I ever saw," said Richard. "When I raced Daddy, he beat me like a dang drum."

Not really. That first year, Richard won three of his 40 races. He finished in the top ten in 30 races and was runnerup to Rex White for the stock car championship. Lee Petty finished sixth.

But one race is memorable. At Atlanta's Lakewood Speedway in 1960, Richard thought he had won his first Grand National event. He took the checkered flag and coasted into the pits and waved to the crowd. Lee kept charging around the track for one more lap, then accused the checkers of miscounting the laps.

The father demanded a recount and he was proven right; the scorers had stopped the race one lap too soon. So they took the trophy from the son, and gave it to the father.

"When he wins, he can have it," grumbled Lee, "but he ain't gonna have it given to him."

One of these days soon, it will be the second and third Petty generations squaring off.

"It was sort of fun to drive against my daddy and I suppose it will be fun to drive against my own son," said Richard. "But I don't dream about dynasties or anything like that." Charity doesn't begin at the Petty home. It never has.

KNUCKLE LUCK

FEBRUARY 4, 1977

The most illustrious citizen of Yazoo City, Mississippi, stopped by this desk a few weeks back to drop a copy of his book, *Ain't God Good,* but as dadratted luck would have it, one of his staunchest fans was not in. This fan and your trusty agent here, which happen to be the same person, was Superbowling or something similiar and missed a meeting with Jerry Clower, the famous footballer from Mississippi State.

Well, maybe that's not exactly correct. Let's try it again. Jerry Clower is comparatively famous alrighty, and he *did* play football at Mississippi State, but there ain't much connection between the two. Jerry is one of those jocks, like Bob Uecker, the former catcher, who has become much better known as a comedian than as an athlete. Jerry is the onetime fertilizer salesman who makes albums and speeches and whoops and hollers on the Grand Ole Opry. He is best known for his coon hunt story, which is frequently punctuated by a ringing shout, "Knock 'im out, J-a-a-w-w-n-n!"

Darrell Royal, who coached at Mississippi State a few years after Clower's day, can still be walking the Texas sideline and hear "Knock 'im out, J-a-a-w-w-n-n!" from somewhere in the crowd and know that his old friend is watching the Longhorns.

Jerry says he never played football in high school because he lived across the road from Graves's Mill, Rt. 4, Liberty, Mississippi, and there warn't but seven other folks in his high school class. But he and his brother Sonny used to listen to the battery radio when McComb would be playing Laurel or Biloxi, and cry because they lived so far out in the sticks that folks thought a football was a watermelon gone outlaw.

"Closest I ever come to playing football in them days was kicking a Pet Milk can in the gravel road at East Fork School at recess," says Jerry.

When Jerry got out of the Navy, he told his mama, "I'm gonna play football. I'm gonna fulfill my life's ambition.

"I wasn't fat in those days," says Jerry, who goes about 270 these days. "I was six feet, 215 pounds and had just turned twenty. I put on one of those tight-fitting Navy t-shirts and sucked myself up where my physique would show real good and I went out to Southwest Mississippi Junior College. When I walked on the campus, folks got to looking at me. When they saw how I was strutting and now muscled I was, they went trying to find the football coach. The coach took one look and offered me a half scholarship. Then he asked what position I played. Sir, I says, I believe I am the man what runs with the football."

Sixteen days later, Jerry played in the first college football game he ever saw. A couple of years later, he went to Mississippi State. "They were patient with me and they let me play in the Southeastern Conference." Long before, Jerry discovered he was not the man what runs with the football. He was more like a tackle.

"I believe I can refresh your memory as to when I played. Auburn had a fine All-America running back named Travis Tidwell. I am the man—the defensive tackle in 1949 before standing room only at the Auburn stadium—that Travis picked up twenty-seven yards running backwards over."

Once, says Jerry, the Bulldogs were playing Kentucky and its great quarterback, Babe Parilli.

"I run to the sidelines and screamed 'Time out!' The referee says, boy, what in the world's the matter. I said Kentucky wasn't playing fair. Parilli had three footballs. He's giving one to the halfback, one to the fullback, and he's chunking one. If you're gonna let Kentucky play with three footballs, you gotta let us play with three.

"The smart aleck referee said, not yet, you ain't doing too well with the one you got."

A Clowerism on coaching: "We tied one game that year. We had a coach who felt like you could catch more flies with vinegar than with sugar. (Head coach at the time was Slick Morton, although Jerry didn't call his name.) It was one of the real distasteful things of my life to see how a coach could treat grown adult men and think he could motivate them when he had just the opposite effect. If you brag on me, I'll kill myself for you, but if you tell me how sorry I am or grab me in the collar and shake me and cuss me, that ain't the way to do it."

14

Clower now has been from ocean to ocean, telling his coon hunt stories and whatever, and he even puts on a tuxedo now and then, but his backwoods nature has remained singularly untouched. He was on the David Frost show with Debbie Reynolds and Nanette Fabray and Pierre Cardin.

"Now can't you see me talking to Pierre Cardin. He's a little Frenchman. He sews. He makes clothes. He had invented some Pierre Cardin cologne for men."

"Jereee, what do you use for cologne in Mississippi?" asked the Frenchman.

"Mr. Cardin, we just slosh on whatever our younguns give us at Christmas."

Jerry is a religious man and frequently delivers lay sermons. Someone said he may be one of the few current-day Christians whose prayers the Lord looks forward to.

DEFENSE SPECIALIST

JULY 23, 1986

A casual note in the copious reporting of the Len Bias inquiry concerned the attorney hired by Mr. Lefty Driesell. Same was identified as Mr. Edward Bennett Williams of Washington, D.C.

Mr. Driesell, as you know, is the basketball professor at the University of Maryland, upon whose campus Len Bias expired in some sort of cocaine seizure. This drug involvement came as a distinct surprise to the coach, he said. A few hours after the death, Mr. Driesell gathered Bias' cronies at his house for a prayer session.

Now the county prosecutor wishes to question the coach about this prayer session, but Mr. Driesell has zipped his lip and engaged himself a lawyer. Of course, this is not your everyday legal eagle he hired.

Ed Bennett Williams, the sports buff will recognize as owner of the Baltimore Orioles, but this is like placing Mr. Benjamin Franklin only as the inventor of bifocals. Williams is one of the world's *super*-lawyers. His clients have included Sen. Joseph McCarthy and that renowned statesman, Adam Clayton Powell. He handled trials of Dave Beck and Jimmy Hoffa, the union chaps. He walked our very own Hon. John Connally on that milk bribery charge and got John Hinckley Jr. an insanity verdict for his attempted plug of President Reagan. Frank Costello, the mobster, was a Williams patron as was Mr. Robert Vesco, the financier en absentia.

Us laymen are not versed in such logics, but to employ high-powered Edward Bennett Williams to advise the legal pitfalls of holding a prayer session seems a bit heavy, like perhaps using a maul to drive a thumbtack. Of course, the county prosecutor hints broadly of interest in any possible advice the coach gave to

Bias' friends, such as stonewalling the fuzz and disposing of any incriminating dope paraphernalia on the scene. I suppose we shall soon see about *that*.

Once on a sports banquet dias we shared in Minneapolis, Williams told a story that returns to mind, probably not apropos to the present topic but mayhap worthy of retelling:

"Several years ago, I got a call from some Boston lawyers asking me to join in the defense of one Mr. Bernard Goldfine, who was having tax problems with the government. I said, send me the files and I would look them over. They said, well, ah, that was a bit difficult for Mr. Goldfine didn't exactly keep files. Then I said I would fly to Boston and meet the client in my hotel. They said that also would be impossible for the client was spending 90 days with the government on a Connecticut correction farm."

Williams knew the warden of that particular resort so he arranged a conference with Goldfine in the warden's office, along with the Boston lawyers also representing the client. One attorney present was not overly endowed with smarts; in fact, he was a sort of valet and chauffeur and handyman. He may have handled some minor claims for Mr. Goldfine, but mostly his duties seem to consist of fetching coffee and sandwiches and putting dimes in parking meters. He was called Ralph the Slob.

After a lengthy conference with Mr. Goldfine and a review of the case, Williams shook his head at the defendant.

"I'm afraid, Mr. Goldfine, that you have no defense," said the Washington expert. The client's jaw dropped and he stared at Williams in disbelief. Then he jumped to his feet and his face was purple with fury.

"Certainly I got no defense!" he roared. "That's why *you're* here! If I had a defense, Ralph the Slob could handle it!"

Years later, as minor stockholder, club attorney and acting president, Williams hired Vince Lombardi as new Washington Redskins coach to replace the fired Otto Graham.

"Vince and his coaches spent days looking at game films," said Williams. "I tried watching, but it bored me to death. They would spend all day on films of one game. Then they evaluated the entire situation. Vince came to my house one night. We went downstairs, mixed a drink and propped our feet up."

Lombardi stared at his glass, then sighed heavily and turned to the lawyer.

"You just have to face it, Ed," the coach said sadly. "You just got no defense."

Quick as a flash, Williams jumped to his feet.

"Certainly we got no defense!" he yelled at Lombardi. "That's why *you're* here! If we had a defense, Otto Graham would still be coach!"

NATURE MAN

MARCH 10, 1982

The bleary early morning sun stabbed gamely through the East Texas chill. It was not yet bold enough to comfort the citified hides of two men in the boat, nor would it be. But the rays glanced from the small angry chops of windswept water and at least brought some promise of future warmth. An empty promise. The two guys shivered and watched the cane poles respond in unison.

On the lake banks, the trees reached high, distressed and brown and lifeless, like oversized sagebrush lodged forlornly against a wire fence. Only the green dash of an occasional pine broke the drabness. The water had color, of course, but the temperature had turned it a frosty blue, like the shattered mirror of a haughty lady.

"Look at that old gator yonder," said Charlie McCool, from the stern of the boat. "Gonna get hisself some sun."

Between the bobbing boat and the east shoreline, a long shadow broke the metallic pattern of the sunned water. It looked like a log.

"Looks like a log," said McCool, cackling as if he had just heard a new joke over his hearing aid.

"How do you know it's not a log?" said a bewildered passenger.

"Because it's been moving since I been watching it," said the guide. "It's an old alligator and he's been hibernating and he's still groggy."

You don't dispute C. McCool, the foremost historian of these particular waters of Henderson County. He has wandered these parts all his life; as a kid, Raccoon Creek was his barefoot playground. And after the creek was dammed and became one of the four lakes in the Koon Kreek Klub, Charlie remembered every nook and cranny of the original channel. Other guides swear Charlie has a mental chart of each bush and tree along the creek banks, now covered by lake waters for almost 60 years, and where the white perch hold impromptu picnics in their shelter.

He has followed the evolution of nature's warfare. The Koon Kreek lakes were threatened by vegetation, so nutria were imported from Florida to chomp at the reeds and sawgrass. Then the nutria multiplied alarmingly fast, like, well, like the big rats they resemble. So the alligators were imported from other East Texas haunts to chase away the nutria population. Something like that. Charlie could tell you.

McCool's existence has been bounded by these singular surroundings.

"All my life," he said loudly, in the fashion of deafened folk. "I spent all my life right here and I'm 79 years old." That's rather a marvel in itself, 79 years among the same trees, probing the same secrets, solving nature's same riddles over and over without much curiosity about what goes on elsewhere.

"I lived all my life on the same farm," he said.

Some wedding partners or business partners who spend long years together are said to become look-alikes. So has McCool become a reflection of his environment, tall and lean and limber and leathery, creased and cured by the elements, fueled by unflagging good humor. Black hornrims are his only concession to modern days. For some odd reason, he wears his Sunday-go-meeting black oxfords with his faded overalls.

Field Scovell, the old Aggie, and I have fished periodically with Charlie McCool, good heavens, has it actually been 20 years? We have filled sacks with crappie and bream and an occasional bass that got in the way. And we have plopped the filets in boiling grease, per McCool's instructions, with flour and meal coating laced with just a tad of cayenne pepper and garlic powder. With a slice of sweet onion and a mess of Henderson County black-eyed peas, as Bro. Dave Gardner would say, it is something nother like glory.

"Retire?" McCool whooped, his choppers unnaturally white against a saddle skin. "Not long as somebody wants to go fishing. When old folks just sit and stare at four walls, the good Lord ought to come and get 'em. I couldn't have much longer, I know that." He grinned widely.

About one furlong away, a boat bounced past. The passengers were a pair of Dallas braggarts, Bud Dalton and Leslie Shults, and they grandly hoisted a whopping black bass for the watching eyes to envy as they chopped off to distant and, I suspect, more caloric surroundings. Weighed out at seven and a quarter, they said later. They are two of the 165 members of Koon Kreek, which was founded in 1900, an exclusive retreat that has refined outdoormanship to a pampered art form.

At dawn, Shults had stepped from his kitchen to toss corn to 20 deer that go from lodge to lodge like wise beggars making the rounds. There are duck and geese calling and giant white cranes flop awkwardly through the reeds and wild hogs root in the thicker brush of the 7,600 acres and varmints prowl at night.

There were not full strings of fish this particular trip. It was windy and out on the water, away from the sheltering bush, it was parka country.

"The white perch are scattered," said McCool, as his companions nodded like schoolboys. (Call them crappie some places; with McCool, it's white perch.)

"Notice the ones we caught were black? They are males. They're out fanning the nests. Almost spawning time."

Still, a half-dozen bass and a few respectable crappie took the minnows as McCool, a thin, sinewy arm wrapped around one working oar like a python, threaded the channels and reedy islands against the bucking wind.

"You fellows have to come again when the weather is warmer and the dern old white perch are back at home," said the old nester, cackling and slapping shoulders. "Hope I'll be here to fish with you." And certainly, when the East Texas woods come back to springtime life and the flora flows into the waters edge like friendly green lava, he will still be there, as indestructible and indelible as the woods and waters that spawned and held him captive for almost fourscore.

COACH OF MYSTERY

JANUARY 17, 1980

LOS ANGELES, CALIFORNIA—There is a standing prank in the press room whenever the Pittsburgh Steelers fill a Superbowl date, which seems more often than not.

Some wag pins a notice on the bulletin board. "Highlights From Chuck Noll's Press Conference" is the heading and below is a large expanse of blank paper.

If Noll has heard the story, it would have all the effect of a BB gun on a tractor. The Pittsburgh coach may be the only citizen in jockdom who changes expression less than Tom Landry, the well-known marble bust who supervises the Dallas Cowboys from Olympus.

There seems to be a major difference, however, between these two coaching giants who have played the Superbowl more than any others. Landry makes a conscious *effort* to participate. At the endless media confrontations and in the probing glare of the electronic interviews, Tom does his level best to enter the carnival spirit. At times, he seems almost outgoing, even if it is contrived like a middleaged bridegroom meeting his in-laws for the first time. But the Dallas coach wants to contribute to the game's buildup, when you know he would much rather be behind locked doors with his beloved X's and O's.

On the other hand, Noll appears to put a deliberate damper on his feelings, if any. The boob toob flacks already have tagged the Superbowl as the second biggest day of the American calendar, behind Christmas but considerably ahead of Easter.

Well, it just might be a trifle smaller than *that* but many NFL coaches would give their upper plates to be here. Whatever Chuck Noll feels on the inside, outwardly he approaches this game like a man sitting down to a breakfast of carrots. That's easy to take, you say, if you're holding all the cards, such as Noll with three Superbowl wins already and a bale of advantages going into this one against the Rams. But the stocky Steeler coach was like this the first time his team made this vaunted plateau and he ain't even changed his cashmere golf sweater. When Chuck gets out of bed in the morning, he puts on his blandness like Liz Taylor glues on eyelashes. His news conferences are short and applicable to dry cereal. One of his media nicknames: Chuck Null. And that's okay with him.

Behind his factual facade, Noll is an enigma. He is a person of many facets. He is a lover of chamber music with his multiplex stereo and tapes. He is a connoisseur of fine wines. He flies his own plane. He goes scuba diving whenever he can spend time at his Florida condominium. He built a personal greenhouse to raise rare tropical plants.

As a college lineback-guard at Dayton, he was known as the "The Pope" by his teammates because he was never wrong in his, or anybody else's, play assignment.

"According to The Pope, that ain't right," a guy would say. "It's the *right* shoulder." The reputation followed into Noll's playing career at Cleveland. Yet when the head coaching job opened at Dayton in later years, Noll was an assistant on Sid Gillman's Charger staff, and he applied at his alma mater and struck out. In another reversal, Don Shula interviewed Noll for a post on Shula's Balitmore staff. "After 15 minutes, I knew he was the man," said Shula. "He was all solid football." It is *not* one of the high spots of Noll's portfolio, however, that he was the Colt defensive coordinator when they were so ingloriously upset by Joe Namath and the Jets in Superbowl III.

His Pittsburgh Steelers have dominated the 1970s, yet somehow Noll is seldom mentioned with the same respect as Don Shula and Landry and the late Vince Lombardi. Why?

"He's not a media person," said Steeler veteran Joe Greene. "That could be the difference."

"He's certainly underrated," according to center Mike Webster. "I think that's the way he likes it."

At one of Noll's fun-filled press conferences this week, a newsman asked if the coach ever wondered how history would regard him; did it irk him that he wasn't mentioned in the category with Lombardi and Shula?

"Not really," Noll said impassively. "I just work for today and leave history for 15 years from now."

Possibly the reason Noll is bypassed by current historians is that Pittsburgh is not known for its finesse, nor innovations and trends. The Steelers are seen as a bread-and-butter *physical* team, one with the old Bear Bryant theory—jist line up and outbutt 'em. And, the scientists say, it doesn't require an overload of coaching skill to win with big overpowering brute strength. You just make good draft choices, teach them how to lace their pads and tape their hands, warn them not to eat the referee and unlock their cages once a week.

It isn't, of course, that simple. While Bryant was shilling the "outbutt 'em" theory, he also was teaching some involved defensive techniques that had him recognized by fellow coaches as the sharpest defensive mind in the lodge.

Noll would have the neophyte media to believe that it's all a basic business. Or perhaps he avoids any technical explanations with the Superbowl crowd because the press dunderheads couldn't recognize a doublewing reverse if it ran through their parlor. And besides, where does it say in the contract that he has to be Dale Carnegie.

"I know I'm not good with the press as an individual," he told a guy recently, "but I don't think that's a bad thing. The ability to b.s. with people, to kid them along and make little jokes, isn't a necessary part of football. Talking a good game isn't a prime requisite for success. You've got to be yourself."

What about the *real* Chuck Noll?

"He's definitely not like any other coach I ever had," said Steeler rookie halfback Greg Hawthorne. "He can communicate better. He just tells you what he wants you to do."

"He's the most disciplined man you'll ever meet," said Webster. "He knows what he wants and sticks to it. He's very strong, mentally tough."

But what kind of guy is he away from football?

"I don't know," said Webster.

CURTAINED OFF

The look is direct and a bit challenging. Some people have called it *arrogant.*

A magazine author describes Ivan Lendl as having a "stony, surly facade." Others of the international gin-and-tonic set see him as a merciless computer, manufactured by Iron Curtain scientists in Czechoslovakia and sent out to put a tennis dent in the capitalistic world.

Courtside journalists here at the WCT Finals complain they can never get a straight answer from the strange import who plays John McEnroe tonight for the big enchilada. Or as they might say in Prague, the big *ruska,* which means, nearly as I can tell, the big sardine, or the big pale yellow cow.

"I asked him 12 questions yesterday," said a bald Briton. "Nearest I got to a bloody answer was maybe or possibly."

"To Lendl, an interview is a contest of wits," says our man Ish Haley, well steeped in the international tennis mannerisms of Texas and the western portion of Arkansas. "I asked what he did with all his money. He said, 'At roulette table, I put all on 00 and always lose. So I don't have money.' "

In the first round of the WCT Finals, Lendl (pronounced LIN-del) was pitted against his great friend and mentor, Wojtek Fibak. A newsman asked if he disliked having to play against Fibak.

"If I say yes, will you change it?" said Lendl, with that hard stare. Or anyway to the reporter, it *looked* like a hard stare.

At first thought, it seemed that Lendl was implying that the reporter would alter his answer. More realistically, the Czech youth meant: What difference did it make if he disliked the pairing, nobody could change it.

Saturday night, an Australian journalist questioned him on the ongoing "war" between Lamar Hunt's WCT program and the Grand Prix tennis circuit.

"War? Are they having a war?" Lendl said quickly. "Did they send the ships to the islands? How many ships did they send?"

He cut a sly glance at his friend Fibak who rubbed his hand over his nose and moustache to hide a grin.

His little joke finished, Lendl said in his emotionless monotone that he thought competition between the two factions was great for tennis and so forth.

Certainly the competition is great for *him* as well as his fellow passengers on the current gravy train. Lendl has sacked $762,500 in WCT monies *alone* this year and it is not yet May. Should he win at Reunion tonight and follow with a Tournament of Champions victory next week (and he will be favored in both), he will have a million bobs of Hunt's gold in his rumble seat, with eight more months to play.

Lendl easily could reap another half-million or so in exhibition money, plus that much in endorsements and fringe loot. We may be speaking of a conservative minimum of $3 million income for this calendar year. And the boy just turned 22 years old.

So we sit in judgment on a youth still in the Pac Man stage, with Ft. Knox in his backyard, with a fantastic winning streak going, apparently operating free of his country's strict bonds, and we ask him to be humble and gratefully tolerant of questions he doesn't *have* to answer. Would *your* kid be?

Remember also, this is a youth from behind The Curtain who probably has an ingrained suspicion of any press and any questioning. And when he hears what he considers an *invading* question, he counters with a defensive retort. A-ha, journalist, you don't trap me! I may be young but I see many movies of your man Bob Hope.

The brash bravado Lendl often shows is sometimes used to cover the fears and impatience of youth. And a youth with a sack of banknotes and unlimited future can often run amazingly shy on patience with elders.

Then, there is another psychological factor. Czechoslovakia, if we are to believe John le Carre and his fellow spy authors, is a land where life's greatest boon is to live three score and seven years without having to answer a single question. Where suspicion is a way of life, as sinus and freeway traffic in this country; where one pulls curtains and checks behind pictures for listening devices and all those instruments of dreaded intrigue; where border guards would make our IRS auditors seem like Mother McCree.

Then Ivan reaches the outside world where reporters ask how much money he has, what he does with it, is he going to defect, what are his politics, do communists really eat their young? No matter if Lendl has been a part of the international tennis world for several years, some genes persist.

The Czechs have a saying: "Do not trust a Hungarian unless he has a third eye in his forehead." Perhaps to young Lendl, in his heritage, we are all Hungarians limited to one eye on either side of our nosy noses.

Fibak was an interested bystander at Lendl's press conference late Saturday night, after the lanky Lendl slaughtered Vijay Amritraj in the WCT semifinals at Reunion.

Fibak is a sharp, charming Polish lawyer, son of a Poznan surgeon, who has ranked in the world's top 20 tennis players for the past eight years. He is recognized as one of the headiest players around, a master of six languages who now makes his home in this country. And he has become recognized as the molder of Lendl, the developer, the mentor, the *burge,* if you will.

"It all started when he was 19," said Fibak. "He began following me around. It was more his admiring *my* game. He would walk with me, bring me drinks, carry my racquets, always asking questions. Maybe it was because I spoke Czech and he spoke a little Polish. He adopted me. After one year, he stayed with me in New York and later at our home in Connecticut. We worked together. Just to practice is not enough. I told him *how* to practice. Other players have the shots, but few know how to use them, especially against certain opponents. Ivan has worked hard to become the optimal player. I wouldn't say I was the reason for his improvement. It has been *his* brain and his legs and his work.

"Now I help him with his investments, tell him how to live, how to travel, what to buy, arrange his schedule. I am not his coach because I don't travel with him. I have my own schedule. But many times we are together. He is my great friend."

As for Lendl's reluctance: "Some people like to talk to the press," said Fibak, who obviously does, "and others don't. He is the other one."

PREACHER'S SON

The bustling waitress, puzzling over a full tray, set the martini in front of Mike Singletary. He stared at it and then cut his eyes sideways uneasily.

At first, you suspected he wasn't sure if an All-America footballer should drink in front of the press. But then there came a stronger hunch, that he actually didn't know what the tomfool it was or what it would make you do. Mike is served a martini about as often as I ain't, which is not often indeed.

The Baylor lineback appeared ill at ease anyway. His luggage had been lost en route to this remote stop in Ohio and he is not your basic seasoned traveler who *expects* to have his baggage lost once out of three times. It bothered him, whereas old wardogs like us shrug and charge a couple of shirts to room service.

Mike was still wearing the t-shirt and slacks that had covered him protestingly during the trip, and *that* made him uncomfortable. He sat immobile, looking down at the tablecloth, answering when spoken to, after he had given each question a thorough inspection. This dinner was in a private room at The Golden Lamb in Lebanon, Ohio, an ancient and revered and rather fancy dining spot where, it was said, a dozen United States presidents had partaken of the fare and perhaps of the martinis, too.

It was the night before a national promotion tour began, featuring six outstanding college players, one from each sector of the land, and Singletary might have been nervous about *that*, too, contributing to his quietness. He is a solemn fellow, a round face behind thick glasses, small sleepy eyes that have almost an oriental cast, a studious appearance that seems out of sync with a thick neck and melon biceps and thighs the size of an East Texas backlog.

The other chaps on the NCAA-ABC tour were more outgoing. Major Ogilvie, the Alabama halfback, is mature, posed and polite as an insurance salesman. Rich Campbell, the California passer, boyish and friendly. Mark Herrmann, the Purdue quarterback, thin, intense, earnest. Hugh Green, the Pittsburgh defensive star, relaxed, with just a hint of swagger. George Rogers, the South Carolina halfback, eager and happy with the national attention.

Singletary could match brains and brawn with any, but he isn't the political type. This stop, at the National Football Hall of Fame at nearby Kings Island, was the first of six the group would make across the country, talking to hundreds of media, taped and filmed and snapped and quoted. It was great exposure, say, for a Rogers or a Campbell or Herrmann, who are admitted candidates for the Heisman Trophy.

Singletary has quietly intimated to his coach, Grant Teaff, that he too wants to win the Heismann. Perhaps he doesn't realize that none but a back or end has *ever* been so voted.

"And I'm not going to tell him," says Teaff.

But first, there was this martini to be dealt with. It sat there, clear and evil and defiant, while Singletary tried to tune to the conversational buzz around him and also to figure out what to do about this thing. He was terribly hungry, as you could later tell by the way he went after some crackers and butter that stopped by.

There were several pressboxers at this particular table, talking of this and that, and Mike watched as they lifted the glasses with the grace of long practice. Maybe this was the first course, a clear fruit juice perhaps, or some kind of Ohio soup? When the waitress had come around and asked for cocktail orders, Mike had said, "Shrimp."

Finally he lifted the glass and took a tentative sip. A convulsive shudder ran through his bulk; he squeezed his narrow eyes shut and quickly sat the monster down. My mind raced back a century, to a small cafe in Jacksonville, Florida, where I tried my first martini and was convinced there had been a horrible mistake and I was tasting the juice of something dead.

"Oh, I think you got my drink," said a press guy, eyeing Mike.

"Here," said Singletary, still stricken, shoving the thing away from him.

"What did you order to drink, sir?" the waitress stopped to ask. Several of the players were pulling at beers.

"Milk," said Mike. While waiting, he drank two glasses of water, quick.

If Mike Singletary is an example of the Good & Clean & Pure, it is but happenstance that he's in college football at all.

As Baylor's middle lineback, he has gained national acclaim as an uncaged monster. In fact, for his first two seasons, Singletary roamed and ranted and raged at such a degree that he was all out of ammo by the fourth quarter. He had hypered himself out. Teaff and his aides spent hours trying to fashion a governor for Mike's carburetor. And even *they* are astounded at Singletary's field fury, considering his peaceful background.

In Houston, Mike's father was a minister at the Church of God In Christ Sanctification and it was a stickler for personal behavior.

"In my religion, you couldn't play football or basketball," Mike remembered. "You couldn't play *any*thing. You couldn't wear shorts, or dance, or play cards. The feeling was that you might get so interested in winning or competing, that you would sorta forget God, that He would no longer be first in everything you do."

When Mike reached the seventh grade, he was 5–5 and 155. "That was *small* at my school," he said. "Leonard Mitchell and some others were there." Mitchell is the giant football-basketball star now at Houston.

Mike asked his father for permission to play football. The answer was no. A couple of days later, his dad reversed his answer, even though it changed *his* life, too.

"He thought, because of my size, I needed to get banged around a little," said Mike. "But he couldn't go on preaching after that, even though we never left the church. In fact, the church changed eventually. Another preacher's son later played for the University of Houston."

Before the NCAA tour was finished, Singletary was *the* focal point for the other collegians. That's the same way he influences the Baylor squad that opens the season tomorrow night at Lamar.

"He's a lot like E.F. Hutton," says Teaff. "He doesn't say a lot but when he does, people listen."

DAD'S DAY

JUNE 19, 1985

In this space anyways, Father's Day crept in and crept out like a cat burglar, all cloaked and obscured by involved doings at the U.S. Open. But perhaps the story is worth a delayed replay.

It is a remnant of chance conversation from a late-night seminar, in aftermath of Andy North's victory in Detroit.

Us learned professors had threshed that topic beyond recognition, and then someone remembered it was Father's Day and wondered idly if there were any noteworthy connections between North and his father and the Open trophy. It was something no one had thought to check out, and now the deadlines had made the question a useless exercise. So one of the congregation rattled his ice cubes for attention and showed an excellent change of pace by telling a Father's Day parable. Ole plagiarist here—like Tom T. Hall did to the talkative waiter in *Watermelon Wine*— borrowed a pen and copied down his rhyme.

This was about 30 years ago and a Mr. W. Hobert Millsaps was principal of Central High in Chattanooga, Tennessee.

Mr. Millsaps was fairly interested in athletics. He was devoted to golf, and he played a little basketball in a muny league. But his teenage son, as most of us in that stage, was a sports nut, especially baseball. Billy Millsaps studied box scores and memorized standings and schedules and knew Sandy Amaros' shoe size and the names of Enos Slaughter's parents. Believe me, it used to happen that way.

Father and son seldom talked sports. In truth, they were principal and pupil during the day, and sometimes those diverse roles are difficult to shut off at 4 p.m.

And so we come to that one afternoon in early October; young Billy was woolgathering in a Tennessee history class, trying to concentrate on Gen. Albert S. Johnston with 40,000 johnny rebs surprising Gen. U.S. Grant near Shiloh Church and getting himself kilt in the process.

(Bill Millsaps is now sports editor of the *Richmond Times-Dispatch* and has a memory for detail. As a matter of fact, he places the exact date as October 8, 1956, and he was 15 years old.)

The teacher was Marion Perkins, the old Tennessee blocking back who also served as assistant coach at Central High. His classroom door opened with a rap, and coach Perkins went to answer. He turned and pointed to Billy Millsaps.

"The principal wants to see you in his office," he said. "Bring your books."

Those were dread words, even to the normal student. You were not called to the principal's office for a popsicle. Such a summons was automatic bad news.

Especially was it a nervous proposition for young Millsaps. His father always went to great lengths to show him no partiality, no favoritism. In fact, the principal's son seemed governed by stricter rules, by higher expectations, than the ordinary pupil. All these dark thoughts raced through the teenager's mind as he gathered his books and hurried to the door. Down the hall, his father already was striding away.

The kid trotted to his side. "What did I do, Daddy? What's wrong?" The parent did not look down. "Just follow me to the office," he said sternly.

A sudden terrible thought struck Billy.

"Is it mother?" he said with a quaver. "Has something happened to mother?"

The father didn't respond, other than increasing his pace.

The principal strode purposely through his secretary's anteroom, stalked through his office, shut and locked the back door. He fixed young Billy with a grim stare and nodded toward a chair facing the desk. Billy sat. The principal returned to the entrance.

"No calls, please," he said to the secretary and shut *that* door. Then he hurried to his desk, sat and wheeled around to the table beyond. He reached to flick on a small black-and-white TV. Waiting for the set to warm, he glanced back at his son.

"You won't believe," he said, "what Don Larsen is doing to the Dodgers."

The Political
Arena

GOALS POSTED

NOVEMBER 4, 1983

Just recently a wealthy and recognized citizen of our town made some statewide recommendations that caused several little mushroom clouds to puff from the countryside.

As chairman of the governor's special education committee, Ross Perot had the temerity to suggest that high schools were primarily intended for educating youngsters and not for winning district football titles. Gracious, to some, Mr. Perot spit on the Alamo.

Now I wouldn't know Mr. Ross Perot if he walked into my backyard and ate one of my prize periwinkles, but he obviously isn't afraid to take a stand. Of course, if you and I had all those millions, we might talk back to a traffic cop, too.

Most of us haven't studied the Perot proposals in detail but when he says educational demands for high school jocks should be toughened, I say bully for him. As we understand it, a high school athlete now must pass three of his five courses in order to participate and it seems to me that we are offering gravy trains.

The last time I looked, roughly a century ago, we had to pass *every* course to play football or anything else. As I recall, there were four years of English and math required, two years of foreign language and two years of science and four years of a combination of history, government, civics and what not. And a failing grade in *any* of these and you sat out for a year while you brought your grades up, or you joined forces with a wheelbarrow or hoe. Studying, in comparison, seemed less conducive to hand blisters and could be done in the shade.

Somehow over the years, these requirements have slackened until now a student must pass only three of five courses and those courses do not necessarily have to be "basic." Mr. Perot wishes to raise requirements to four passing grades and I do not see how any discerning citizen can object to this. We all know many schoolboy (and college) jocks do classroom work at the minimum. Raise the minimum and he will somehow match it.

What Mr. Perot suggests is akin to Proposition 48, which has been adopted for the future by the NCAA. This new rule requires incoming jocks to show a C average in basic courses (English, math, science, etc.) before they qualify for college scholarships. What happened is that college presidents were embarrassed when some of their products showed up on the teevee unable to grunt intelligibly.

A select committee on athletic problems-higher education, appointed by the NCAA, has just issued a report. It found, in part: "Academic standards for student-athletes should be more demanding than they are now . . . . Pre-college education must be strengthened so that all students receive educational experiences necessary for success at the collegiate level . . ."

There will be objections from those who say some football jocks will be discriminated against, that tougher requirements will prevent some youths from attending college and therefore qualifying for the livelihood of a professional footballer. The answer there, it seems to me, is that colleges weren't established to groom pro athletes. A pro jock should not be forced to attend college if he is not qualified. Let the football pros sign him out of high school, if they wish, and train him themselves, as they do in baseball or basketball. Or maybe lease a ranch and breed their own.

If Mr. Perot is saying that football is overshadowing the main purpose of high schools, it says here he is right again. There was a time, before other interests were available, when Texas towns were focused solely on their high school football teams. It was the rally flag. The smaller the town, the more emphasis. The high school coach was the most important figure in the community, the most admired or most maligned.

The high schooler became popular and respected in direct proportion to his talent as a football player. Not basketball, understand, nor saxophone nor physics, but football. Players acquired exaggerated ideas of their own eminence. They became overbearing. If a lad did not play football, he was a second-class citizen, a role he seemed to accept. He was tolerated maybe, but not admired as was the halfback who scored twice in the district playoff, despite the fact he was an 18-k crumbum.

Perhaps it's not that way anymore. In my little Texas hometown, too late we became smart. We eventually learned that football talent does not necessarily make big men. The biggest man we had, it developed later, was a Czech lad, quiet, fair, short and slight of build. He wasn't around too much, because he hurried home after the last class to grub on his pa's farm until dark. He joined the National Guard, not from any sense of patriotism but because it paid $2 a week for the drills and $2 was a bundle.

He was mobilized with the 36th Division. Ernie Pyle, the correspondent, was there when they brought his body down from a mountain in Italy and wrote a story about him and the story won a Pulitzer and somebody made a movie out of it, with Robert Mitchum. Henry Waskow was the biggest hero our little town ever had—and he couldn't, or didn't, throw a football from here to there, and that's how it should be.

GRAND INTOLERANCE

FEBRUARY 3, 1986

The groundhog surfaced yesterday and either did, or did not, retreat to his couch, signifying we will, or will not, have another six weeks of sniffles. The details are fuzzy.

Sorry, but I have never bought the groundhog, nor the Easter bunny nor the tooth fairy and over the years, I never have been *really* convinced that Ms. Brigitte Bardot wasn't some sort of pleasurable figment. Yet I find it easier to swallow those tales than to believe there is a single pro basketball, football or baseball team on these shores *without* a "drug problem."

It depends, of course, on the definition of "problem."

Obviously, Raymond Berry thought his New England Patriots had a "problem." He called it "intolerable," which indeed is a strong term.

Raymond is a resolute, devout man with basic inalienable values. A single joint, puffed hurriedly in a men's room cubicle, might be "intolerable" to this particular coach. Other coaches might shrug it off and order another scotch on the rocks. Still others might close eyelids, clap hands over ears and draw X's and O's before leading the squad in the Lord's Prayer.

Certainly Raymond is not so naive as to be stunned to hear some of his hearties were stuffing powder up their heroic honks. He has been around pro football for a quarter-century. Back in his playing days, he must have seen the "greenies," the pep pills that some trainers used to dispense like jelly beans.

The old-timers thought no more of these artificial boosters than of the team doctor plunging a long needle of Novocain in a knee joint and running it around under the skin like a snake under a bedsheet. It was all so commonplace and so very legal. Some will see only a thin line between these practices and the so-called recreation drugs that have become so public and prominent within The World of Perspiring Arts.

Looking back on it, when Berry seemed unenthused and stoic about his team making the Superbowl for the first time, we all attributed it to his low-key nature. But it also might have been that he knew this drug business was going to pop open after the game, certainly a cause for worried preoccupation.

Berry said he first learned of drug use on the Patriots shortly after succeeding the fired Ron Meyer as coach October 25, 1984. But he had visited players in the off-season, given warnings and maybe even thought the situation was cool. He was disheartened and disgusted to hear differently, but he never would have gone public with the story, unless he was forced. This is a guess, but it seems likely.

The sitation was "intolerable" to him, Raymond Berry, because he simply does not feel compelled to coach in that sort of climate. And so he informed his team after the game: *You agree to a drug test program, or I'm gone. I don't need this.*

Hooray for Mr. Berry, it says here. As for names being made public, so be it. Frankly, us reformists are a bit weary of this "invasion of privacy" balderdash player unions are spouting. Let the narcs bust them, and see how much influence "invasion of privacy" has with a police blotter.

Likewise we are fed up with claptrap about sports being a "microcosm of society," that there are no more jocks using dope than salesmen or lawyers or authors. Some of us are old-fashioned enough to believe jocks are role models for youth and, as such, are *obligated* to live as such. It should be as much of the contract as the zone block and the double play.

The players' unions say no. They see drug-testing as a negotiable item.

And the football union head, Gene Upshaw, asked, "Why don't we have drug testing in all parts of society? Why is it so important in sports?" Any person who has to ask that question shouldn't be walking around loose.

SEEING RED

JULY 14, 1980

Even at the risk of forfeiting jounalistic history, it is probably just as well that the 1980 Olympics begin this week without some of us pressbox crusties. Personally I had rather be right here, creating exotic omelettes on the sidewalk, than participating in The Great Moscow Adventure.

Of course, some of us homelovers are never too enthusiastic about traveling *any*where a passport is required, for there is always the possibility of losing same. You are talking to living proof of that stupidity. Ole stoop here once became disassociated with his passport in Cologne and was forced to quiver noticeably for several days in Munich before the thing mysteriously reappeared, thereby sparing me a lifetime in bondage or worse. But that's another story and I expect any day now to dicker over the screen rights.

Misgivings over the Moscow trip have lurked all along, but they surfaced during the Winter Olympics at Lake Placid. I must admit, some were based on raw envy of Soviet forcefulness.

In the Lake Placid high school building, where press headquarters was located, most of us were packed into working space that only a sardine could appreciate. Too, we all were bundled in our little snow outfits, with quilted jackets that bloated one to the size of a San Diego Charger, and huge foul weather boots that Christopher Columbus could cross the Atlantic in. This made it even more crowded. But the Ruskies, oh, they had a swell spacious room all to their own. They probably *demanded* it, and if you demand something in loud enough voice, you are apt to get it. The Ruskies are masters at this.

There were about two dozen TASS reporters on hand, stolid middleaged guys who ignored the subzero temperatures like it was capitalistic propaganda. Their pressroom was maybe 30 by 50 feet. You could have played half-court basketball in it, if the Reds had gotten around to inventing same.

TASS people went en masse to Olympic events, came back to

their personal gym to file reports and then went to their sleeping quarters in a body.

One American columnist, Jerry Izenberg, thought he made friends with a TASS guy. This fellow promised Izenberg an interview with some Russian hockey players who, like others of the USSR contingent, would talk to no press. Izenberg was to report to the TASS office at 4 p.m.

At 4 p.m. Russians in the TASS office had never heard of Izenberg's contact and were openly scornful of his story. In midst of the squabble, his contact walked in. Jerry yelled at him and waved for help. The fellow gave no sign of recognition. Izenberg was firmly invited to depart.

One frigid night in the area behind the high school there was a personal experience. It was maybe 10 o'clock and transportation service was even more laggard than usual, which is to say there was none at all. A couple of us wretches had waited for more than an hour, noses numb from sleet acupuncture, stomping in the snow, clapping gloves, to keep circulation astir. There were maybe 50 other miserable, frozen press, students, workers, waiting for transportation to other towns of that miserable, frozen county.

The Pinkerton guard, a young miserable, frozen lady with frosted glasses and nose like a cherry, took pity on the two of us because we had been waiting so long for a mythical van to take us to Wilmington, a miserable, frozen outpost where we laid down each night. The next van that happened along, she promised, would be dispatched to Wilmington.

Sure enough, within an hour, this lonely van slid wearily down the hill into the parking area, like a pioneer scout reeling back to the wagon train with an Apache arrow in his loticimal. The Pinkerton guard spoke briefly to the driver, who slid back the side panel of his van. She turned in our direction and beckoned.

"Wilmington!" she called, like a sweet Joan of Arc. We hoisted heavy briefcases and started the treacherous route over the ice. Then it happened.

Just before, about 10 members of the Russian press corps had exited the school's rear door and were striding toward the curb. In the middle was a huge guy, maybe 55 years old, six feet and 300 pounds. His head was completely bald and uncovered, even in that biting snow and bitter cold. He wore a bulky, fleece-lined greatcoat but it wasn't buttoned, the flaps tossed back as if this giant were disdainful of capitalistic weather. He looked like a fierce old wrestler on the Orpheum circuit. We had not seen him before. He could have been one of those KGB watchdogs that Red delegations are never without.

The Russians saw the waiting van. They heard the young Pinkerton girl call out to the two American popsicles.

There came a hoarse cry from one of the Russians.

"VILMEENGTON!" And they broke into a charge like you have never seen before. Jerry Kramer and Fuzzy Thurston, leading the interference on the old Packer Sweep, never plowed through opposition as these squatty, middleaged fire-plugs attacked the crowd surrounding the van.

The two frozen Yanks, stepping cautiously on the slick surface, had about reached the open van side when the force struck. It was like a Galveston tidal wave during Hurricane Carla, heavy shrimp boats borne aloft and thrust aside by mystic power. We were flung yards away, really unaware of what hit us until we looked back at the wreckage.

The big bald wrestler had not reached the van with the first wave, but now he was there, at the rear of this scramble of humanity his massive arms parting bodies as a swimmer doing the breast stroke. Friend, comrades, foes, all were flung aside without prejudice. He cleared a mighty path, pushed himself through the door and plunked down in the middle seat, staring impassively ahead like a victorious buddha.

His comrades flowed in around him like wet sand filling an East Texas post hole. The Pinkerton turned helplessly to us and spread her hands palms up. You couldn't budge these bullies with a derrick. There wasn't a shotgun handy.

"Go!" the big guy said in a powerful voice. The van vent Vilmeengton.

The girl driver of a later van, hearing this, told of a pack of Russians commandeering her vehicle earlier that week, jamming themselves in, refusing to move. They ordered her to drive to various stops, kept the auto tied up for most of the day. She was actually terrified, with no choice but to obey. Mind you, this was in *our* country. This week, they have the home court advantage. It says right here they are welcome to it.

DUNCE CAPS

Now that the shock waves have simmered off to the horizon, the world has been cleansed again from smears against the purity of college athletics. Swords have been beaten into plowshares and the voice of the turtle dove is heard throughout the land and The Great Academic Institutions shall go and sin no more. And if you swallow that, I got some nice oceanfront property for you on the outskirts of San Saba, Texas.

Of course, that would be nice to believe, just as Santa Claus and Snow White made pleasant thoughts back when we were in rompers. The NCAA disciplinarians seem confident they have struck a blow for integrity by severing the SMU hamstrings, and good for them. There is naught hypocritical nor prejudiced nor self-serving in the punishment they assessed. But the jurists are incredibly naive if they think the drastic sentence will stop, or even slow up, cheating in recruiting. It will just lead recruiters to hone their art. You can't stop college cheating any more than you can pick up mercury with tweezers.

The cheaters, and this could well include maybe 40 percent of football factories, will study the SMU situation with passing curiosity, but they will refuse to accept possibility it could happen to them. Mr. Bruno Richard Hauptmann was executed, as your grandpa can tell you, but it didn't exactly stop the practice of kidnapping. The death of Len Bias didn't bring an abrupt cease to doping on campus.

This is not a jaded outlook, but a realistic view from a working scaffold. Some folks will never, ever learn. That's the way it shall ever be in big-time college football, where so much money and ego and, yes, lack of adult intelligence, is involved.

That's actually what SMU was punished for: Dumbness. That's what it should have said at the top of the NCAA charge. Not Illegal Payments, not Excessive Entertainment, not Extra Inducements, not Alumni Involvement. The writ should be emblazoned with old English script: Dumbness.

How else do you explain a gotrocks booster pulling the old "bedspread trick" while the school was *already* on probation? That's the term for the ancient recruiting caper when you get a poor boy in a motel room and toss $1,000 in small bills in the air, scattering carelessly on the bedspread, the floor, wherever. The kid never saw that much money, of course, and his eyes would swell into saucers as he made a mad grab for the fountain pen.

In essence, that's how Sean Stopperich told the NCAA he was recruited by an SMU highroller in a Pennsylvania hotel room. While the school was *already* on probation! Moving parents to Dallas, a free apartment, a job for papa, leaving a trail a blind goose could follow. Dumb. Keystone cops.

When the touted recruit, already pledged verbally to Pitt, "changed his mind overnight," and Bobby Collins, without batting an eye, said, "Oh, I'm not surprised. Basically, this is where he wanted to come all along." Sorry, Bobby, this was dumb. Either the coach knew better, or *suspected,* or he's too naive to let past the gate without a nanny.

When President Donald Shields displayed what many judged an arrogant, challenging attitude toward NCAA charges before he knew their validity, claiming "selective enforcement"? Threatened a suit against the NCAA? Dumb.

When Collins and Bob Hitch let alum gotrocks bully them to the extent they shut their eyes and turned their heads? Double dumb. For Hitch to blame SMU exposures on a local newspaper circulation war? Dumb, dumb.

Then, when one axe already had fallen, to keep up payoffs to certain players because they might rat to the NCAA if cut off the payroll? Oh, brother. You know brussels sprouts with more sense than that.

Of course, that's another big reason the SMU experience will not deter other cheaters. They cannot imagine themselves operating as dumb as SMU and they are probably right.

BUCK STOP

College presidents are great ones for soapboxes. In fact, if you locked a dozen college presidents and a dozen U.S. senators in a room with just one television camera, somebody would get hurt.

Why, just the other day, the head guy at Florida found access to a dais and declaimed, by gollies, we are going to have to clean up college athletics. I fully expected him or one of his peers to take a firm stand also against pellagra, snakebite and the Red menace in South America.

For some reason, it reminded me of a statement once uttered by Mr. Lyndon Baines Johnson from his platform in the White House. The memorable words came during the Watts riots in Los Angeles, the start of a great American heritage.

"Killing, rioting and looting are contrary to the best traditions of this country," said Mr. Johnson. Apparently, Mr. Johnson or his underlings had done considerable research on the subject and could find nowhere in the Constitution where our founding fathers endorsed high-tailing it with somebody else's television set.

Anyway, the Hon. Marshall Criser was here in town for the College Football Association meet and told his audience that "we are going to have to clean up our acts." He said it was about time to get started, by gum.

Mr. Criser is a newcomer to the college presidency business, having recently left a law practice to assume command of the listing Gator craft. Therefore, he may be excused for a decided lack of originality. This thought was first expressed, I believe, by Mary Baker Eddy or perhaps it was Pliny the Elder.

However, Mr. Criser is understandably disturbed because his school, for acts performed *before* his arrival, has been severely flogged by the NCAA disciplinary committee. And just last week, his fellow members of the Southeastern Conference stripped the Gators of the league football championship. This hurt doubly, of course, because it was the first one Florida had *ever* won, dating back to Ponce De Leon. This was like finally managing a social engagement with Miss Dyan Cannon and discovering she had just won a garlic tasting contest.

College athletics has been crying out for sanitation for the past, oh, quarter-century. This possibly coincides with the influx of big television bucks into the picture. The bigger the pot, the stronger the temptation to palm an ace.

There's nothing wrong with televising sports, you understand; it's just that the heavy revenue thereof does magnify problems. We must admit that right now the need for Athletic Reform has reached new proportions.

The college folk face four main dangers to their public image. Never mind what is right and wrong *philosophically*, it is the public image that causes most concern among college administrators. The problems: (1) illegal recruiting and later sustentation of jocks; (2) lack of educational progress of jocks; (3) possibility of tampering with point spreads because of gambling interests; and (4) drugs.

You *know* that the college public image has been severely tarnished because the college presidents have finally dealt themselves a hand. For years, the good doctors have smiled benignly and looked the other direction, as a commodore might stand in his wheelhouse and gaze at the beautiful sunset, while below, the crew flails each other cross-eyed with belaying pins.

It always *should* have been the presidents' problem. Hell, don't ask the coaches themselves to police their ranks. Most of them are too busy trying to survive. The presidents have every authority and every chance. Two years ago, an NCAA committee recommended much, much higher educational requirements for jocks, to go into effect after a five-year preparatory period. Immediately the detractors started screaming, as the critics quickly attacked President Reagan's tax reform proposal.

The presidents can hold fast or they can bend, back into the old blindfolded pattern. The decision is in their lap and nobody else's.

STARE GAZERS

SEPTEMBER 23, 1983

Now that the Chicago White Stockings have won the American League West by nine lengths over a sloppy track, you may expect an alteration in major league rosters next year. Each team will have its own hypnotist, listed right along there with the equipment man, the clubhouse boy and the bullpen catcher.

Sports outfits are the greatest of copycats, or at least they rate no worse than a place bet against television producers. Especially where gimmicks are involved.

Let a golfer win the U.S. Open, putting with a ball-peen hammer, and immediately there would be a stiff run on hardware stores.

Just recently, "stretching" was the rage in pro football. Most teams hired a "stretching coach," who was usually a small Oriental in white ducks who taught all manner of weird positions for elasticizing the muscles. It was indeed an unforgettable sight, before a game, to see all these behemoths lumber on the field, line up for calesthenics and assume the motionless pose of a Pontiac hood ornament. Supposedly this flexed the *gluteus maximus* so that you could shoot spitballs with it, to say nothing of the *latissimus dorsi*. If you can't say anything good about a muscle, say nothing, is the creed of the presscoop.

Anyways, this fad passed and now we are back to the old-fashioned American jumping jacks and duckwalks.

The Cowboys fancy themselves innovators of this sort of thing. Why, a couple of years ago, the highdomes of Expressway Towers decided their lads' concentration would be enhanced if each player was secreted in a dark tank, buck naked and floating in salt water, while listening to a muted recording of Tom Landry singing Amazing Grace. This, in effect, retired D.D. Lewis from football. While laughing hysterically, he swallowed so much salt water that he grew dorsal fins that were ruled illegal by Art McNally and his NFL inspectors.

46

Still, had the Cowboys won the Superbowl that salty year, every other team would have roofed their bathtubs and laid in a supply of brine.

The word is now well circulated that the White Sox have been employing a hypnotist since June, and consequently have won the pennant with an aggregation that, on paper, wouldn't have finished third in the 1953 Sally League. Chap's name is Harvey Misel and he has an office, a dim bare room, in the bowels of Comiskey Park. He gives 30-minute individual sessions with the taped theme from "Rocky" throbbing in the background.

"You can hit any pitcher," he croons. "You can see the baseball beautifully plain. It is large and white with flaming red seams. You will drive that baseball back to the pitcher's head!"

Since Tom Paciorek started his sessions, he has increased his batting average 40 points. Floyd Bannister has won 11 of his 12 decisions since he went under the spell.

Misel is a portly 51-year-old gent who went broke selling electric rodent repellers, took a short course in hypnosis and opened his own couch in St. Paul. He has 200 clients among major league players and first came to attention when he talked Rod Carew out of a pulled hamstring in 1976. According to his new contract with the White Sox, he cannot recruit new clients in the American League, which rules out Eddie Chiles shipping his Texas Rangers north en masse.

Of course, hypnotism is not exactly a new drill, but it may be the first successful *baseball* use of the same. We realize the technique is used in medicine and whatnot, but still most of us associate hypnotism with night club acts in which a visiting deacon from Falfurrias is persuaded to roll up his trouser leg and crow like a Dominique rooster.

More than three decades ago, Bill Veeck hired a hypnotist to convince the St. Louis Browns they were pennant winners. His name escapes memory but unfortunately, the Browns' finish does not. It was last.

Leo Durocher once engaged a performer named Arthur Ellen who put Giant pitcher Sal Maglie under and talked him out of a hip injury. Ellen later claimed to have worked with Tony Lema and "many other professional golfers I am not at liberty to name," according to his modest recollection. Ellen also said he had hypnotized seven members of the 1962 Houston basketball team before they played the Texas Aggies, who had thrashed them soundly two months previous. Houston won by eight.

We all remember when Craig Morton admitted, in retrospect, that he had visited a Dallas hypnotist named Edward J. Pullman and that the chap had induced a hypnotic state that could be triggered by the key words "Black Salt." Before home games of 1970, the Cowboy quarterback would visit Mr. Pullman and receive his transmissions. Before road games that year, Craig would telephone the hypnotist and hear "Black Salt" over the wire and then accept his post-hypnotic suggestion.

Tom Landry, the noted poker face, received news that his starting quarterback had been in a hypnotic trance, with no change of expression. But I heard later, on good authority, that Landry went calmly home, locked the doors, sealed the windows, entered a cedar-lined closet and gave vent to the first and only scream of his long and illustrious career.

BAD MIX

OCTOBER 31, 1986

You are listening to a dedicated supporter of Mother Nature. Take my lawn, for example. Please.

Nature meant for grass to grow green and tall, knee high if it bloody well wants to. Nature also decreed that trees shed leaves, falling on the green grass and laying there, pelted by winter rains until they decay and distribute vitamins and minerals into the soil to help the green grass grow tall. This was the original plan of the forces who put together the Garden of Eden.

Now us civilized tribes, in our infinite wisdom, take over from nature. We rake the lawn and scoop the leaves into green plastic bags and place them in the alley where they are picked up practically every year. Then we skin the grass one-half inch high and spend $40 on fertilizer to strew about so the grass will grow higher so we can whack her down again.

If we let the green grass grow tall, as it was meant to, then the neighbors glower and eventually sign a petition and The Man knocks on the door with a paper in his hand.

Dang it, grass was not meant to be mowed and leaves to be raked, and if that be treason, make the most of it.

And neither was the female woman meant to play football, he said slyly, after lulling the audience into his corner.

It is not this milquetoast intent to anger anybody, such as the Civil Liberties Union and them. I certainly do not wish Ms. Gloria Steinem to burn her bra on my stoop, nor do I intend to stretch out in front of stadia ramps in Yonkers or New Jersey or Austin, Texas, where women of the female sex buckle pads on their shoulders and bang into young fellows. I merely wish to make a political point.

Late in the summer, a New Jersey teenager named Ms. Elizabeth Balsley was given court permission to draw football pads from the Hunterdon Worth Lions. The judge overrode a school board's unwritten ban against female girls of the opposite sex.

A Yonkers lass named Jacqueline Lantz filed suit in federal court so she could punt for Lincoln High. Her case, of course, was backed by the New York Civil Liberties Union who argued it was rank discrimination that the young lady was not given an equal chance to get her leg broke. Ms. Lantz is 4–10 and weighs 116 pounds.

And in Austin, Tina Rejo just finished a season for Bedichek Junior High under a temporary restraint against the University Interscholastic League. Here again, the state civil liberties union pushed the case.

Now I know naught about law, nor much about civil liberties. Women are tops in my book. There is nothing like a dame, and someday I shall write a song to that effect.

It's just that I do not believe in disputing nature. And nature did not intend for female ladies to play football. Heck, I'm not even sure the original planners meant for *males* to do football. It was designed for robots and small livestock.

There probably is a humorous aspect to females tackling males and vice versa. Ms. Phyllis Diller once said, "Fang's ancestors were all bronco busters, bear hunters and lumberjacks. And the men were all bookkeepers." So if these civil liberties chaps are doing it for a joke, well, that's another matter. But I have a hunch they're serious.

One hopes, doesn't one, that the young ladies in Yonkers and New Jersey and Austin are not being used as ploys by zealous advocates desperate for causes to bear.

It seems rather silly and unnecessary to point out that female bones are smaller and muscle mass is less dense than the male counterparts, so let's don't even go into that. I mean, we're not being actually serious about this. What we're being is a crochety old curmudgeon. It was earlier just this year when the Playboy Club, doubtlessly fearful of civil liberties zealots, changed its practice and hired male "rabbits" to supplement its "bunny" waitresses. Come to think of it, I was against that, too. Harumph.

Stadium Noise

ZERO IS HERO

NOVEMBER 24, 1980

It will never be recorded, of course, that Larry Cole is a rank traitor. Nowhere will history list him alongside Brutus and Benedict and Shoeless Joe Jackson. Nevertheless it is known to a few discerning observers that the Cowboy mossback has betrayed a dignified, dedicated group.

Were this Abraham Lincoln's time, it would be the firing squad for Bubba. In Rome, it would be 15 rounds against the lions, winner take all. In Cuba, he would be hanging by two of his 10 thumbs.

The reason Larry Cole will escape the everlasting stigma is that the outfit he betrayed is really not an organization at all. It is an unbrotherhood, a non-lodge. To be organized would destroy it.

This, of course, is the exclusive Zero Club which was fermented a dozen years ago in Cowboy training camp. Charter members were three large flaxen linemen named Larry, Pat and Blaine. Their last name was Who. They were swathed in anonymity and gloried in it. (Actually, there is very little else you *can* do in it.)

The Zero Club was just that. The members met occasionally in the dorm room of Cole or Pat Toomay or Blaine Nye, assumed a prone position and did nothing. To do *something* would have violated their by-laws, if they ever had any. Their motto was *Apathy uber alles,* which you immediately recognize as the famous old German cry "Apathy above everything."

Occasionally Toomay or Nye would speak forth on the healthgiving qualities of inertia but Cole rarely said anything. Mostly he would lie on his back and roll his eyes and, over his 13 seasons, became quite proficient at this.

These meetings were faithfully chronicled by our man Frank Luksa, who himself is not adverse to sprawling horizontally and studying a fleecy cloud or two. Says it affords him deep insight about the mystery of professional football and also is pretty good for the sinus. So *he* says. Frankly I have never found it so, especially about the sinus.

The Zero Clubbers were never asked for autographs nor photographed nor interviewed.

They were convinced they were destined to spend their football careers unrecognized by the public and maybe even by coaches and teammates and this was quite all right by them. In anonymity, there is peace. Not much money, but peace.

In a way, I presume, all three have betrayed their fraternity. Toomay deserted oblivion when he wrote a book and put his own name on it, an act that frequently calls attention to oneself. He lives in our midst, has a raven on his windowsill and is writing like mad on other tomes.

Nye quit the Cowboys in his prime, making modest headlines that destroyed his anonymity. This surprised him greatly. He thought no one would notice his *absence,* because they never noticed his *presence.* Blaine had all sorts of graduate degrees, in physics and things, and he is off in California probably making nuclear bombs, hopefully for our side.

But Cole's fall is the topper of all. He pulled it Sunday, flaunted it even, there in the Cowboys' lethargic 14–10 edging of the downtrodden Washingtons.

Bubba is going into the *record* book, for heaven sakes. He will never be anonymous again. His name will live forever. I mean, this is like having a disease named for you.

L-a-r-r-y C-o-l-e, scrubbed of its incognito, will be inscribed in Cowboy history right there alongside Bob Lilly, the founder of defensive football as we know it today.

Most touchdowns by a defensive lineman: Four!

The fourth came in the fourth quarter at Texas Stadium, and it was decorated with distinction. When Randy White jerked Redskin passer Mike Kruczek groundward and the ball plopped pitifully into the air, suspended and helpless like a clay pigeon, there was our man Bubba careening along in White's impressive wake.

He captured it with a rare technique. First he butted it with his face guard just to show the dang thing who was boss. Then he bounced it off his taped hands.

"I finally trapped it with all my thumbs," he said, forming a bushel basket with his hams. And then he seized the thing in his right paw like a loaf of Mrs. Baird's finest rye bread and set a course of approximately 345 degrees.

He was forced to demonstrate 187 times for all us serious historians who assaulted him in clustered shifts after the game. He thought it rather amusing that so much ado was made of his deed. His words were polite enough but there was laughter just under the surface. After all, he said in an aside, it's not as if it were the *first* time it's happened.

Cole ran his prize 43 strides into the end zone, much in the manner of a logging train.

"The first thing I thought when I saw those old bow legs start moving," said Randy White, "was HE'S GONNA MAKE A TOUCHDOWN!"

"When I got to the 15," said Cole, "I thought, 'Could it be? Could it be?'"

Next, his biggest concern was dodging congratulating teammates so he could make his almighty left-hand spike. "I thought about doing one of those Billy Johnson waddles in the end zone," he said, "but I probably would have thrown my back out."

Larry's fourth touchdown is even more memorable because it sent Dallas ahead 14–3, a cushion that survived a late Redskin score.

And even more—because all four of his touchdowns have come against Washington. The first three came in his first four games against the Redskins, a century or so ago.

"I'd like to hear the Vegas odds on *that*," he said blissfully. But then Larry realized he was in the spotlight.

"Hey, I'm out there with all those studs—Randy and Harvey Martin and Ed Jones. I'm just an old dog picking up their scraps. That was Randy's play today."

His act brought a gruff appraisal from a betrayed Zero Clubber.

"Any time Bubba Cole scores the winning touchdown for the Cowboys," said Toomay, "things aren't going right."

He was correct. It was not a day for the Cowboy scrapbook. It was sort of a nothing game. Somebody suggested, indeed it was a game for the Zero Club. It could be its highlight film.

"This is all entertainment business," said Cole. "I shot J.R., right?"

But it was no special surprise, even though it has been 11

long scoreless seasons since Cole pulled his last touchdown shenanigan.

"I had an eerie feeling all day long that I was going to score a touchdown. It's crazy to say that, but I did have this really eerie hunch. I guess because it was the Redskins."

Have you ever had that eerie feeling before?

"Yes."

And . . . ?

"It didn't happen," said the traitor.

LATE ARRIVAL

SEPTEMBER 19, 1979

When Roger Staubach outraced the clock on Sunday last, it was the audience's clue to go ho hum. So what else is new. Wouldn't you think it's about time he broke in some new material?

Hairbreadth Harry in another of his goosebump episodes. Your time to go for the popcorn. You didn't actually think for a moment that Little Nell, beloved by all the village, would be run over by the 7:14 to Memphis, did you? Does the burning fuse *ever* reach the dynamite when old Joe Clean is in the saddle? Was there ever a doubt that Roger K. Staubach, patched but clean, would swing in on a grapevine and kick Black Bart off the trestle?

By now, you should recognize the pattern. Only the newcomers, the ones with fingernails bitten off to the elbow, take this thing seriously. Us ole seasoned Staubach watchers are the cats with the yawns, the cool hands who keep the binocs on the cheerleaders until the last five minutes, and then venture a casual look at the scoreboard to see if this is the day for Roger's act. He winds it up, you know, after the jugglers, the musical seals, the boy violinist and the yodeler from West Virginia. Here comes Our Hero, crooked smile, straight teeth sparkling like dewdrops in the sunrise.

If it ain't Chicago he's knocking looplegged, as it was Sunday, it's Minnesota or Philadelphia. Or St. Louis, for goodness sakes. The Cardinals have never been so sick of one man. Five times in Roger's eight seasons as a regular Dallas quarterback has he passed St. Louis into defeat in the last *two* minutes.

After Staubach's last-gasp strangulation of the Bears, a bolt of curiosity struck nearby. Just how many times had Roger performed this particular act, how often had he passed the Cowboys to victory in the last two minutes of play? In a sly manner which would have brought shame to Tom Sawyer and his whitewashed fence, I mentioned the project to Bruce Jolesch, the club's designated bookworm. Two days later, he surfaced, paddling furiously, a parchment held carefully in his teeth. Would you believe Sunday was the 12th time for Staubach's highwire stunt?

Of course, we all remember the two Staubach masterpieces. First, when he came off the Cowboy bench in the 1972 playoff against San Francisco, after sitting out the season with a broken shoulder, and passed for *two* touchdowns in the last 78 seconds! Run that one by your memory and you'll *still* go out and bet against it.

Dallas was all but eliminated, you recall, trailing 16–28 when your stumbling locals gained possession with 1:18 remaining. Many eager beavers had already left the pressbox, to find early stations outside the victorious 49er lockerroom. Enter Staubach. Four plays, 55 yards, the last a 20-yard pass to Billy Parks. Next, a beautiful onside kickoff by Toni Fritsch and a Dallas recovery. This time 50 yards in three plays, the capper being a 10-yarder to Ron Sellers.

"I would think that game stands out as the greatest," Tom Landry said yesterday, asked to review Staubach's climactic rallies of the past. "Mainly it was great because his team was playing so badly that day. One of those late drives is not as hard when your team is playing well, but that day, we played lousy."

"And then, of course, there was the Hail Mary pass in Minnesota," said the coach, and you could almost sense a note of fondness.

This was in the 1975 playoff against the Vikings, with Staubach and mates behind 10–14 with 1:27 left and 85 yards away and, it seems to this memory, just one timeout remaining. There were several Staubach heroics on that one unbelievable drive, but the payoff was a desperate 50-yard heave to the Viking five where Drew Pearson and Nate Wright were rooster-fighting for the world champeenship. Pearson somehow stole the ball away, trapping it finally between the back of wrist and his hip, and reeled across for the winning points.

"That was the one great play that sticks out," Landry was still combing Staubach's thrillers, "because it was against an excellent defense."

There also was a little luck involved, a guy suggested.

"Well, I don't know. It was a great throw and a great catch."

Well, said the guy, if the Lord had intended folks to catch footballs with their hips, He would have put hands down there.

"I guess that's right," said Landry, happy at the memory. "There *may* have been a little luck there."

In four of those dozen rescues, Staubach won the game with a touchdown pass. Once, he ran for the winning points. Seven times he passed the Cowboys within range of a winning field goal.

Two were in overtime. Two, of course, were playoffs. And in those 12 games, Staubach hit 60 percent of his passes for 2,800 yards and 19 touchdowns. His three greatest passing days of his career were included. Each game has a little plot all of its own. Against Philadelphia in 1975, for example, Staubach engineered a touchdown *and* a field goal in the last 70 seconds.

Most of these dramatics were conducted in the framework of the Cowboys' "two-minute drill," the hurryup offense each team uses just before the half-time gun (if it's in proper field position) and right before the end of the game (if the team is behind).

"We expect to score on 40 percent of our two-minute offenses," said Ermal Allen, the researcher who counts such items. "One year (1966) we scored points on 57 percent. Last year, it was very low. That's the reason we worked on it so much in training camp." Allen wouldn't give last year's figure. Some unidentified bird said it was below 25 percent.

But those percentages don't tell the full Staubach story. His 12 games were lost until the last two minutes. This doesn't include rallies just before half-time. These were for all the chips. And, remember, the Cowboys haven't trailed in a whole lot of games at that point. Until someone comes up with a covering set of statistics, you could assume there is none better than Staubach at jerking a lost cause from the coals, and hasn't been in years. Maybe never. Maybe you could look it up.

STAR STRUCK

AUGUST 6, 1980

KINGS ISLAND, OHIO—The stain is unfortunate, but permanent. It's like an unsightly birthmark on a beautiful woman, a blemish which becomes more noticeable as the lady grows older until that is *all* you see.

Dick Maegle wishes he had never heard of Tommy Lewis, that there was no such impulsive bungler. *Then* maybe the college football researchers would record that January 1, 1954 with proper respect for what it was—the greatest offensive show ever in a major bowl game.

Instead Maegle finds he is remembered mainly for a freakish goof in which he was the innocent victim.

Roy Riegels, too, is branded in memory for a boner in a bowl game. Riegels was an excellent California center and linebacker. But in the 1929 Rose Bowl, he snatched up a Georgia Tech fumble, lost his compass and ran 75 yards in the wrong direction. But this was Riegels' doing, nobody's fault but his.

In comparison, Maegle was a bystander struck by the bandits' getaway car.

There he was, galloping along in the wide open spaces of the Cotton Bowl, minding his own business en route to his second long-range touchdown of the second quarter, when an Alabama highwayman burst from the ambush of his own bench, ran on the field and cracked Maegle with a blindside collision that *could* have crushed the Owl halfback like a sopapia.

Then this Tommy Lewis, the skulking trespasser, rushed back to the bench, sat down, buried his head in his hands and started crying. He didn't even look to see if Maegle was in two pieces or more. There are folks doing three to five in the state joint for less.

By his sordid act, Tommy Lewis entered history. You would never have heard of this obscure fullback, were it not for his misdeed. Now he's a famous trivia question.

You *would* have heard of Maegle and probably in more impressive terms, for his performance that day alone would have engraved him in marble. He was awarded a 95-yard touchdown run on Lewis' action. Earlier, Dick had reeled off a 79-yard touchdown sprint. In the third quarter, he scooted 34 for Rice's third score of the day. In only 11 carries that afternoon, Maegle gained 265 yards, unmatched ever in a major bowl.

And yet when Maegle was inducted into the College Hall of Fame here this week, the conversation centered around Lewis & Maegle, rather than Dick as a solo act. He didn't especially giggle over it.

Quite frankly, Maegle is a bit sour on the subject.

"I've never brought this up because it might sound selfish," he said. "But it took away from the rushing record that day. My rushing total was the highest ever for a major bowl game."

Some Southwest graybeards attending the rites here remembered the Ed Sullivan blotch of the event. Sullivan had the biggest television show of the time, a variety show on Sunday night, and he loved to introduce figures in current news from his stage and in the audience.

The nation was abuzz over Lewis' illegal tackle which, of course, was featured over and over on the national toob. The game was on a Friday. Sullivan called Maegle, his coach Jess Neely and Lewis and wanted them for his show a couple of days later.

"Coach Neely was already in New York for a meeting," Maegle recalled at a Hall of Fame chitchat. "This was in the days of the prop planes, and I flew six or seven hours from Houston to New York, two or three stops. I went straight to the theater that afternoon for rehearsal.

"Backstage there was all this confusion, there must have been a circus on the show, too. There were guys juggling all over the place and other guys turning flips. I remember a bear standing on a ball. I never said anything to anybody, and nobody said anything to me."

The same held true for the live television show. Ed Sullivan called Lewis, Maegle and Neely on the stage and introduced them. Then he talked to Lewis.

"Mr. Sullivan asked why he had done what he did. And Lewis said (Maegle lapsed into a thick Southern accent) 'Why, Mistuh Sullivan, ah gess ah wuz jist so ful-l-l of Alabama.' "

Some of us remember that Sullivan then turned to the audience in that commanding style of his and said something like, "Let's hear it for this fine young American!" and everybody cheered like Tommy Lewis had just rescued the *U.S.S. Pueblo.* Maegle and Neely were asked no questions, never uttered a word.

After the show, Maegle recalled, Ole Smiley said, "Thank you boys very much. Now we got you a fine room at the Waldorf. Everything furnished."

"I still hadn't said anything," said Maegle. "But I waited around a while and went back up to him. 'Mr. Sullivan,' I said. 'I don't want this to sound wrong, but would you mind if I got my own room?'

He looked kinda surprised and I said, 'Just two days ago, this guy came off the sideline and knocked me out in front of all those people and now he's on national television. You can't tell what he might do if he woke up in the middle of the night. He might throw me out the window.' Mr. Sullivan stared, and then he snapped his fingers, 'Get this boy a room of his own!' he told somebody."

The following Thursday Sullivan called Maegle in Houston.

"He said he wanted me to come back to New York and be on his show again Sunday," said Dick. "He said they got 6,200 letters from people mad about the way he paid all the attention to Lewis and none to me. He said he wanted to apologize to me on the show for the way he had handled it.

"But there was that six-hour plane ride and besides, I had midterm exams coming up and I had to study. I turned him down."

Of course, Maegle returned for a big senior season in which he led the Southwest in rushing, scoring and punt returns and gained consensus All-America recognition. And then he went on to a seven-year career as a defensive back in the NFL. This week, as he became the 24th Southwest Conference player to be recognized by the Hall of Fame, Maegle found some things stay the same for a quarter-century. Like conversation topics.

GIMMICK MART

Jocks are not the only portion of the populace with eccentricities. Most everybody has a screw loose somewhere in his makeup and it was ever thus.

Peter the Great, who stood six feet, eight inches, had a great feeling for midgets and dwarfs and once gathered all the little people in Russia, the ones who didn't run hide, and built them a snow village. Catherine the Great had 300 lovers, although not all at the same time, and Henry VII was a devoted pole vaulter and wore a big gold whistle around his neck. Edward II loved to pull chairs from under his queen, Isabella the Fair, and Lucrezia Borgia washed her hair with a mixture of saffron, cumin and wood shavings. Honest to pete. Made it yellow.

It's just that jocks get more attention for their unorthodox behavior and this is quite all right with them. The more notice you attract, the more merchandisable you are. Many jocks are not flaky by nature; their quirks are acquired.

A pioneer practitioner of this theory was a middleaged chap named George Wagner, who was built more like a baker than a jock, but he took a bottle of peroxide and some hair curlers and parlayed them into a fortune under the billing of Gorgeous George.

"You got to have a gimmick," Hacksaw Reynolds was telling fellow linebacks the other day. Jack Reynolds is an old-time ruffian for the San Francisco 49ers, and he received much credit for the 49ers' Superbowl defense last season. Also he received much publicity, called *ink* in the trade, for an old folk tale off the campus of the University of Tennessee, where Hacksaw received his higher learning. As the legend went, Jack Reynolds was so enraged when his Vols lost a big football game that he tore his old 1953 Chevy in half, or ate half of it or something. The story varies.

When Reynolds reached the Superbowl, this parable was rehashed so much that he had a circular printed, telling the story of his taking a hacksaw and making a trailer out of an old Chevrolet—not in anger. Simply because the car wouldn't run anymore and he wished to salvage part of it.

Anyways, the story earned him the nickname of Hacksaw and a certain amount of attention among the imaginative authors always looking for such. It is much easier, as you realize, to write about a king who jerks the chair from under his lady than it is about some deadpan who lives by the book.

In attendance at Prof. Reynolds' lecture was a young man named Bobby Leopold from Port Arthur, by way of Notre Dame. Bobby very much would like some of the notoriety being handed to Reynolds. So in the future, he wishes to be known as Bobby Black Shoes Leopold.

"After that session with Hacksaw, I began brainstorming about gimmicks with taste," said Leopold. "I mean, there're not that many gimmicks still unclaimed. There are only so many '53 Chevrolets available for sawing in half. So I came up with the black shoes."

This means, we must presume, that Leopold will shoe himself in black, which, in these days of white footwear, will make him stand out like a mink coat in a nudist camp. The gimmick is a steal, of course, from Billy White Shoes Johnson, an itinerant punt returner who wore white shoes when everyone else wore black and also performed disco gyrations on occasions he made it to the end zone.

Foremost along this line on the Cowboy roster, of course, is Butch Johnson.

For seven terms now, Johnson has been the most frustrated of players. Maybe not the *most* frustrated, but the one who gave most voice to it. Johnson is convinced he should be starting in the place of Drew Pearson or Tony Hill, a conviction somewhat unshared by Tom Landry.

Johnson points out, with some justification, all the clutch catches he has made, the impossible snags that glorify dramatic moments of big games. Periodically, Johnson demands to be traded, but then he will sign a new contract, and he hears arguments that Landry's offense often uses *three* wide receivers so he is, in reality, a starter. Then later on, he realizes he is a definite third on the list, has always been and probably will remain. This is a bitter pill for Butch, who loves the limelight as few will admit.

Johnson seems to have balmed himself with one resolution. If he is to remain a backup receiver, then he will be the best-known backup in the league. He courts attention.

Butch now does tv interviews for Channel 4 and loves it. Recently, he did a split-screen interview with himself—the questioner in tie and jacket, the interviewee in sport clothes—and was proud of his production as David O. Selznick. There's a Butch Johnson poster and a Butch Johnson disco dance, patterned from "the California Quake," which is one of those showy end-zone maneuvers after a touchdown pass.

It ain't something you usually connect with the straightlace, businesslike Dallas Cowboy approach. It is pure Butch Johnson and admittedly hotdog or showboat or whatever you call the attention-seekers.

In the second quarter last week, Butch cut a square pattern across the Buffalo middle, took a 22-yard pass from Gary Hogeboom. He was dropped but jumped up immediately, put his feet together and did a little crisp Chinese bow.

"I just like to get the fans involved," Johnson said afterward. "I just thought I'd show them we appreciated the cheers."

It wasn't planned?

"Oh, no, just something I thought of at the moment," he said with a giggle. "No, I didn't rehearse it. I don't rehearse anything but the Quake."

Will it be an addition to the BJ act?

"I dunno. You'll have to wait until I catch another one," said Butch *"If* I ever catch another one," he added, back down to earth.

MODE BLOCK

Over a period of one hour after the Pittsburgh exhibition, there were at least two dozen microphones stuck in his perspiring puss and the same questions asked.

"This contract dispute, Randy, has it affected your concentration?" That was usually the opener. And then, "Is it possible you might walk out before the season opener?"

Randy White had rather been in prison camp. These postgame interviews are not his cup of tea, anyway, even under normal circumstances. He cooperates, for that is his nature. He leaves the sanctity of the Cowboy locker room to cross the passageway to the big hot hall, where players perch on metal chairs on small individual platforms like geeks outside a carnival sideshow doing the come-on bit, while us media types mill as Ellis Island imports, from post to post, asking the same silly questions over and over.

The tackle sits there uneasily, a strangely unmarked collar-ad profile atop a weightlifter's torso, and does his polite best.

There are players who leave a game with a comprehensive overall picture, but Randy is not one of them. Charlie Waters can explain the big view, the theories and blueprints. Lee Roy Jordan could do the same, and back in the old days, Larry Stephens was good for an incisive lecture.

But Randy White's football world is limited to a few square yards, what he can see between the iron bars of his helmet cage. A half-hour after the game, it's still a blur to him, a disjointed cacophony of crashes and collisions and thudding forearms and clutching hands and awkward falls and growls and gasps and grunts normally associated with a Kenya waterhole at dusk.

Pardon a personal metaphor, but Randy White on the field, to me, is a colonial field musket, one of those shortrange, wide-bore muzzleloaders. He is tightly wadded and primed and when the ball is snapped, he explodes in a fearful clap of smoke and slug, rattling and ricocheting and echoing until finally the dust dies. And then he quietly reloads, no demonstrative tribal dances, no Tarzan gestures, no backslaps or High Fives. The play before is gone and forgotten; his whole concentration is on the next snap.

If I could guess, I'd think the entire game to White is simply a chain of these explosions, like a string of firecrackers going off, each one individual at the time, but indistinguishable one from another in afterthought.

Pressboxers ask him, after a particularly outstanding performance, some brilliant question like: "Was this your best game this year?" And White squirms slightly and answers with pure honesty: "Oh, I don't know about things like that. I just try to play every play."

Just as he wrestles with the overall game explanations for the mawkish media, trying to give answers they expect, Randy was doing the same in his contract hassle with Cowboy management.

He didn't want to talk about it—you got the impression it was embarrassing to him. His game is banging into the guard, not trying to overpower some contract term. His arena is grass, not office carpet. You feel he goes through life waiting for the next snap.

A more sophisticated jock, a Tom Seaver or a Fran Tarkenton, would have planted calculated remarks to influence the negotiation, or maybe refused to even discuss it. Certainly they wouldn't have repeated and repeated the same answers for this guy who came in late with his tape recorder, or that chap who had been elsewhere in the room with his pad during the original answers.

"I really wouldn't want to comment on it," he would say. But when the questioner persisted, Randy didn't blow his top like so many would have.

"I would like to sign before the first season game," he said again, patiently. "Sure, it's on my mind, but I try not to let it affect me on the field. No, we haven't talked about it in three and a half weeks." He said it over and over, as more perspiration popped on his brow under the hot lights.

"I just enjoy *playing*," he told a guy at his elbow. "This is one side of the business I don't like to deal with. But I guess it's a part of it."

"Will you walk out of camp if you don't sign?" said another

latecomer, pointing his microphone like a district attorney's forefinger.

White turned to face him. "I really don't know what I'll do," he said politely for the 35th time.

A politician like, say, Reggie Jackson could have made a public pitch. He could have told of enlightened disappointment in his 1978 contract, after he found his $120,000 was nowhere near other top-rated tackles. He could refer to the compliments of Tom Landry and Ernie Stautner, ranking him at the top of league defenders, comparing him to the incomparable Bob Lilly. He could have recounted his All-Pro plaques. He could have mentioned the $230,000 contracts of Alan Page and Joe Greene, and wondered aloud if he were in their class, why not their income bracket.

He could have mentioned that he lived with his old contract, without whimpering or demanding "renegotiation" as so many have. With White, a contract was a contract, but now it was expiring and it was a different ballgame. He could have reminded how he had played with a foot injury that would have kept most on the sideline. He could have put a yardstick to his career, and realized he had passed the halfway point.

"It's gone by so quick; I can't believe it," he said the other day. "It seems like just yesterday I was in college. I look at the game program and there by my name it says 'Seventh Year' and I think, where did it go?"

But White is not a complicated man nor a manipulator. Whatever he felt about his situation, he kept it inside. He didn't go public with it. Cowboy negotiators could fault him for nothing. To rap White would have backfired with the populace. To find a villain, they had to center on agent Howard Slusher. This they did, of course, especially at the last.

As for "walking out of camp" as several Slusher clients have done, well it's doubtful that possibility led Cowboy brass into buying White's signature Wednesday. Randy might have actually taken his uniform off, but, it says here, he would had rather fought sharks.

PEPPER AND SALT

JANUARY 14, 1986

NEW ORLEANS, LOUISIANA—Batten down the hatches. Button up your overcoat. Get ready for the big blow. You are preparing to be buffeted about the ears and eyes, perhaps even nose and throat, with enough Superbowl words to give a severe hernia to Mr. Funk and Mr. Wagnalls and Mr. Noah Webster and the dray they rode in on.

Within the next fortnight, your household will add new proper nouns, like Refrigerator and Bam Bam and Sweetness and Biscuit and Hog and Nellie and Big O and Danimal and Jumbo. You will learn how many pigs William Perry has for breakfast and the toothpaste used by Craig James. You will hear Mike Singletary's views on the Libyan situation and Brian Holloway's judgment of the President's tax reform. And prominently, in this media overkill of Superbowl XX, you will be inundated with comparisons of the two head coaches. And this, friends, could make a mini-series.

First off, there are the common points. Both Mike Ditka and Raymond Berry were passcatchers by trade and standouts in the NFL and they both served as Dallas Cowboy assistants. Right there, she ends.

Take the exteriors. Even the name Mike Ditka denotes something blunt and forceful and *physical.* A longshoreman would be named Mike Ditka, or a sandhog. Raymond (never Ray) Berry is a name for your high school principal or dentist.

Ditka has a bowling ball face and bold eyes and a thick stern moustache. He once got his hair permed and dared you to smirk. His normal look is half-glare and his stance is bent forward belligerently from the waist and his stride as though he is stomping out cinders. Berry, behind his mild contacts, has a drawn, long face with practically no expression. He may be the only NFL coach who owns an old-fashioned hair brush, and he walks as though he doesn't want to wake up the baby.

It would be impossible for Ditka to be in a crowded room and not be noticed. If he were listening, he would be the one standing tall and glancing impatiently over the heads of others. If he were talking, he would be the one jabbing his finger and jerking his head.

Berry would be in a corner with his back slumped against the wall, looking down and nodding politely. If he spoke, he would bend toward your ear and his move would be slow and deliberate. In a conversational cluster, Ditka would be in the center, Berry on the fringe.

If someone asked you to pick out the football coach in the room, Berry would be in the bottom 10.

If they were tobacco, Ditka would be a chaw, Berry a pipe. If they were material, Ditka would be canvas, Berry tweed. If they were transportation, Ditka would be a locomotive, Berry a glider. A weapon: Ditka a blackjack, Berry a snare. If they went to a current movie, Mike would choose *Rambo*, while Raymond might opt for *101 Dalmations.*

If this makes Berry appear a softy, then the picture is out of focus. There is a certain resolute hardness to Raymond; I think maybe it's the way his neck sets on his shoulders, if that makes sense. (The cut of his jib, as old bluewater sailors said.) If you had to play poker, you had rather play against Ditka.

Likewise, if the portrayal of Ditka comes across as a muscular mule, then again, it's a misfire. The forthright Ditka has learned much control in a couple of years' time. There is still the temper, of course, fairly close to the surface. It will break out a few times under the tremendous media pressures and demands during Superbowl week. Be assured of that. But only a few.

Both Superbowl coaches have worked extremely hard at their trades. As players, Ditka had natural talent, Berry built himself. Ditka always has been furiously impatient with talented players who operate at less than full throttle. Berry, while in college coaching at Arkansas, was thought not to be the greatest talent evaluator, perhaps because he himself would have been bypassed by most talent evaluators.

I'm not sure Mike Ditka ever wanted to be anything other than a football coach and I'm not sure Berry ever has made up his mind exactly what he wants to be. Ditka campaigned for his job. Berry's job plopped in his lap while he was relaxing on his patio.

With both Superbowl coaches, as you will read and hear many times next week, what you see is what you get. With Berry, perhaps you have to look a little harder for it.

LAB COURSES

In a brilliant effort to spike the Gator Bowl telecast the other day, one coach was wired for sound. As misfortune would have it, the ratings still fell somewhat below *Bowling for Dollars*.

Next year, the show may be banned in Boston, which should jazz up the attraction considerably. Pat Jones, director of the Oklahoma States, used dialect of a deacon for most of the game. But eventually, just as you knew he would, Pat spouted a basic four-letter word familiar around boiler room and corral. It came forth into your living room, loud and clear. Upstairs in the ABC booth, Al Michaels and Lee Grosscup chuckled uneasily and quickly introduced another topic, like what their good friend Joe Morrison said at dinner last night. Pass the salt, I think it was.

Of course, this is not an original gimmick. There have been numerous other instances. Directional microphones have trespassed into bench territory during hot action, shoved by a buttinsky under orders from a teevee emperor, while coaches and players were shouting at opponents and zebras. These tactics frequently pick up graphic phrases that would sour milk at nine paces. And you cannot tell *me* that it displeases the producers; the contraband dialogue provides many a chortle over martinis at the next production meeting.

But it isn't the language that raises objection from ole dad here. Almost any night on cable teevee, you are privileged to hear talk as purple as you please. No, it ain't the words. It is the *mechanization* that brings growls from us old grumps.

Now we hear that the Progressive Party, under the stalwart leadership of Texas E. Schramm, wishes to wire NFL coaches and players with two-way radio. Signals may be sent and received, recipes exchanged, whatever.

Well, sir, this is just another step in dehumanization of football. Already we have erased most of the recognizable element. We have these huge padded faceless *creatures*, arms jutting out like oars on a dinghy, stalking in jerky movements of science-fiction robots. I defy you to see any human parts.

Eyes? Forget it. A sewer grate, bolted to a hat the size of a thundermug, hides all facial features. Skin? Huge neck rolls and bicep pads and elbow pads and forearm armor and wrist bands and gloves. I think I saw a finger last season, sticking out from a tackle's mitt, but then it might have been the sun glancing off the brass knucks.

These automatons are graded by computers and interrogated as to the last time they wet the bed and if they hated their mothers. They are stuffed with scientific formulas and bulked with steroids until they travel one to a bus. In wartime, each would be drafted as a pontoon bridge.

These things waddle between plastic goalposts onto a synthetic rug inside an air-conditioned, heated edifice. If perchance they slip a cog, they undergo surgery at halftime and return in the third quarter.

They squat or kneel or bend and the ball is snapped and there is a fearful fracas of maybe five seconds duration. Then eight guys run off the field and four run on and then three and then one and they stand around while some coaches hold committee meetings and others, wired to headquarters, send frantic semaphores.

After a minute or so, the hulks assume another stance, and we have another five seconds of warfare. It's as if they are using muzzleloading muskets, where they have to ram powder, then shot and wadding and then tamp and cock and sight and balooey. Pro football, anymore, has all the spirited continuity of call-shot pool. And now we're going to equip these creations with walkie-talkies, for goodness sakes.

"I feel that sports should take advantage of modern technology," said Schramm.

It follows that the college draft is doomed. What do we need, receivers? Hey, Gil, ring up Texas Instruments and have them send over a batch. Try to get stainless steel this time. Brillo doesn't grow on trees, you know.

MR. HYDE

WASHINGTON, D.C.—Every time he does it, Danny White cops a plea of temporary insanity.

When the brainstorm strikes him, he says, his judgment blacks out and nature assumes command. Danny is back there to punt, see, and his intentions are right out of the Boy Scout manual. The ball arrives and suddenly the devil takes over. Through this strange fog, he senses laxity in the punt rush or a carelessness, and his fangs grow long and a fearsome growl comes from his corded throat and, in a flash, he is dashing downfield, like Count Dracula leaping off the balcony and bounding across the moonlit greensward in the form of a wolf.

After such an experience, Danny seems shaken by the memory. His eyes are big and somber and it is as though he is describing someone else. He's a stricken witness of a street crime, or Butterfly McQueen after seeing a ghost in the hallway.

Example: Sunday the Cowboys were clinging desperately to a 17–10 lead over the rallying Redskins, and White stood on his own eight-yard line, fourth down, a young cleancut American male in complete control of his faculties.

By every tenet of traditional football, he knew he should punt the ball. Every weighing of possible gain or loss, every fiber of football logic says kick it 45 yards downfield and get it off your doorstep.

Instead, Danny turned into a werewolf and ran 13 yards to reach the line of scrimmage and 20 yards beyond and, as Washington tacklers neared him, he slid down and wondered who that fool was.

"I didn't even think about what I was doing until I was getting up off the ground, and then I wanted to kick my butt," said the quarterback.

What if he had tripped on the wet, torn turf as runners had done all afternoon? What if he had fallen short of first-down yardage and yielded possession to the aroused Redskins? What if they had then ridden their momentum to the winning touchdown?

"I would have had to buy a house in Washington and stayed. They would have loved me in Washington, but I couldn't live in Dallas," he said.

"It was pure reaction. There was nobody on my left, so I just took out. They didn't expect it because it was a crazy thing to do. I guess I just went crazy there for a moment."

What makes White's success more remarkable is that he has a history of such. There should have been no surprise element. This must infuriate Joe Gibbs, that his Redskin punt coverage team was *aware* White frequently pulls these rash tricks.

Or maybe Gibbs doesn't realize the extent of White's, uh, shall we say eccentricity.

"The fake punt was a darn good call," Gibbs said afterward, apparently thinking it was a *planned* play. He must think Tom Landry is a bit weird also.

"I couldn't believe it," said Landry. "If he failed in that situation, the game could have gone their way. But Danny has the option to do what he wants, and believe me, he was doing what *he* wanted." In other words, it dang sure wasn't what *Tom* wanted.

Later, after Landry had stopped quaking, he rationalized in his artful fashion. "What makes Danny a great quarterback is he's got the courage to do things. Fortunately he seldom gets caught."

What made it even more risky is that Dallas was not behind. It was not a *desperate*, shoot-the-works situation. White didn't have everything to gain and nothing to lose. Just the opposite.

"It was a tremendous gamble," said Landry. "If he doesn't make it, we're liable to be 3–2 right now instead of 4–1."

How long and often has White had these seizures? In interest of science, a curious soul took a high dive into play-by-play history of White's seven seasons as Cowboy punter. The findings:

It all began in a Chicago game of 1976. With Dallas ahead 29–7, punter White got a high snap from center. Danny glanced at the two outside rushers (the *contain* men) to see how much time he had and noticed they already had peeled aside and were heading downfield. So White ran 14 yards for a first down. Later the same season, he did the same against the Giants, running eight yards for a first down that led to a go-ahead field goal.

In all, White has gambled on 16 fourth downs in his Cowboy career. He has won 13. He ran 12 times for necessary yardage. Once he saw he couldn't make a first and punted on the run for 60 yards. He tried this maneuver against Pittsburgh this season and got the punt blocked, putting the Steelers in position to score the winning touchdown. He lamented his judgment on *that* one.

Against Miami last season, he was tackled after a three-yard gain, short of a first down. But the loss was not harmful to the Cowboy cause.

Against Pittsburgh in 1979, White sinned with malice aforethought. In a punting huddle, he warned Jay Saldi he might *throw* to him. He did, unsuccessfully, giving the ball away on his 31, a boner instrumental in the Cowboy's 3–10 loss.

Apparently a split-second decision to *run* is okay with Landry, but a *planned* pass is not.

"I don't like surprises," the coach said afterward in a passable imitation of an iceberg. "I thought it was understood that these plays are not called in that situation, unless by the coaching staff.

"It won't," said Landry, "happen anymore."

White was strangely unmoved. "We had to get something going," he said, with a shrug. "I don't regret it. I'm sure I'll hear about it, and I'm sure it will be a long time before I call it again. Next time, it will probably be in Green Bay." White meant, he would probably be traded to Green Bay as a result of the goof-up.

However, he has not called a pass again. There really is no need as long as he can stand off to the side and watch some foolhardy stranger do the stuntwork.

DEFENSIVE RALLY

JANUARY 23, 1985

The plea here, Mr. Don Shula, is not guilty.

When the powerful chorus of the press shook you and your associates, this feeble little tenor was in the kitchen with Dinah. Ole buster here was then, and remains now, a member of the abandoned minority, discriminated against at almost every turn. Bob Lilly and me and Ernie Stautner and Deacon Jones and the like.

Shula was explaining the new liberalized blocking that has turned the NFL into a beanbag toss. The Miami coach is a member of the "competition committee," the powerful group that considers everything from rules to replays.

"Two years ago, the competition committee got a mandate to open the game up," said Shula. "A mandate from the media, from coaches, owners, fans—it came from everybody but defensive backs."

Not true, Don. Several of us hidebound fogies of the media would have protested strenuously against any such mandate, had we known the dang thing was running around loose. We were taxed without representation. As a consequence of that presumed "mandate," the competition committee recommended changes in blocking rules and limitations on defensive tactics. (The entire league votes on rule changes but usually follows committee recommendation.)

Anyways, the offense was handed a license to rape. Cornerbacks now are limited to a polite wave at receivers at the line of scrimmage. Defensive linemen are not permitted to breathe heavily on the passer, especially after an Italian meal. And offensive linemen are allowed to carry ice tongs in each hand.

So now we have us a game of catchball. One tall guy throws, while his blockers clutch every defender in range, and a platoon of basketball players spring to dunking height, catch and sprint into the end zone and go into celebrating seizures that would shame Jerry Lewis. We have touchdowns in clusters, like radishes.

In confabs last week, the two Superbowl coaches discussed the new liberties accorded the offense.

"I like the game the way it is now," said Shula.

"The game had become so stymied, so neutered," said Bill Walsh, the other Superbowl professor. "Three yards and a cloud of dust."

Hogwash, says our brave rebel band.

We preferred the game *before* it became a touchdown orgy. We saw nothing wrong in a 14–10 result, if any of you can remember *that* far back. We considered defensive skills just as intriguing as touchdown gallops.

My favorite Cowboys play, through the quarter-century memory, is *not* the Hail Mary pass against Minnesota, nor the Butch Johnson catch in Superbowl XII, nor even Tony Dorsett's 99-yard scamper against Minnesota two years ago. The one action that stands out most prominently is Lilly's sensational sack of Bob Griese in Superbowl VI. With pal Larry Cole riding hazer, Lilly herded the Miami passer backward 29 yards before dropping him with the biggest loss in Superbowl history. That play was the story of the game, perhaps of that particular Cowboys era. But under today's rules, Lilly would never had made it. He would have had three blockers clinging to his underpinning like fiddler crabs and nary a yellow flag to be seen.

Another personal gripe is that the new offense offers too much of a good thing. Now *that* sounds like an old goat grumbling just for the sake of it. Perhaps it's an eccentricity, but when I leave a game, I like to remember one or two offensive plays that carried the dramatic plot. The Immaculate Reception of Franco Harris. Dwight Clark's leaping playoff catch against Dallas. Max McGee's rearview juggle in the first Superbowl. Clint Longley's heroic heave on Thanksgiving Day. The Hail Mary pass. But under the liberalized rules there are almost *too many* noteworthy throws and catches. They all fade into a memory collage, one indistinguishable from the other.

Example: San Francisco's first touchdown in the recent Superbowl was a splendid catch by Carl Monroe, a nifty maneuver, a 33-yard touchdown. But if The Great Unwashed remembers it at all, it will be just another pearl in a large collection of offensive gems, several of which would not have been possible under stricter old rules.

You got no mandate from here, Mr. Shula. It probably came from the boob toob folk who need the touchdowns for commercials. It's not the defensive line they worry about, it's the bottom line.

JOY BE CONFINED

SEPTEMBER 22, 1976

Near as anyone around here can remember, this was a Pittsburgh rookie receiver named Dave Smith a half-dozen years ago, on the verge of scoring his very first professional touchdown. He was fleeing far in advance of his pursuers, so he had ample time to consider the proper demonstration of his glee.

He decided to *spike* the ball in the end zone, a practice becoming quite popular at that time. This act consists of spiraling the football into the ground as hard as possible. Psychiatrists have never been able to discern exactly why this particular action is especially chosen over, say, turning a handspring, or doing the split, or taking a bite out of the ball, or running over and giving the nearest pom-pon gal a smooch that would water a horse. But then, psychiatrists have never figured out why Tarzan chose to bellow through the jungle, scaring the bejabbers out of parrots and pythons and goodness knows what else, after putting the shiv to some dangerous beast.

Anyways, this Smith, if indeed that was his name, misjudged his position on the field, much as Willie Shoemaker misplaced the finish line as he led the 1957 Kentucky Derby. Smith mistook the 10-yard line for the goal line so he did his little spiking act on the five. The bouncing ball, of course, was ruled a fumble and the pursuers recovered it for *their* team and Smith dug a hole in the ground, jumped in it, zipped it up after him and the last anybody heard, he was pulling a rickshaw in Rangoon, still blushing like a sunset.

There was a similar occurrence in the Southwest Conference last fall. Ike Forte, a fine running back for Arkansas, seemingly was off to a banner afternoon against SMU. Four times he carried the ball, for a total of 71 yards. His last gallop covered 38 yards for the Razorbacks' first touchdown. Apparently Forte thought he had safely outdistanced all defenders, because the last ten yards of his run, he went into gaudy theatrics, holding the ball high above his head in one hand and taking those lofty, springing steps of a ballerina, or a barefoot man running from a bull in a grassburr patch.

Forte was well into his victory prance when an SMU safety, Mickey Early, made a desperate dive from behind. Somehow his outstretched hand slapped Forte's celebrating heel, causing the Porker to stub his foot in the synthetic turf, dislocating three toes, putting him out of action for the rest of *that* game, all of the next, and he did not regain full speed, in fact, until the Cotton Bowl.

Now certifying for membership in that dubious society is Travis Crouch, a large, enthusiastic defensive end for the University of Texas. He's the lad wth crutches and a rosy complexion. Real rosy.

Texas had gone ahead of North Texas State, 17–7, late in the third quarter last Saturday evening, and the Longhorn defense seemed particularly inspired to hold that advantage.

On the Eagles first snap, quarterback Glen Ray was dropped for a four yard loss by Tim Campbell. On the next play, the Eagles tried a tricky double reverse with flanker J.T. Hollins winding up with the ball and swinging wide around his own left end. Most of the Texas defense was fooled by the play, but not Crouch. He met Hollins with a smashing openfield tackle on the line of scrimmage. Then Crouch leaped to his feet and went into a victory dance. He jumped in the air a couple of times, brandishing his fists, and seemed to shiver his legs from side to side like old Elvis, while airborne. Suddenly he arrived back on earth, grasped his left knee in agony and collapsed on the ground and threshed around like a man who had just discovered a scorpion in his bedclothes. Several teammates gathered around and stared at Crouch, thinking this was a continuation of his celebration gyrations. But no. He was finally carried from the field, writhing in agony. Medical report yesterday: two torn knee cartilages. Out for the season.

After the game, someone asked Darrell Royal for an injury report. "We had one guy hurt celebrating," he said, shaking his head slowly. "I don't know how you coach that."

The defensive showboating is a comparatively new act. Perhaps the defenders resented seeing the halfbacks and the ends doing their tribal rites in the end zone. Now, when a defensive tackle recovers a fumble, he leaps to his feet, stretches the football high above his head in one hand as if to say, "Here it is! I did it! No. 73, Slugger Bochak in your program!"

And when a defender makes a particularly good solo tackle, he is apt to slam his hand into the ground in a fierce gesture of triumph, or jump up and swing a vicious fist through the air at some imaginary opponent.

Royal's offensive guys don't do any hotdogging. He tells them, "Don't act like it's the first touchdown you ever scored." But the Texas defenders are as openly exuberant as the next team.

Royal hastened to defend Crouch. "He hurt his shoulder early last year and he never got back in and nobody ever worked harder or ever was more faithful. Now he's playing again and I can understand his excitement at making the play."

But about the wild celebration rites?

"People didn't used to do that," said the coach, still shaking his head. "This is a different age we're living in."

Someone suggested a cure for the future. Take that segment of the game film, when Crouch's victory dance ends in embarrassing agony, and show it over and over to the squad. That would put a stop to it.

"Thanks," said Royal, as if he hadn't already thought of it.

GIANT STEPS

JANUARY 28, 1987

Once upon a time a large mercenary from Argentina named Luis Firpo came to this country and placed Mr. Jack Dempsey on the seat of his pants. As a matter of fact, the crude chap downed the heavyweight champ thrice and once whapped him through the ropes into pressrow where he did not have a ticket.

Mr. Dempsey quickly wearied of this treatment and when he got his bearings, knocked the senor bowlegged and went back to his hotel. The entire affair lasted less then two rounds, but it entered history books as a crackerjack event.

There was almost the same scenario a couple years back in Vegas when Marvin Hagler and Tommy Hearns staged the wildest slugfest in modern history. This one ended in the third round and it, too, was branded a classic.

The 1927 Yankees dusted the Pirates in the World Serious and oldtimers call it a great achievement. The tournament was over in four games, yet that sweep is remembered as a premium thrill of that era.

Now we have a Superbowl ending late in the third quarter and the critics call it a rum show. A stinkeroo. A dud. One-sided as a turkey shoot, said the wits. "It turned out to be another stinker in what is becoming an endless string," typed one L.A. critic.

Your quavering milquetoast here, clearing throat and squaring tiny shoulders, begs to differ. Actually, Superbowl XXI was a jimdandy for two quarters. In itself, that makes it a bargain.

Hey, the Dempsey-Firpo fight didn't go seven rounds, did it? It was a heckuva lot more one-sided than the Giants' victory over Denver and we made *it* a museum piece. Us lofty critics didn't badmouth Hagler's victory because he didn't stretch it to the limit and win in the closing rounds. In reality, Denver made the Superbowl a lot closer than the '27 Pirates made the World Serious.

Superbowl XXI was a corker for the first 35 minutes; for the last 25, it was *interesting*. It was a concert by a team that was superb, on that particular day, place and situation.

Denver didn't lay down or fold up or mutilate the field with mistakes. There was but one turnover the entire game. The Broncos simply were overwhelmed by an exceptional team of that one moment, running exceptional plays with exceptional execution. New York was a textbook.

The Giants may never—*probably* will never—reach that plateau again, but at Sunday dusk, we were seeing a classic team. That seems somewhat of a privilege.

There is one impudent Superbowl tradition that appears to be fading, and hooray for that. There was a time—and the Vikings and Cowboys and Colts and Chiefs remember it well—when the Superbowl *loser* was immediately clamped in dock on the village square and pelted with ripe eggs. The winner was lauded, but not as much as the loser was condemned.

Yet no one seemed to ridicule the Broncos. It was more a friendly pat on the head and a reaction of, hey, sonny, come back in a couple years when you've grown a little. Like a Marine recruiting sergeant might treat a resolute 10-year-old.

Perhaps the Giants also will improve, but somehow one gets the impression that the champs—given their peculiar personnel and their *location*— will self-destruct like most Superbowl winners. Any number of players will write books and there will be controversy therein. They'll make videos and appear on David Letterman and host cruises and endorse hamburgers and get divorces and make speeches and vie for attention and discover jealousy and buy longer belts and throw alarm clocks in the trashbin.

As you have noticed, it is easy for Superbowl winners to disintegrate. It will be even easier along The Great White Way. But for one afternoon in the California hills, as the saying goes, the Giants truly caught lightning in a bottle and it was interesting to witness.

Malice In Wonderland

EYE WITNESS

MARCH 29, 1977

ORLANDO, FLORIDA—The sequence was all so incredibly swift, maybe four, five seconds at the most, and yet in afterthought, it hung there suspended in time, like slow motion or instant replay or the old newsreel films of the Hindenburg breaking apart reluctantly in dark Jersey skies.

There was the tableau of Frank Lucchesi and Lenny Randle talking, calmly it seemed to these witnessing eyeballs some 40 feet away—the Texas manager and his embittered player, once again debating Randle's past, present and future with the Rangers. They stood maybe 18 inches apart, Lucchesi in his blue flowered shirt and gray slacks (he had not yet dressed for the game), Randle in his uniform, some 20 feet toward the Ranger dugout from the pre-game batting cage.

There was no raising of voices, or even these jaded ears would have picked it up; no animation, no gestures, no jabbing of forefingers, no distending of neck veins. It seems to this memory that both men had their hands on hips, not belligerently but naturally as a couple guys on the street corner argue the respective talents of the Longhorns and Sooners. Three, four minutes and conversation continued while your eyewitness here watched it idly, only vaguely curious at what appeared to be another review of Randle's discontent that he wasn't getting a full-scale chance at retaining his second base job from the challenge of rookie Bump Wills.

(The debate surfaced angrily last week when Lucchesi exploded that he was "sick and tired of some punks making $80,000 moaning and groaning about their jobs." The word *punk* was the fuse.)

Lucchesi had walked on the Minnesota spring diamond, said hello to a few fans, walked away for a private chat with Jim Russo, the Baltimore superscout. (Trade talk?)

The 48-year-old manager was en route back to the dugout tunnel to the lockerroom to get dressed when Randle approached. So the two men talked while Rangers took batting practice behind them, a cluster of players awaiting turns at the cage.

Suddenly with unbelievable quickness, Randle's right hand shot forth. No wild drawback nor windup, as a saloon brawler might use, but a straight strike from the body and here was Lucchesi falling slowly, turning to his right from the force, and there came a left with the same terrible rapidity. This was probably the blow that fractured Lucchesi's right cheekbone. Then another right and a left, all before the victim finally reached earth some 10 feet from where he was first struck. In personal reference, I have seen the handspeed of Sugar Ray Robinson and the cobra strikes of Muhammad Ali, but the flurry of Randle's punches, all landing on the manager's face, must have broken all speed records.

After Lucchesi hit heavily on his right hip, his left arm curled above him in some helpless defense attempt, there were other Randle punches, maybe they landed, maybe not, before Bert Campaneris reacted from four strides away. He had frozen at first, probably as others stared in disbelief, but sprinted quickly to the scene, leaped astride the fallen Lucchesi and stretched his hands out, palms up, to fend off Randle. The furious player backed away, yelling, "Leave me alone!" while Jim Fregosi and others reached the dazed victim.

Then, while players carried Lucchesi to the dugout tunnel, his right eye already blue and puffing, blood trickling from his mouth, Randle preceded them to the dugout, pulled a bat from the rack and held it briefly, then dropped it and trotted to the outfield where he began to run wind sprints all alone. This was maybe the only positive move of the day, for who knows what player emotions might have followed. Ken Henderson, especially, had to be restrained when he saw Lucchesi, sitting propped against the tunnel wall while trainer Bill Zeigler tried to administer aid and judge the damage.

No witness could remember any similar baseball incident. Fights between players, surely, even spats between players and coaches, but never a player felling his manager. Eddie Robinson, the Ranger vice-president arriving later, couldn't think of one. Sid Hudson, the veteran coach, shook his head. Burt Hawkins, the traveling secretary who watched Babe Ruth, also flunked.

So what prompted this unprecedented explosion? Randle, seemingly composed afterward, said Lucchesi had called him a "punk" again. Lucchesi, from his bed in Mercy Hospital, said this was a lie.

Was the Randle violent, savage action triggered by a remark in the apparent calm conversation? Was it a buildup of Randle emotions, of frustrations bred when he thought he was not being given enough chance to play?

A day earlier, Lenny had told Channel 4 interviewer Allan Stone, "I'm a volcano, getting ready to erupt."

"But," said Stone, "he was smiling when he said it."

If Randle's was a calculated action, would not a single punch have sufficed? What pushed him across the line into uncontrollable fury, an outburst that might end his baseball career forever? Probably no one will ever know.

In a corner of the dugout, by the bullpen telephone, while Ranger players milled about in stunned aimlessness, a small white card glared from the wall. It was the lineup for Monday's game. The second line read: Randle, 2b.

SKULL SESSIONS

JUNE 4, 1982

The week past was not one for logic, not as us straightlaces learned it at the feet of our forefathers.

In Ohio, a politico paid a prostitute with a personal check. In New York, George Steinbrenner began his second month without strangling anyone. At Buckingham Palace, Prince Charles got his royal lip split in a polo match, and in Wisconsin a man did a mating dance with a whooping crane and it worked. In Pennsylvania, two Pitt students started a rugby game by rolling several human skulls on the field.

The last event interested some of us older professors as we chatted over tea at the faculty club. We are not much on fertility aspects of the whooping crane, and we have forgotten the nuances of credit with ladies of the street. But skulls on a rugby field struck a familiar chord somewhere in the dark reaches. (Familiar chords, you realize, seldom show up in the *light* reaches. It has something to do with astigmatism.)

These Pitt students, unnamed by authorities, resigned from the university after their prank. The skulls, said the university report, were seven in number and were stolen from the dental laboratory. The report referred to the stolen property as "anatomical materials," but witnesses to the match said the objects were pure and simple human skulls.

Pitt officials were most secretive about the entire caper, stressing that the Oakland Rugby Club involved students but was *not* affiliated with the school, and that the match was not a Pitt-sanctioned activity. Goodness knows why the university was so gun-shy, unless the dean and his associates feared any publicity might launch skull-rolling as a new campus fad, like swallowing goldfish and panty raids back in prehistoric days.

Back to the skull-rolling. The components rattled around fruitlessly in memory and finally led your addled prof to a history book.

Sure enough, there it was. The Pitt students, unrecognized

by dean or opponents or even teammates, merely were commemorating. You have perhaps heard of re-enactment of buccaneer assaults in the Tampa Bay Gasparilla Festival each year. The battle of Bunker Hill is re-created as a part of some regional celebration. There is the Passion Play each Easter, staged on a thousand hillsides around the country.

These two students, by rolling the purloined skulls about the greensward, were celebrating the glorious start of soccer and/ or rugby, and the eventual birth of American football. The dean wasn't up on his history; he probably thinks, like the Great Unwashed, that American football was invented by Grantland Rice and Earl Campbell, under a grant issued by Alvin Rozelle.

There have been attempts to tie football to both China and Greece in a couple centuries both preceding and after the birth of Christ. And surely the Russians will claim its origin, as soon as Roone Arledge signs the Moscow league to a summer contract and puts it on the toob.

But most researchers credit football to 11th century England. The Danes had occupied England for about 30 years, and they were rather rough on the Tommys, kicking them in the pants frequently and occasionally lopping off a British head or two. After the Danes went back to their own shores, some English workmen were digging in an old battlefield and unearthed a skull of a Dane. History doesn't say *how* the workmen knew the skull belonged to a Dane, so it is to be assumed that it had a sardine in its teeth or some other identifiable mark.

Anyways, the Briton gave a whoop and kicked the skull forthwith and it rolled merrily on the grass and another workman booted the thing, and soon the work project had halted and the employees were happily kicking the gong around. This later became known as the WPA.

Small lads, watching their elders at play, dug up a Danish skull of their own and began kicking it around. But small lads usually went barefoot or, at the most, wore some flimsy foot cover and the hard skull was not a comfortable target. Some innovative youth substituted a cow's bladder and the kicking proceeded at much the same fervor, because the object was still regarded as the head of a hated Dane.

Early in the 12th Century, some basic rules were established and games were played between neighboring hamlets. Men would meet at a halfway point, the cow bladder was tossed down and the kicking commenced. The winner was the team that kicked the ball into the middle of the rival town.

Sometimes there were hundreds of players on each side and when a player couldn't get position for a swish at the old bladder, he simply kicked a player from the other town. This led to magnificent civic fun and many great bleeding welts. Players came charging through the streets of a small town, kicking at stray pedestrians and occasionally knocking over small buildings. At the time the game was still called "kicking the Dane's head."

Eventually, city dads wearied of having their property kicked full of dents, so they moved the activity to urban fields. And somebody even came up with the name of "futballe." It became so popular that King Henry II finally banned it because his subjects were spending too much time kicking that silly bladder, when they should have been practicing with their bows and arrows in case the Danes came back. After a couple of centuries, futballe crept back into English culture. And there, or course, it remained until Knute Rockne brought the game to this country on a vessel captained by the late Leif Ericsson and Tom Landry localized it with the Flex Defense. Those Pitt students should be lauded, not scolded, for recognizing history.

TIME AND PLACE

The basic fault, in all probability, has been compounded through the years. From the very beginning, your trusty correspondent never had a real solid working knowledge of mathematics. I was always getting the hypotenuse mixed up with the oxymoron and goodness knows what else.

Anyways, from those timorous beginnings, it got worse. I could never undertand why, if one ship could cross the Atlantic in seven days, that seven ships couldn't cross in one day. That one still brings on a throbbing in the temples, to tell the truth.

Through the years, the deficiency has grown so that I no longer understand simple distance, like in yards and feet and this newfangled thing, meters. This became noticeable some time past when I was confronted with a situation in San Francisco. In a baseball enclosure there, a chap named Juan Marichal took a stick of wood and tried earnestly to rend the skull of another fellow named John Roseboro.

It was no mere happenstance, like stepping on a rake and having the handle smite a neighbor on the honk. It was not even one angry spasm of reflex, as when a medic taps a patient on the kneecap.

Mr. Marichal, wearing the garments of the Giants, was at the plate, bat in hand, and Mr. Roseboro was doing the hindcatching for the Dodgers. One thing led to another and suddenly, the former took a hefty cut at the noggin of the latter. Not satisfied with the glancing result, he took yet another swing, this one landing more solidly and causing tears to come to Mr. Roseboro's eyes.

My childish frustration was this: I simply couldn't fathom the distance factor. Of course, that has been two decades past and you naturally assume I have learned better since. You are wrong.

As I understood it, had this incident occurred just 50 yards away, then Mr. Marichal would have been seized by the scruff, handcuffed and hustled off to the hoosegow where he would be allowed to make one phone call.

Fifty yards away would have been on the parking lot of Candlestick Park. Indeed there are strange happenings on parking lots throughout the land, many of them legal. But banging another citizen on the pate with a deadly weapon ain't one.

But because the assault happened *inside* the park, *on* the playing field, Mr. Marichal missed two pitching turns. That was his total punishment, assessed by Judge Warren Giles of the National League. Presumably if his blows had proven fatal, the guilty party might have missed an entire season, subject to appeal before arbitration board, of course.

It was noted recently there is a city councilman in Boston who also has this childish confusion with distance. When two hockey groups, such as the Bruins and Canadiens, start banging each other with sticks and spill off the ice into entrance ramps, whanging away with deadly intent, as they did last November, Councilor Bruce Bolling wishes to see somebody jerked up and jammed into the Black Maria for a trip downtown. He doesn't grasp the difference in distance.

According to the highdomes who run the NHL, an eye poked out intentionally on the ice is entirely different from one poked out intentionally in the $10 seats or on the parking lot outside.

There have been more and more bloody brawls in hockey, which often incite dangerous melees in the stands, and Mr. Bolling has his dander up. If gendarmes are called in to halt mayhem in the stands, why not on the ice just 15 feet (or 4.57 meters) away?

"If the league and owners and players want local, state and federal authorities to stay out of the arena, they're going to have to strengthen the rule and procedures that will curb the level of violence we've been witnessing," our fellow said stoutly.

He introduced a civic proposal to that effect. The poor man was voted down by the rest of Boston councilmen who obviously are much better educated in significance of distance.

FIRST BLOOD

NOVEMBER 1, 1979

The key phrase for this week, I suppose, is *Sucker Punch*. This supposedly is what Billy Martin struck one Joseph Cooper in a Minnesota pub, costing the latter a split lip and the former, his job.

Possibly the phrase needs some exploration. Too often, us esteemed journalists just *assume* the reader understands all the idioms which leak from quill to foolscap. A listener also, unless he asks questions, may be silently befuddled by nomenclature simple to others. You yourself have known children who reached puberty before they realized the hymn they sang on Sundays was not *Jesus, The Cross-eyed Bear*, but actually *Jesus, The Cross I Bear*.

Likewise, I remember a court case in Austin years ago when Bobby Layne, then a Detroit quarterback, stopped off to indulge in some heavy research with scholarly friends. Late that evening, Bobby was driving to his hotel, innocently enough, when he was sideswiped by several empty cars lurking at curbside. At Layne's hearing, the arresting officer testified that Bobby could barely talk coherently at the time of his accident.

Layne's lawyer explained that his client merely had a case of laryngitis.

"What?" the cop said incredulously. "A whole case?"

Anyways, there may be those out there, hearing *sucker punch*, who can picture Billy Martin hoisting a huge lollipop and pasting Mr. Cooper in the chops with same. Or perhaps, Martin dropped a mickey in the bowl Mr. Cooper was sipping from. And there are debonair men-of-the-world who think *sucker punch* is something you buy b-girls in joints along Bourbon Street.

In this Martin incident, however, the phrase describes a blow delivered to the teeth and gums while the recipient's attention is directed elsewhere.

94

"Oh, look, the Goodyear blimp!"

"Where?"

Pow!

The sucker punch probably began as the old shoestring gimmick. There's a yarn about a sneaky fighter named Kid McCoy, who knew all the tricks. One of his favorites was to clinch and say in his opponent's ear as follows:

"Hey, Gus, your shoestring's untied."

And when Gus glanced down, Kid McCoy would whang him on the button with all the force he could muster.

Once, however, he was boxing Gentleman Jim Corbett, who also knew some old verses.

In the third round, McCoy looked down and quickly said, "Jim, Jim, your shoelace is loose!" Whereupon Mr. Corbett fetched him a clout that put McCoy on the seat of his pants.

"While you're down there, Kid," Jim said politely, "I'd appreciate if you tied it for me."

The sucker punch became even more refined when Bob Hope and Bing Crosby made it standard equipment for all their Road movies, when they would do their pattycake, pattycake, baker's man routine and wind up double-parking some Mongolian ox on his prominent jawbone.

I can remember eons ago, while serving a Shore Patrol hitch in Astoria, Oregon, being aware that nightclub bouncers usually kept a cigar or a toothpick or match in their mouth in stressful times, so they would have excuse to keep one hand around their own face to block any sneak blows, or sucker punches, from belligerent customers.

Any barroom fighter will tell you the first punch is the biggie. And if the other guy ain't expecting it, if he's distracted or relaxed, so much the better. He's not braced nor prepared. There used to be an old honky-tonk brawler down in Central Texas named Poe Smith and he allus said, "Jist gimme the first one, and you can have the rest."

There was a scene in a movie called *Hooper* when Burt Reynolds and his pals knew they were in for a beer joint donnybrook. Reynolds pulled an old stunt. In a face-off with the rival leader, Burt turned his head to trade a joking comment with a friend and in the middle of his comment, he whirled and copped his Sunday on the guy's jaw. The guy didn't flinch.

"Fellows," Reynolds said wearily, "I think we are in trouble." If the first one didn't work, help!

When Billy Martin punched that Reno sportswriter, Ray Hagar, last winter, the victim explained it something like, "We were talking and he turned away, and suddenly I was down." The old Burt Reynolds turnaway.

Mickey Mantle once said of his pal: "Billy don't argue long."

When Joseph Cooper was hit, he said he was following Martin to the parking lot when the Yankee manager suddenly whirled and smote him in the mouth. "If I'd got to the parking lot, you're damn right I would have fought him. But I'm sure he had his plan that he would hit me before I ever got there. I assume all of his fights have been sucker punches."

So now you know about sucker punches. The Marquis of Queensberry never approved, but the technique is most effective if fistfighting is your kick. Unless some day you happen across a guy with a cigar in his face and a tire tool.

THE BRUISE BROTHERS

AUGUST 7, 1980

It is much the same as if you station a former Marine in a jungle path and hand him a Springfield Thirty Ought Six.

"In a matter of minutes," you tell him, "a rabid water buffalo will tear down this trail and attempt to rend you asunder. But do not shoot him with this gun."

So it is when you allow a defensive lineman to gird his arms with tape and padding and plastic and boxing gloves and then ask him please not to swat the gentleman on the other side of the line. *Certainly* he's going to club the bloke, with whatever haymaker force he can muster.

It has long been the contention of us old fogies that if you remove all that armor from a fellow's arm, he ain't going to be too eager to swat you with his own personal skin taking the brunt. You can remember hearing about Ernie Stautner, master of the forearm shiver, taking pains to avoid his own pain when he whacked a blocker under the mandible with his radius. Ernie would split a tape container and cup one half of the hard surface around each forearm and tape it in place. Probably Pudge Heffelfinger, an eon past, did the same thing with a copy of the *Saturday Evening Post.* Now linemen have special molded hard plastic forearm guards, the better to crack your dimple.

Just a few weeks ago, in conversation with Dave Nelson of the college football rules committee, a couple journalistic graybeards pressed the point. In fact, they found themselves waxing fairly warm on the subject. Furman Bisher, the Atlanta author, has a special chemical makeup that allows him to wax warmer than most. He made his point so strenuously that he flecked bystanders with a light froth.

"When you let a guy pad himself up like a gladiator, you invite him to slug the other guy," Furman roared intelligently.

"Well, what would you do about it?" asked Nelson, the Delaware athletic director and foremost authority on college rules.

"Outlaw all padding on the arms and the hands, by golly!" Bisher thundered smartly. "You see these guys with armor plating from shoulder to fingertips and all they do is use those arms like clubs!"

Nelson glanced at the other pressboxer.

"Me too!" the fellow yelled wisely.

Of course, the debate concerned reduction of football injury, the constant objective of the rules committee. Nelson had solicited ideas from a media group gathered at the Hall of Fame induction rites in Ohio.

"Heck, you see it in junior high!" Bisher continued in high key. "They watch the pros do it and they got to do it too.

"Some of these pro linemen wear leather boxing gloves, better protection than Jim Kilrain had when he fought 75 rounds with John L. Sullivan!"

"Jake Kilrain!" his partner corrected thoughtfully.

"Jake Kilrain!" Bisher recovered loudly.

"Well, the other man is all padded up," said Nelson. "How can you hurt him?"

"You can still hurt him with a *club!* You can jar him! Hit him on the helmet and bust his eardrums! Hit him on the side and bust his ribs! Cut out all tape, all padding! Make the rascals play barehanded! They're not going to club anybody on the helmet with a naked hand!"

"We have legalized soft casts for broken bones," said Nelson. "Are you going to tell a guy he can't play with a broken finger?"

"I don't know!" Bisher bellowed brightly.

Nelson said there is a much heavier problem in helmets.

More injuries are inflicted by helmets and because of wearing same than any other equipment. Head injuries, neck and spine injuries. And million dollar lawsuits, aimed by victims against helmet manufacturers, are a drug on the dockets.

"There are only seven companies still making helmets," Dave said. "Most helmet manufacturers are just a small part of a big conglomerate, and they represent a tiny part of their profit. And if they get soaked with a $2 million damage judgment, some fellow in a bottom-line office way up in that conglomerate, he'll say, hey, who needs this? Drop the helmet division.

"It may come to a point when we'll all have to get together, high schools, colleges and pros, and make our own helmets."

You might have fewer injuries, a guy said, if you played without helmets.

How about boxing headgear, suggested another, outlaw the hard plastic helmets and play in boxing headgear.

One of the college rule changes this year is to enlarge the facemask penalty. Some medics claim the facemask is a prime cause of neck injury, with opponents grabbing the bars or the plastic guards and wrenching the poor fellow's neck. This year, the penalty will include grabbing *any* opening in the helmet, grabbing under the side, under the forehead, under the back.

"There are always going to be injuries in football," said Nelson. "And players are getting bigger and faster than ever. I can see, within five years, we'll have 300-pound players."

"Has any coach ever thought that they're just building big muscle robots?" said an Iowa pressbox theorist named Maury White who still has lumps on his being from days as a 175-pound halfback at Drake. "I mean really, they do all this stuff with weights and vitamins and they actually manufacture massive muscle men. Their bodies are not the way God intended for them to be or He'd made them that way in the first place."

Nelson said it was a valid point.

"The human skeleton is not going to change," said Dave. "You can put 220 pounds on a skeleton designed for 185 pounds and you're building antagonistic muscle. It is not normal. It may work against you."

But that part of college football is not going to be altered, no matter how many necks are broken or how many femurs are splintered. Not as long as winners get raises and losers get fired. As Tarzan said to Jane when she greeted him with a martini: it's a *bleeping* jungle out there.

MUFFLED DRUMS

JULY 6, 1987

It was early on the Seventh Day and us savages hunkered around the campfire, gnawing our pemmican and jerky with a side order of chipped beef on toast. With occasional grunts of approval and disapproval, we kept keen eyes fixed on a small rawhide screen, where two palefaces slapped a white pellet across the sunburnt grass.

Suddenly from the contraption, there was a faint outcry in the background, such as a native child might emit when hunkering on a prickly pear. The action halted while some straw bonnet on a highchair sternly rebuked the offender. A second offense, he warned, would result in stitching of his lips.

Later on in the match (for this was an electronic transmission of the Wimbledon finals between Ivan Lendl and Pat Cash), activity again ceased while our trusty rebuker scolded customers who were fanning themselves with programs.

The day was hot in Londontown, and the poor blokes were trying to bestir a bit of breeze. But their waving cardboards were in Mr. Cash's sight range as he prepared to bat a pellet to Mr. Lendl, and it was most disconcerting to the former. The rebuker somberly informed the fanners that theirs was a disgraceful breach of etiquette and if the distraction continued, the culprits would be burned at a Centre Court stake as a part of the post-match rites.

It was enough for us savages. With a mighty grunt, we kicked ashes on the fire, mounted our cayuses and went looking for some buffalo to torment. I don't mind admitting, we gave a few yelps along the way. In derision, I suspect.

Of course, us primitives are always hard put to understand the enforced reverence of European games. In tennis and in golf, two regal pastimes originating across the big pond, on-lookers are sworn to ghostly silence.

At Wimbledon, uncouth vocalisms are out. Appreciation is limited to polite smacking of the palms, as us savages are wont to do when a mosquito flies between.

If a sainted golfer bends over a putt and some oaf rattles a couple dimes in his pocket two furlongs away, his nibs slowly straightens, rolls eyes to the skies and gives a sigh worthy of an unharnessed mule. In the gallery, heads swivel, shooting murderous stares at the coin rattler, who is expected to slink to the nearest grove and swallow hemlock. Let a photographer click his shutter while his nibs is on his backswing and USGA rules allow the plaintiff to remove a Smith & Wesson .38 from his bag and put a hole in the coarse fellow.

These two activities have been imported to these shores, I regret to say, with all their pompous regimentation. We go along. Years ago, at another newspaper, I recall a stripling named David Casstevens, assigned to cover the World Championship of Tennis at Moody Coliseum. During one of the royal matches, some fancied blueblood thought he heard the faint peck of a small typewriter. Heavens! Young Casstevens, piteously protesting his innocence, was summoned before the regal tribunal, his typewriter torn from his trembling grasp and a felt pen substituted with a supply of soft paper. The ignominy was too much for the shaken youth and the last I heard, he had changed his name and joined the Border Patrol.

In contrast, look at our own native games. Darryl Strawberry at bat at Shea Stadium, last of the ninth in the final game of the World Series, two outs, bases loaded, Mets down by three runs, count 3–2 and 60,000 gooks splinter the heavens with a din that causes tidal waves in Bermuda.

Larry Bird, time expired, at the free throw line of a tied rubber game in NBA finals. Behind the backboard (in Mr. Bird's sight range), they ain't just swishing cardboard fans. They're waving huge flags, shooting off howitzers, flash bulbs, smoke bombs and a couple attackers have fired blow guns.

Mark Moseley prepares a final field goal attempt in the Super Bowl. Does some celluloid collar command quiet?

But what do us savages know about combat manners? Heck, those proper lads of Cornwallis and Howe, when they marched through New Jersey woods, shoulder to shoulder, wearing bright red coats, they were behaving as true sportsmen, even in warfare. On the other hand, the poor Colonial farmers, shamefully ignorant of battle etiquette, chose to squat behind stone fences and fire their squirrel rifles and yell when they bloody well felt like it. Ugh.

Teed Off

LIVELY MIKES

MAY 9, 1980

On one of the next few days, Commissioner Deane Beman will send a stone tablet down from Mt. Sinai and inform his golf multitudes whether they shall be allowed to wear microphones around their necks while performing their work chores. "Miking" this is called, and it has come in for considerable golf tour conversation of late.

Miking is hardly a new item. Ever since Roone Arledge invented television, every director has this mad itch to stick a microphone in the White House powderroom or the sports equivalent. Let the viewer hear how it *really* is in the trenches.

Perhaps you remember the first Monday Night Football telecast with Dandy, Howie and Keithie. The game involved the Vikings and Fran Tarkenton was the Minnesota quarterback. This was an exhibition, and it was used as a trial run for the new Patti, Maxine and Laverne of the tv booth.

Tarkenton was not scheduled to play in this meaningless game, but he was in uniform on the sideline. ABC producers persuaded Tarkenton to wear a microphone, although this hardly required a filibuster, and ole Dandy and ole Howie carried on a jovial revue with ole Franny during the game. It wasn't a threat to Kukla, Fran and Ollie, but it was a novel approach.

The print media did a double flip off the high board. A typewriter guy would never be allowed to interview a player during the course of a game, so why should the boob toobers?

"Well, any time newspapers want to pay us $8 million, maybe they can do the same," said the Cowboys' Gil Brandt, a remark that now is engraved in the Newspaper Hall of Fame.

Pete Rozelle professed great indignation at this television invasion of bench privacy. You got the impression, rightly or no, that the commissioner had not been asked permission. Of course, he may have been reacting to the newsprint scream, but anyway, Pete bade immediate halt to such liberties.

However, tv producers are a dogged lot. You might as well try to halt a locust blight with a Louisville Slugger. They will strive and strive again. You shut the doors, they come in the windows. Shut the windows, they come in the door. The next time the Marines want Mount Suribachi, never mind the riflemen. Send a platoon of tv producers and they'll have the flag up and four Japanese privates underneath, singing *Jesus Wants Me For A Sunbeam,* while there's still enough sunlight to film.

To the tv producer, the prospect of a live microphone amid sports action is like heroin. The practice has infiltrated college football ranks. Coaches are leery of the distraction during the regular season, but several have permitted themselves to be wired up during bowl games. And for the post-season All-Star games, like the Hula Bowl and the Shrine, you can stick a bug in the huddle for all anyone cares.

It is not without some risk, if you wish to call it that. Two seasons ago, UCLA's Terry Donahue wore a mike in the Fiesta Bowl and he cut loose with one of those picturesque folk terms used around every barn lot in the land.

In a recent NBA playoff game, some tv guy jabbed his mike into a sideline conference and picked up some rather interesting twelve-word nouns that originated, I believe, in the British navy.

The announcers usually react with something brilliant like: heh-heh, the boys are pretty excited. And in the control truck, the producers are giggling at the added "flavor." The FCC may issue a harumph or two, but who cares. The horse is out.

There has been concern, among networks and the PGA itself, over declining ratings of golfcasts. The brains search desperately for ideas to spice the show, and still leave the sainted Game of Golf on its blessed pedestal. It was remembered that, years ago, on the old CBS Golf Classic and the like, those series filmed especially for television, the players wore microphones.

"What do you think this is, Arnie?"

"Well, Jack, I tell you. It looks like a five-iron to me."

I mean, this was realism! This was like the big boys talk in a regular tournament! Hot spit.

Commissioner Beman, from whom all edicts flow, gave a reluctant permission to experiment with live microphones in four tournaments. In the Heritage, the tv audience heard Tom Kite criticize the slow play of John Schroeder. (Tom didn't realize his mike was hot.) Heavens, what a brouhaha. You'd thought Kite had busted a stink bomb in the Vatican.

In the Tournament of Champions, Tom Watson was heard offering advice to Lee Trevino, his playing partner. A viewer remembered that was against the rules and called a complaint. Watson was penalized two strokes, but he had won the tournament by five. You wonder about the ruling had he been leading by one, don't you, you troublemaker?

Anyways, this has created a regular scandal and as a result, Beman probably will negate the live mike from now on, despite the fact that the two picayunish incidents have created more talk about golfcasts than anything in years.

Heck, if Beman *really* is disturbed about lack of interest, he *could* make the mike pack 'em in. Don't censor the eavesdrips.

"Hey, Joe, is that Albert on the seventh fairway? He's walking pretty brisk for a guy who got in at six ayem. You know the gal at the rent car counter at the airport, the redhead? He says she's got a tattoo of a cactus on her *bleep*."

"Fred told me that in Atlanta, the night I got him out of jail. By the way, he caught his old lady with Sammy the night he won the Hartsboro. Right after Ernie McGonigle bounced that check at Charlotte."

"Bobby is in big trouble anyway. Beman caught him cheating in Knoxville. Palmed a ball. Beman saw it on television. By the way, you got a cigarette?"

"Take one of these. They have less tar than any filter on the market, a doctors research institute says. They're mild, yet they have a man's taste."

"Thanks, what would really go good right now is a Natural Lite beer. It really does have less calories. Incidentally, you're away."

IN DEFENSE

JUNE 15, 1983

PITTSBURGH, PENNSYLVANIA—Whenever U.S. Open history books are cracked, Johnny Miller jumps out like a jack-in-the-box, worse luck.

Especially this week in this particular place, Johnny Miller will wear a festoon of fetching asterisks. It was here on Oakmont's exalted acres that J. Miller became a member of the Yes-But Association. You know the drill. Larry Holmes once kayoed Muhammad Ali. "Yes, but Ali was long over the hill." Roger Maris broke Babe Ruth's home run record. "Yes, but his season was eight games longer." Forward Pass won the 1968 Kentucky Derby. "Yes, but Dancer's Image finished first and was disqualified."

Johnny Miller shot 63 on the final round of the 1973 U.S. Open at Oakmont. "Yes, but horrendous thunderstorms had left the fairways soggy and true and the slick treacherous greens became gluey pussycats. The dangerous minefield on the Pennsylvania Turnpike became a sandbox for toys.

"With greens like that," wrote the noted Herbert Warren Wind, "it was more like darts than golf."

Even Gen. A. Palmer, a decorated veteran of several Oakmont campaigns, was scornful of his old battlefield.

"That's the only time Oakmont has ever been knocked out and if you take a look at it, nobody in the world thought that could happen," said Palmer. "But when the rains hit and they had the course set up a little easier than normal, it took everyone by surprise."

Miller's blasphemous deed was a first, of course. No one shoots nine birdies on a U.S. Open course, not after the USGA sadists finish with their evil alterations. Since then, both Jack Nicklaus and Tom Weiskopf have shot 63s, but theirs came in the first round of the 1980 event at Baltusrol and lacked the theater of a 26-year-old stripling going berserk on the final round, coming from six shots off the pole, leapfrogging 12 golfers, including five former Open champs, to win the whole brisket.

Mention any freakish aspects of that adventure 10 years past and you will still get a bristle from Miller. Here on the scene of his most spectacular day, he points out one established statistic of that particular round of golf. The national weather bureau will back him up. It did not rain just for Johnny Miller that night. Benevolently enough, the heavens opened for the whole crowd.

"To make excuses for that round is asinine," said Miller, typically blunt. "It irritates me the way people talk about it. The course might have been softer but it was still super fast and I still shot 63.

"Ask the guys who played that day. Only three guys broke 70. Is that easy?"

Of course, Palmer is one of those guys. In fact, he thought *he* had the blamed title in his sack, until Miller leaped out of the bushes and bit him on the flank. Palmer entered that final round tied for the lead with John Schlee, Julius Boros and Jerry Heard. Miller, who was six strokes behind, teed off one hour before Palmer. For some reason, Palmer was not aware of Miller's arson as the general played the front nine.

Not until Palmer was approaching the 12th hole did he realize he was *not* leading the tournament by one shot, but trailing one Johnny Miller by a stroke.

"Where did *that* blankity-blank come from?" he asked Schlee, staring at an unobscured scoreboard.

"He was shocked and so was I," Schlee said later. "When he found out he wasn't leading, it took all the fire out of him. He lost his drive right then." Palmer bogeyed the next three holes.

That one particular round changed Miller's career. "I have a tendency to be like Boros or Gene Littler," he was saying yesterday after an Oakmont practice round. "The Open made me reach a new dimension, made me raise my goals a rung or two. Before that, I was just one of the so-called young lions."

Miller, the prototype of all those blond, slimbellies who overran the tour in subsequent years, is now quick to point out his lethargy, his lack of drive. But he remembers very well those four straight opening birdies on that 1973 Sunday, those following approach shots that zeroed on the flagstick. And how the resulting confidence catapulted him into a fabulous 1974 season, in which he won the first three tournaments of the year, and five more before the calendar was torn off. "I went crazy," he said.

Now he makes a "nice living" playing golf, winning a couple times a year, going fishing when he chooses. It may come as a slight surprise to realize only Jack Nicklaus and Tom Watson have won more tournaments than Miller, in the last decade.

He gives himself no chance this week; a gall bladder attack has him on stomach tranquilizers. "I'll probably be the only guy this week smiling after a double bogey," he said with a shrug. He may have an operation next week, but that doesn't bother him either.

"I would have liked to have done more in golf but I don't deserve more because I haven't worked hard enough at it the last few years. Chi Chi Rodriguez says Nicklaus became a legend in his spare time. Well, I became a semi-legend in my spare time. I won't be remembered with the Hogans, Nicklaus, Palmer and those guys. I'll be rememberd with Middlecoff, Mangrum, and Boros. I don't have that special ego that drives a Nicklaus or a Watson. My ego says, hey, let's go fishing."

UNCLE JACK

APRIL 14, 1986

AUGUSTA, GEORGIA—This was the American doughboy marching down Broadway. All we needed was ticker tape and leggings. George M. Cohan's tears streaked his makeup. Old Glory whipped from every trellis, for it's a grand old flag, a high-flying flag.

This was heroic old John Wayne, played by Jack Nicklaus, bleeding from a dozen wounds, slashing about him with rifle butt and bayonet until the last foreign devil fell at his feet.

Who better, pray, but the gallant old Golden Bear, arrows stuck in his ancient backside, to fight off the young invaders? Who better than the greatest golfer ever, to protect these shores from alien forces who threatened to overrun our proud fairways and violate our pristine greens? Even if he's 46, creased and perhaps a bit bald under that yellow shag, it had to be our grizzled warrior defending the fort. Our main man. Perfect.

The Yanks are being pushed from the golf bulwarks, as you know, by all these chaps with strange hairdos and accents. They are from friendly nations, as far as we know, but there is naught comradely about their golf scores.

Foreigners have won four of the last eight Masters, our most saintly golf possession. They were threatening to completely bury the fading Yanks in this one. Seve Ballesteros, the Spaniard, swashbuckling as any buccaneer. Nick Price, the South African with bold disregard for Augusta's holy annals. Bernhard Langer, the German sharpshooter. Tsuneyuki Nakajima, the rising son, Tze-Chung Chen, also from the Pacific, Greg Norman, the great cruising shark from Australia. Will somebody, for God's sakes, call the Marines?

When the international Masters bunch swept into the final round, four of the five leaders served other flags. Norman was leading, Price, Langer and Ballesteros were back a notch. Only Yank among them was Donnie Hammond, who still gets a week on a disposable razor. You don't send a kid up in a crate like this.

Nicklaus held stoutly that he was in the hunt, but he was four strokes back, in golf's twilight zone and he had not won in two years, only once in *four* years and he had not won a *major* tournament since 1980. Frankly, if the foreigners were to be denied this prestigious plum, it would have to be someone like Tom Watson or Tom Kite to man the ramparts.

During the week, there had been countless theories on the advance of foreign forces. Ballesteros says the European tour is strengthening, and there were at least a dozen of those gents who deserved to be among the Masters field.

Price thought the adoption of the larger, more difficult American ball a dozen years ago is finally being utilized by foreign golfers.

Gary Player thinks perhaps the Yank golfer is getting too complacent because of relaxed qualifying rules and the abundance of prize money. There are, realize, 58 millionaires on the U.S. tour.

Others think foreign golfers benefit because the courses they learn on are pinched and shy of practice facilities, so the spacious American layouts, once the aliens become acclimated, are like a paid vacation.

Whatever, Ballesteros seems to win in this country whenever he puts mind and body to it. Langer and Norman have established U.S. bases in which they stack their American dollars. Come on over, boys, the loot's fine.

So this was the invasion Nicklaus thwarted, or at least delayed, in one of the most exciting Masters ever.

He did it, of course, with a spendid run of birdies on the back nine—taking only 30 strokes to tie the course record—en route to a splendid 65, spiking the flagsticks and sinking the putts. As as tribute to this remarkable man's longevity, consider that 20 years ago, he won the third of his six Masters, with a score nine shots *higher* than his 279 total last week.

The foreigners fired and fell back. Chen, the Taiwanese, was never a factor on the last day. The kid from Zimbabwe, Price, wilted under Nicklaus' birdie barrage. So did Langer, the German who won here last year.

Ballesteros, the pre-tournament favorite, played strongly until his approach shot caught the guardian brook on the 15th hole. Playing ahead, Nicklaus caught the noise from the prejudiced gallery that greeted Ballesteros' misfortune.

"It was a cheer, yet it wasn't a cheer," said Jack. "It wasn't a cheer that said somebody holed a shot, but that somebody had done *some*thing." At that point, Nicklaus and Ballesteros were knotted. Two holes later, Ballesteros caught another bogey while Nicklaus made birdie on the 17th.

During these adventures, the sounds were rocking the Georgia skies. "The noise was absolutely deafening," said Nicklaus. "When I walked from green to tee, I could not hear a thing."

There was a final foreign survivor to make a run, of course. There seemed no end to them. This one was Norman, who birdied four holes in a row and stood an excellent chance to tie the game old grizzly on the final hole, until he pushed his last approach shot into the crowd, trundled on the green and missed a 15-foot putt that would have sent the hectic day into a playoff. It really wouldn't have been just, to have any other finish. Or certainly not as dramatic.

After raising Old Glory again to its rightful standard, old John Wayne said, well, he guessed he showed them pilgrims he wasn't all washed up and he was tickled pink about it. Somehow the color didn't fit.

In Passing

THE TALLEST ONE

NOVEMBER 23, 1977

Maybe a half-dozen years back, the phone jangled and the voice dispensed with introduction or preamble.

"How come you never write anything about me anymore? Have you forgotten what a hero I was?" said the guy. "Get a pencil now. The name is O-B-R-I-E-N. There must be a lotta lies about me you haven't told yet."

Well, said the listener, *it is a well-accepted fact in my circles that you are nothing but a has-been and a popcorn has-been at that and a pressboxer does not help his image writing about pappy guys all the time. But,* said the callee, *there is this record somebody laid down the other day, Jim Brock, I think it was. That in 1937, you actually handled the ball on passes, runs, punts, and kickoff returns, interceptions, on 562 plays.*

And this was quite true. An average of 56 times a game, this 147-pound runt had teed himself up for monsters to mash.

"Did I do all that?" said Davey O'Brien. "Just a minute until I write that down."

Also, you missed only 14 minutes of action that entire season.

Grantland Rice watched the TCU quarterback and wrote, "The lad must be stuffed with scrap iron."

"Well," said O'Brien, "I must have been stuffed with something or other."

What O'Brien was *really* calling about embarrassed him. Any talk of his storied career at TCU, his all-time honors, his two fantastic seasons with the Eagles, his career as an FBI agent, he kissed off with a wisecrack.

For example, you'd ask him about his FBI days and he'd tell you about when he was a rookie and went with a raiding party of other young agents to a motel where a dangerous criminal supposedly was holed up. It was a simple operation and once

114

there, the G-men spread out and took cover in professional fashion, only to learn that no one knew how to load the shotguns.

O'Brien would never mention that he still holds the pistol marksmanship record at the FBI range in Washington.

Anyways, on the telephone, Davey hemmed and hawed about this or that or the Cowboys or TCU or having lunch sometime, and finally, got down to tacks. Just before Christmas, he and Janie left their Fort Worth home for a dinner party and when they returned, the Christmas tree lights had shorted out and part of his house had burned.

Included was the den, where a zillion O'Brien football awards were shelved—the Heisman Trophy, the Maxwell Trophy, the Sullivan Trophy, All-America certificates and statuettes, Hall of Fame plaques from pro, college and Texas groups.

"Melted that Heisman down to a lump," he said with a laugh.

Lightning probably struck it, said the listener, *proving you were never meant to have it in the first place.*

Anyways, O'Brien asked with sort of a nervous giggle, reckon how could he get some of those darn things replaced?

It was the first time, in two decades of hoorawing and hogwashing, I had ever heard O'Brien even hint that any of his fabled past had left a proud spot or two.

Oh, he would play the game with you, with only a hint of a smile on an ageless, impish face. One TCU season, he fielded and ran back 63 punts, an incredible average of six per game.

"I caught everything I could see," he'd say with a twinkle. "I never did like to see a punt hit the ground. You lose yardage, probably 25 yards a game, and it gets the ball dirty."

Still, that's an awful lot of punts.

"Don't forget, we had a great defensive line in 1937. The other teams had to punt a lot."

Well, they didn't kick out of bounds much, so they must not have been too scared of you.

"I thought you'd take it that way," he'd say with a frown. "They tried to kick out of bounds a lot, but I'd run up in the stands and catch 'em and run 'em back. You could do it in those days. Caught every thing I could find. Wasn't safe to put a ball in the air."

You ever fumble?

"No, never," he said. "Or maybe my memory is a little bad about fumbles."

Well, one time you punted 24 times in one game and that's another record.

"Yeah, but the reason wasn't very flattering. It was in 1936 and we played Mississippi State at the Fair Grounds in Dallas. The rodeo had just closed down and it had rained solid for four days and they couldn't clean the field. And all those horses . . . well, you can imagine what all was floating on the field. Sam Baugh was the starting quarterback, of course, but somehow they thought he might slip on something and get hurt. I played the whole game. If the field hadn't been covered with horse stuff, I wouldn't have played a down. That's how you get in the record books.

"Hey," he said, "you got any more records you want to talk about?"

Well, there were many more, most td passes in one season, only four interceptions during the national championship year of 1938, leading the conference in five different departments, shortest football player ever to be honored by a Wall Street tickertape parade, all those passing marks with the Eagles.

"Say, you got a stack there," said O'Brien. "That's more than enough for one lousy newspaper column. Why don't you do a series on me?

"I'm sure," he said, "that we could get together on price."

At the time of Davey's merciful death last week, there were many of us who thought of doing a series or *something* about the little rascal, but no matter how many records you tabulated, the honors you listed, the testimonials you solicited, the dang thing would come out a love story and who reads that mush anymore.

MAN OF LA MASSES

JANUARY 3, 1986

Regrettably, Bill Veeck will be recalled most for sending a midget up to pinch-hit for the St. Louis Browns. This is like remembering Robert E. Lee because he rode a gray horse named Traveller.

Oh, Bill did the midget stunt alrighty, signing Eddie Gaedel to a legit major league contract and, on the last day of the season, sending the little guy to the plate with the bases loaded. Gaedel, with a strike zone about the size of a Prince Albert can, walked on four pitches and forced a run across. It was one of the few the Browns scored that season.

With Veeck's death, the Gaedel Caper will be eulogized as a typical harebrained stunt of "Baseball's Barnum." Actually, it was much more than that. Veeck was anything but harebrained. He was mischievous and *fun* and bright and inventive and he read other than box scores. In fact, the midget stunt was a steal from a James Thurber short story. Anyone who is a James Thurber fan, of course, rates a special merit badge from this forum.

In Thurber's yarn, the manager sent a cocky midget to pinch-hit *the* game of the year, and the midget got carried away with the drama and *swung* at the last pitch and popped it up. The story closed with the midget waddling frantically over the horizon, pursued by a purple manager with a baseball bat. Veeck's active imagination was snagged by the plot, and several years later, he brought it to real life.

"I try not to break the rules, but merely to test their elasticity," he said with a wink. He made other owners, well, he made them uneasy.

What Veeck was, to this notion anyway, was the toughest old goat around. It was a bit of surprise to learn he had bought it.

Most of us had come to believe he was indestructible and would be there to hoist one of his beloved beers at the wakes of everybody else.

I remember Veeck at the 1982 World Series, on a bitterly cold Busch Stadium night. He sat in the row ahead, in a makeshift outdoor press box, with an old clackity portable typewriter balanced on a plank workbench. He was writing Series observations for a paper, *USA Today* or somesuch, and it was far from some typical jock stunt, with a ghost writer doing the composition. Bill wrote his own stuff, and it was professional and clever and dotted with classical allusions.

The rest of us were bundled like South Pole explorers and stood and stamped frequently and clapped mittens to get circulation going. Veeck was crowding 70 then, and he wore a wool shirt and a heavy cableknit cardigan sweater with a shawl collar. His head and hands and great flapping ears were bare and bloodless, and he never moved except to peck away at that antique keyboard. Hell, he didn't even *complain!*

He was the foremost example of fending life's ills with a sense of humor. He left a leg on a Pacific atoll, and he scorned the cosmetic advantages of a fancy prosthesis in favor of a plain peg leg right out of Long John Silver. Every few years, surgeons would whittle a little off the stump and Bill would get a longer peg and hump off to the tennis court. In 1960, doctors said he was dying of a nerve disease, so he sold the White Sox and moved to a Maryland farm to raise flowers until his time came. To nobody's surprise, he beat whatever illness it was and bought his way back into baseball for another term.

His promotions were many and storied, and others will recount them with delight. But he was first a baseball man.

"Nobody is more aware of the fact that a ballclub must sell baseball and win games," he said. "But you don't sell baseball without dressing it up in bright colored paper and red ribbons."

But there were other reasons Veeck reached pedestal status with some of us. He refused to wear a tie, for one thing. To heck with it. He preferred the lunchpail crowd over silk stocking row. During his games, he would be found sitting alone in the far bleachers.

"I have noticed, in my years of moving around a ballpark,

that the knowledge of the game is usually in inverse proportion to the price of the seats," was another Veeck wisdom.

Another thing, he married a raving beauty from Oklahoma City, Mary Frances Ackerman, whom we once knew as the advance publicist for Ice Capades. We all figured that if a homely, creased, freckled, balding, peglegged old camel could charm a doll like Mary Frances, then he must be pretty much a work of art his ownself, which, of course, he was.

PICTURE PERFECT

JANUARY 17, 1986

And then there were none. Some cynics say there never *was* any.

Some saw The Four Horsemen as commercial products of a giant publicity stunt, but don't come around here with that noise. Ms. Sophia Loren got her share of ink also, but she also was very much a real-life doll and, if you must know, a warm personal friend of mine, and I count it an irritating quirk of fate that she mislaid my number last time she was in town.

Certainly there was publicity involved in The Four Horsemen's place in football history, as they were first to admit. Jim Crowley, the old, slick-haired, laughing Irisher who died this week, loved to relate the Horsemen legends, if it included attentive ears and a wee spot of the pinchbottle.

Some years ago, at the opening of the Football Hall of Fame, a few attentive pressboxers sat around a festive board until early light, listening to Crowley and Don Miller, the surviving Horsemen. Gosh, they were 75 or so at the time, but they were delightful long-stayers. They had told the stories so many times, their timing was perfect as they passed the narrative back and forth, never looking at the other when they dropped a disparaging quip, as Fred Allen and Jack Benny might do an old vaudeville routine.

It so happened, one Friday night in 1924, that Grantland Rice and a couple pressbox pals took in a film. *The Four Horsemen of the Apocalypse,* probably starring Rudolph Valentino with mascara and flour on his face. The next afternoon at the Polo Grounds, as the Notre Dame lightweights raced through West Point tacklers, a guy nudged Granny.

"Like that movie we saw last night," he said.

"What?"

"The Four Horsemen," said the nudger. Granny nodded thoughtfully, and started pecking away. *Outlined against a blue-gray October sky, the Four Horsemen rode again. In dramatic lore they are known as Famine, Pestilence, Destruction and Death. These are only aliases. Their real names are Stuhldreher, Miller, Crowley and Layden* . . .

In those days, that was pretty heavy stuff. Now, of course, the pressbox abounds in Greek scholars and such, who may quote liberally from the works of Mr. Mick Jagger and Mr. Jackie Sherrill.

Rice's syndicated column was published in several hundred newspapers and by time the Irish finished their train ride home to South Bend, The Horsemen were known coast-to-coast. An enterprising Notre Dame student named George Strickler (later sports editor of the *Chicago Tribune*) borrowed four horses from his pop's livery stable, hired a photographer, posed the backfield, in full uniform, atop the steeds.

"When I was a kid, I had a pony," said Crowley, "so I knew something about horses."

"Is that the reason you used a stepladder?" said Miller.

Strickler sold prints for $1 and sacked $60,000 for his part. It became the most famous sports photo ever and is still reprinted 60 years later.

The Horsemen also cashed in. Once college eligibility was finished, they joined barnstorming pros. "One week, we each made $4,000," Miller remembered." "They would advertise The Four Horsemen would play with such-and-such team. Sunday, we played with the Hartford club against Cleveland. On Wednesday, we played with Pottstown and so on. Then we made individual deals. Jimmy and I would play with a team for $500 and they would still advertise all Four Horsemen. Once I got $500 to play against Red Grange and the Bears. Jim made the same deal, but he would agree to play only one quarter. I had to play all 60 minutes for my money."

"Yes, but I scored all 13 points before I left," said Crowley.

There was not a bum among them. All got degrees and all did some coaching before entering private ventures. Miller became a federal judge in Cleveland. Crowley represented the municipality of Philadelphia. Layden was vice president of a transportation outfit. Stuhldreher was vice president of U.S.

Steel. They made hundreds of appearances together, the four of them, then three, then two and finally there was just Crowley, who lasted 83 seasons.

"We certainly never thought the Horseman thing would last as long as it did," said Miller. "There were other Notre Dame backfields better than us."

"Not so," said Crowley.

VANISHING BREED

Everyone will have a favorite Abe Martin story. Everyone, that is, old enough to remember when it was a sign of hard times to wear faded jeans and tennis shoes to school.

Abe was a vital part of the relaxed Post-War era in the Southwest Conference, the last of the Old School coaches with their cigars and spittoons and ashes on their vests and thatched creases on the backs of their sunburnt necks and broadbrim hats pulled low over squinting eyes. These were the clannish rivals—Matty Bell, Dutch Meyer, Jess Neely, Homer Norton, Morley Jennings—who warred fiercely every Saturday during the fall, and fished and played dominoes together in the off-season. And trusted each other enough to shoot dice over the telephone.

Ole honest Abe was the last in that particular fort before it fell to the invasion of the Royals and Broyles, the crowd in shortsleeve, white buttondowns with striped ties, the whippersnappers who dashed for the golf course and wouldn't know a domino from a barndoor crappie. Oddly enough, Abe was the last of the pocketwatch bunch and one of the first to depart. Only Norton preceded him in death. The rest of those tough old eagles are still around and will mourn Abe in the manner of oldtimers, a slight shake of the head, a remembered incident or two, a trip to the closet for the black suit, and then a change of subject. When you've passed 70, you've won already.

Anyways, the Abe Martin entry from this collection goes back to some forgotten TCU game when the Frogs were getting beat in the fourth quarter. Abe got down from his favorite sideline perch (he liked to sit on the back of a folding chair with his feet on the seat) and motioned to a substitute on the bench. He put his hand on the lad's shoulder.

"Jackie, you see what ole Billy Bob's doing out there? That No. 76 is eating him flat up. Ole Billy Bob's trying to take him to the inside and No. 76 keeps going to the outside. Now I want you to go in there and block No. 76, put him on his pants, Jackie, do you hear?"

"I'll try, Coach," said the player.

Abe dropped his hand. "Go back and sit down, Jackie," he said. "Ole Billy Bob's *trying!*"

For some reason, Abe always reminded me of a fictional character in the distant past named Scattergood Baines. He was the central figure in a series of magazine stories written, I believe, by Peter B. Kyne, either in the old *Colliers* or *Saturday Evening Post.*

Scattergood Baines was a crackerbarrel philosopher who ran a general store and he was a great one for sitting in a rocker and whittlin' and solving all the neighborhood problems by applying old-fashioned horse sense.

Farmer: "I got a horse that walks normal sometimes and then sometimes he limps like his front right leg was broke. I don't know what to do about it."

Scattergood: "Next time he don't limp, sell him."

Abe Martin wasn't the world champion philosopher but he had that oldtimey Jacksboro way of reducing things to the lowest common denominator. When Bear Bryant and Royal and Broyles came in the league, there was much coaching talk about "pursuit" and geometrical "lines of pursuit."

"Shucks, we allus had that," said Abe. "Only we called it chase-um."

Abe didn't get the attention with his downhome homilies as Royal does, or Abe Lemons, but he did have a language all his own, sometimes ridiculed by younger wise-alecks around him. If Abe heard their laughter, he never acknowledged it, knowing that all young know-it-alls grow up some day to have doubts of their own. He kept on using words like shistlepott (we never knew what *that* meant) and peckerwood. "Yew bet" was his favorite expression. Football was pronounced foo-et-ball.

Another favorite memory was of Abe's television show during the TCU foo-et-ball season. Jim Brock, the Cotton Bowl boss, was the TCU publicity man at the time and he served as Abe's interlocutor. It may have been the worst television show of all time, or the best. We wouldn't dare miss it.

On one show, TCU game films were being shown and Brock called attention to a particularly good block by a Froggie.

"Eye dogies, you're right, Jimbo!" said Abe. "Ah'm gonna hafta buy that peckerwood a cream cone!"

Now how long has it been since you heard somebody say "cream cone." Like that oldster used to say in the chili commercial, well, it's been *too* long.

It's not the most pleasant topic, but one revealing story about Abe happened back during the season of 1966. His brother was felled by heart failure. During the first week of training, two oldtime friends, Dr. Sadler, the TCU president, and Amos Melton, a former sportswriter, went the same way. An English professor visited Abe's family and became a heart victim on the way home.

Abe's elderly father was stricken by gangrene and placed in a Fort Worth hospital in critical condition. His mother was ill in Jacksboro. Abe handled all details. He rushed daily between the Fort Worth hospital room, to the Jacksboro bedside of his mother, then back to the practice field. His Frogs had won only two games of seven and talk was beginning again that the modern game had passed Abe by. Abe started getting midnight crank calls.

At dawn the Saturday of the Texas game, Abe sat on the edge of the bed and made a quiet phone call, careful not to wake his family. He dressed, let himself out of the house quietly. On the porch, he put on a pair of dark glasses, pulled his hat brim low over his eyes, walked to the waiting car of basketball Coach Buster Brannon. At the hospital, they told Abe he'd had a heart attack. He beat that rap and got a dozen more years out of life before his next one and we're all grateful for that.

RARE SNAPSHOT

MARCH 13, 1987

To my recollection, this place was on the east side of the Loop, not far from where you disembarked the elevated from Comiskey Park, near the headquarters Sherman Hotel. It was big and dark, of course, and had an oval bar in the center. On the way back from a White Sox game, some press whippersnappers stopped in by chance, after intriguing music drifted through the door and onto the sidewalks.

It was during College All-Star Week in Chicago, once the grandest football gathering of the year, for college and pro coaches, press, former players, hucksters and whatnot. It was like a political convention, only for the football crowd.

Inside we found why the music was strangely tempting. On a side platform was a band called The Dukes of Dixieland, an outfit some of us had long attended at the Famous Door in the French Quarter of Noo Awleens. So we perched at the bar to heed *Rampart Street Parade* and *Muskrat Ramble* and such delights.

After eyes gained night vision, we noticed a rugged, stocky, bullneck fellow in a neat beige suit sitting directly across the oval, eyes fixed on the band. He was all alone, empty stools on each side, an ignored glass in front of him.

The guy looked most familiar and there came one of those dreadful nagging questions, so worrisome that we couldn't concentrate on the music.

Finally it dawned. None of us knew the guy personally, but we placed the face. It was Woody Hayes, who even then, more than three decades past, had the reputation of a man-eating terrapin. And there he was, completely out of character, unattended, unrecognized, a beatific smile, eyes half-closed, forefinger firmly thumping the rhythm.

Oddly enough, when the bulletin announced that Woody Hayes died in his sleep at a stricken shrunken 74, that was the first image that popped into personal focus. Not the tyrant who raged the sidelines at Ohio State, who shoved photographers and slugged opposing players and bullied media.

There is another memory, at another All-Star week, Woody as speaker at the annual Football Writers Association luncheon. The talk was superbly constructed, with a beginning, middle and end and with historic, even classical references, and delivered with only an occasional glance at notes.

Football was only a vague theme in the speech; philosophy took over. Woody quoted from Ralph Waldo Emerson: *For every strength there is a consequent weakness. For everything you have missed, you have gained something else. And for everything you gain, you lose something.*

I was no goggle-eyed hero-worshipper even then, but I was fascinated at the way this renowned ogre put together words and theories and presented same. He could have been addressing the United Nations, instead of a profession for which he had little patience or respect.

Woody was a devoted student of military history and his hero, as you would guess, was George Patton. He found football connections all over the place. An Ohio State quarterback, Rex Kern, was from Lancaster, Ohio.

"Do you know another great leader from there?" Woody once asked. "General William Tecumseh Sherman. He's the man who ran an option play right through the South in the Civil War. If you study your history, you'll find Billy Sherman's march to the sea used the *alternative objective approach,* striking over a broad front. The defense never had a chance to dig in. Then a hundred years later comes a fellow from the same little town, Rex Kern, and the way he ran that option play gave our Buckeye attack the same offensive versatility Billy Sherman had."

Well, I don't know about *that.* Sounds too deep for a press-box mind. Most will remember Mr. Hayes, as was often said, "indomitable in victory, insufferable in defeat." But I never witnessed him as an arrogant monarch, but rather one who could close his eyes, spread a grin over his broad face and keep time to *Basin Street Blues.*

MAIN SPEAKER

MAY 7, 1986

Parking space was still available and coffee was a nickel with free refills, which makes it maybe two eons ago, give or take an era. The scene was Mission Stadium in San Antonio, where the Fort Worth Cats were opening their first series with the locals. The visiting press—all two of them—were a bit curious, for this was their first look at Baltimore's young prize, a teenager infielder from Arkansas who was being polished in the Texas League.

Mission manager Joe Schultz used the phenom at shortstop that particular game and the big, sorta awkward lad booted a couple ground balls and looked unsure on a couple more. A tall, skinny chain smoker, a Baltimore executive on inspection tour, watched silently from the roof pressbox.

"*This* is your hotshot?" a Fort Worth reporter kidded.

"Don't worry about him," said Paul Richards. "He'll play 10 years in the major leagues and he'll be a great one."

The kid was Brooks Robinson, and Richards was short in one respect. He played more than 20 seasons en route to the Hall of Fame, and some say he was the greatest ever to play third base. This was Richards' strong point for 60 years in baseball: His evaluation of talent.

In a casual conversation after his retirement, Brooksie said Paul Richards knew more baseball than any man he ever met. Paul read that compliment in a Dallas column, and it pleased him greatly. He was not without ego, nor opinions nor time for the baseball theory discussions he loved. He probably had more buddies among pressboxers than any baseballer ever; he read all their words and he seemed to prefer their company, which made him an odd duck in many opinions. And, of course, they loved his stories and his memories and his frankness.

We all had about decided that Richards was indeed the indestructible man. He had survived several serious operations and a bypass or two, and for 20 years, you wouldn't have taken even

128

money he could climb a flight of stairs. He was skin and bones, but he could go through a platter of babyback ribs like a liberated POW. And if you accompanied this 77-year-old codger to the golf course, you would come home considerably lighter in the wallet region. It was entirely fitting that death came Sunday as he sat in a golf cart on his beloved Waxahachie home course. If perchance he had just finished taking a sawbuck or two from his cronies, it would be about the perfect exit.

Paul had many assignments in baseball, of course, from player to general manager. In between deals, he frequently was a consultant to baseball interests hereabouts.

In 1969, when Lamar Hunt and Tommy Mercer sought a franchise, Richards accompanied them to the Chicago meeting, bluntly said the asking fee—I think it was $10 million—was highway robbery and they would be suckers to pay it. He said this, even though he probably would have wound up with a big job in the new franchise, right in his own backyard.

A few years later, Paul was playing golf with Eddie Chiles, who had just added the Rangers to his extensive oil empire. A check for soft drinks arrived and Chiles suggested that Richards, a close man with a dime, stand treat.

"After all, Paul's got more money than the rest of us," Chiles joked.

"I will have," Richards said dryly, "if you insist on staying in baseball."

In 1965, Richards wrote a treatise on the ills of baseball, on the union troubles ahead and made several radical suggestions. He would make *all* players free agents after their eighth season. And from then on, a player would become a free agent after *every* season.

Under that plan, a veteran's value would depend on his most recent numbers and this would spur maximum efforts and eliminate the lethargy suspected in many performers under guaranteed multi-year contracts.

Another time, when union chief Marvin Miller skinned the owners out of their breeches, Richards proposed shutting down major league baseball for five years and starting all over. Take bankruptcy, like, and then reorganize. This would eliminate the weak sisters among owners, he said, and restore some financial reason to the business. The fact that most owners greeted this idea with horror illustrates what a solid plan it was.

Richards loved to talk strategy: the finer points of running a game, the managerial maneuvers sometimes called "inside baseball."

"Once when I had the White Sox, after a game in Yankee Stadium, a guy came to me and said there just wasn't enough good "inside baseball' anymore, nobody used good old-fashioned strategy.

"Well, I told him I thought we had used pretty good strategy that day. We moved three runners up without a bunt or hit-and-run. We scored from second base on a passed ball. Minnie Minoso stole three bases.

"I told the guy I thought we played pretty good inside baseball until Casey Stengel brought in two guys named Mantle and Maris and starting playing *outside* baseball."

I don't recall Richards ever refusing an opinion on any subject. You could count on one hand the times he ever said, "I don't know."

A favorite example came a few years back when Eddie Chiles called a special press conference. The Rangers had been in a big slump, and there was talk this and that guy might be fired or benched or whatever.

Chiles got all the penpushers and the goldythroats together at Arlington Stadium and gave a dissertation on exactly nothing. I mean, there were a lot of words but all added up to a long string of noughts. The whole statement, broken down, amounted to about a half-pint of froth.

Richards listened intently and afterward turned to an old pressbox chum. "Whatever Eddie said reminds me of the slogan we used to have on the old *Waxahachie Light,* printed right under the masthead every day: 'We are for an early spring and against the boll weevil.' "

Hoops
And Hollers

AIR BORNE

MARCH 7, 1983

The other night, these very baby brown eyes saw Darrell Walker perform a big fat lie. People have been impeached in public office for less.

Walker and his Arkansas mates were toying with Texas Tech and the senior guard went skyward for a layup from the right side. The ball was grasped like a pomegranate in his right hand. A Tech paw was somehow in his aerial path, so Walker switched the ball to his left hand. Another opposing palm showed up in *that* route. Walker flipped the ball back to the original hand and just as he was about to come back to earth, he flipped an under-hand spin at the backboard and the ball somehow banked in.

This, of course, is impossible. It is about as close to a false-hood as things get in his league. Not the shot. There is no such item as an impossible basketball shot. But the length of time Walker spent airborne was a lie.

This was like the prisoner who addressed the court after his sentence was pronounced as a $10,000 fine and 15 years in the joint.

"Judge, I just can't imagine no way I can raise $10,000," he said stoutly. "And as far as the 15 years goes, that's simply out of the question."

There was no mathematic that could explain the successful shot, and Walker's hang time was simply out of the question.

If you'll pardon personal reference, I remember the first guy I saw hang from a sky hook. This was at a little Navy air base in Arlington, Washington, where things were so pleasant that the enlisted men's chow hall had a salad bar, but that's another story. It was at a pickup basketball game on an outdoor court that this stubby New York turret gunner with a ducktail haircut took the ball and sprang approximately eight feet in the air and tucked his feet under him and remained for oh, a half-hour or so.

Other clods on the court stopped and stared at each other.

Most of us were vaguely familiar with Sir Isaac Newton and his falling apple. Yet here was this jerk from the Bronx playgrounds suspended in the air like a Houdini assistant. Obviously someone had repealed the law of gravity while we were in the boy's room.

Several years later I threw ignorance to the winds and asked some basketball coach, I think it was Buster Brannon, how come these new players could hang in the air like a balloon. Did they drink helium in their milk or some darn thing?

"They don't hang any longer," said Buster, looking at me curiously. "They just jump higher and it takes them longer to come down."

Maybe so. Obviously these guys are jumping higher, just as they run faster and lift more weight and make more money. So we probably should be considering height rather than hang time.

There were others before, but David Thompson brought national recognition to jumping ability while leading North Carolina State to the 1974 NCAA title. Here again, it didn't seem to be the height that was so impressive (because all these guys congregate above the rim) but the length of time he stayed up. This became more noticeable when Thompson and his fellows started faking one shot, then switching the ball from hand to hand, or changing positions and approaches or whatever while still suspended. The more hand action taking place, the more noticeable the time elapsing.

Vertical jumps are measured now, of course, by football as well as basketball prospects. Rick Sund of the Mavericks says there are two types of measurement at two different sites for prospective pros. The sites are the Aloha Classic all-star game in Honolulu and the NBA tryout camp in Chicago. Also, players are first measured from a standing stance, and next they are allowed to take one step and *then* jump, which supposedly makes a lot of difference.

Bob Griffin of the Cowboy scouting force says vertical jump measurements are conducted by putting chalk on the player's fingertips and having him touch the wall with upstretched arm. Then his fingers are chalked again and he leaps as high as he can and touches the wall again. The vertical jump distance is the difference between those two marks.

"For football players, anything over 30 inches is pretty

good," said Griffin. "Around 35 is really exceptional. Rod Hill is probably our highest jumper and I think he was about 35 inches."

On the other hand, David Thompson supposedly had a 42-inch vertical jump! Marvin Delph, the Arkansas springer of a few seasons ago, was measured at the same height. Mike Cooper of the Lakers and Sidney Moncrief of Milwaukee are in the 38–40 range. The Mav's highest are Elston Turner, Kurt Nimphius and Bill Garnett, all in the low 30s.

Then there was that little runt from Wilmer-Hutchins High two years ago, that 5-2 Spud Webb who could dunk a basketball! Now if you figure his arm could reach an abnormal 25 inches above his head, young Spud would still have to leap about 45 inches to get the ball high enough above the rim to dunk it.

This Houston Cougar bench, heck, they spend more time a foot above the basket than they do in the classroom. They must *all* be 36-inch jumpers or more.

Still there seems something spectral in watching these flesh-and-blood creatures float above the earth for awesome instants. I never believed it when that smart aleck from the Bronx stayed airborne in Arlington, Washington, and I don't believe it now. Max Schulman once wrote about taking his girl friend to the beach, where she left him for a divinity student she saw walking on the water. She later discovered the chap was wearing history's first pair of water skis. That's why you see old Sam Spade here forever snooping around under the backboards. There must be a pogo stick around here somewhere.

DREAM DUEL

MARCH 26, 1979

SALT LAKE CITY, UTAH—At courtside, Jud Heathcote is an angry man, or an unreasonable facsimile.

He's the stocky guy in the dark green blazer with a green polka dot tie, thinning strands brushed forward in a Napoleon hairdo. He's forever smacking fist against palm, shouting firece unintelligibles into the din that engulfs all NCAA basketball playoffs. He glowers when his Michigan States are behind, he glowers when his Michigan States are in front. When his Spartans swept 15, 20, 30 points ahead of Penn in the semifinals, Heathcote looked like he had just been given a traffic ticket by his mother-in-law.

Off the court, the Michigan State coach is pleasant and composed and he talks somehow like a circus poster. His tone may be lacking in animation, but the wordage is there.

"I am caught up, like everybody, in the idea of the confrontation between The Magic Man and the The Bird Man," said the coach, previewing tonight's championship game in the Utah arena. He sounded like a broadcast goldythroat had written his script, but that's the way he speaks.

Most coaches hesitate to use the theatrical nicknames applied to their charges, and also to admit they have one star far above everybody else wearing his uniforms. Not Heathcote.

He was plugging the duel between his Earvin (Magic) Johnson and Indiana State's Larry Bird. In their respective semifinal victories, both were slightly sensational.

"I could not believe The Bird," said Heathcote, in his press agent's idioms. "I was amazed. I said that's not a Bird, that's a whole flock."

He spoke in glowing terms of The Bird's scoring proficiency, his wide variety of shots, his showy passing—behind the back, around the neck, between the legs, looking starboard and passing port, all the tricks the big blond delights in pulling.

"We still believe we have the best *complete* passer in The Magic Man," said Jud.

Then he speaks of Greg (Special K) Kelser, the target of The Magic Man's passes. Honest, he calls him Special K, just like the pressboxers. These two, Heathcote admits frankly, are his superstars. The rest of the team he refers to as "the supporting cast," a reference most coaches had rather choke than make.

After the Penn carnage, Heathcote said, "Our two superstars were super. Our supporting players continued to play well."

Even the two focal points of the finals joined in the billing. When Bird first considered the so-called duel, he demurred.

"We don't match up," said the reluctant Bird Man. "We're different players. I'm a scorer, he's a passer."

Later, however, Bird said, "Well, I guess this is what the writers all dream about, two guys like us in here."

"I guess I could say there's two of the best passers in the game in this match-up," said the younger, eager, more talkative Johnson. "It's what the whole world wants. Everyone wants to see the Magic Man against the Bird Man."

This particular individual match, the dream of any television huckster, seemingly has been the ideal goal of the entire NCAA playoff procedure. With each progression came added excitement. Saturday afternoon here, while Michigan State was burying Penn early in the second half, the Spartan cheering section began a chant: "WE WANT THE BIRD! WE WANT THE BIRD!" Two students held a big banner: "The Bird can score, but Magic does more."

Actually, both players do a lot of everything: Johnson is not heralded as a great shooter, but he hit nine of his ten field goal attempts against Penn, made 11 of his 12 free throws, leading his team in scoring was well as rebounds and assists. Bird also is a strong factor on defense, sweeping the defensive boards with almost brutal power.

Mostly, the pair has been compared as passers. Bird is more the trickster, with his Harlem Globetrotter passes. Magic zips the ball from his chest with stunning velocity. Or he will palm the ball in one big hand, flip it like a softball pitcher to any range. Or his favortie stunt, lobbing the ball high so that it comes down just short of the rim, where it is met by a rising Kelser, who then dunks while witnesses go quite wild.

When Johnson completes a pass that results in a basket, he glories in it. He leaps in the air and strikes out with his clenched fist and yells like Tarzan signaling lion for supper.

Bird said he learned his passing in high school in the great metropolis of French Lick, Indiana. "I grew up all of a sudden," said the 6–9 senior. "I was a guard as sophomore and junior in high school, before I grew up and we had some great shooters. I tried to get the ball to the great shooters. Passing is so much part of basketball it's unbelievable. It don't matter who scores the points. It's who gets the ball to the scorer."

Off the court, the comparison ends. Bird is big boned, strong, a blond with a mature body, a childish face with a wispy white moustache that looks like a little boy wearing his father's trenchcoat.

Johnson is but a sophomore, but appears older than the normal college soph. He's one of those loose black kids whose legs start right beneath his sternum.

Johnson is as effervescent as Bird is reticent.

"I love it, I love all this attention," Magic told reporters here. "I just eat it up. As long as you got the questions, I got the answers."

Bird put the press off-limits during the regular season. The interviews were taking up too much of his time, he said, and none of the media was talking to his teammates, only to him. "It got to a point where I wasn't having no fun in college," he said.

But he is making what appears to be a sincere effort during the Final Four tournament. He is talking to the press, although he said he still doesn't like it. "If you all were paying me, it would be a little bit different," he said in jest, or maybe not.

Bird would love to find himself a cave in the neighboring mountains, emerge only to play a game, and then returning immediately. Johnson would lead songs in the hotel lobby if someone asked him.

"I strive on pressure," said The Magic Man. He probably meant "thrive" but again, maybe not.

OPPOSITES ATTRACT

MARCH 26, 1982

NEW ORLEANS, LOUISIANA—What we have here, obviously enough, is a game of cops and robbers.

In this corner of the Superdome, we have the cops, played by the North Carolina Tarfeet. Disciplined and stern and unbending as any military policeman you ever saw drag a tipsy Pfc out of a jeep. Every hair in place, every button polished. Experts in close order drill. By the numbers, hut, tuh, three, cadence count!

At the troops' side is the commander, disciplined, stern, unbending Dean Smith, sword balanced on epaulet, whistle clenched between straight white teeth. Squads right! Squads left! His game plan for this semifinal encounter would fill the back of a weapons carrier.

And then we have the Saturday matinee opponents, the Houston Cougars. Hell, it's a moral victory if they all show up in the same uniforms. Hair bristling out like a Brillo pad with glandular trouble. Slouching around, unconcerned. Their only senior, Lyndon Rose, wearing a double 0 on his shirt for theatrical purposes. Leading rebounder Larry Micheaux, a light black with a strange sort of strawberry complexion, staring into space with expressionless eyes. Their foremost sub, Eric Davis, eyebrows cocked quizzically and eyelids lowered to halfmast as if this were a total bore. Yawning yet. A towering, awkward youth entitled Olajuwon which no one can pronounce, grinning like the village dolt and occasionally breaking into Nigerian dialect. A skinny guard with parenthesis legs planning his individual press conference to announce his professional intent to a world somewhat underwhelmed by the news.

No offense intended, but these Cougars wouldn't look out of place with a pillowcase full of silverware slung across their back. Heck, when the Houston reps approach midcourt for tomorrow's pre-game ceremony, you almost expect North Carolina to read them their rights.

Just as Col. Smith fits the rigid pattern of his Tarfeet, so does the Houston coach reflect his motley charges. Smith will wear a dark suit of conservative cut. Guy Lewis is apt to show up wih yellow shoes and a purple jacket with white stitching. He will look like an aging matinee idol until he speaks, when his East Texas idioms twang like a bent juice harp. Smith will be mostly unflappable in battle, while Lewis will frantically wave his trademark red polka-dot towel and gulp so much water that he outsprints even his fastest player to the men's room when the whistle sounds.

North Carolina is *supposed* to be in the Final Four every blessed year. This is the seventh trip for Col. Smith, more than any coach with exception of the mythical John Wooden. The colonel's troops have vowed to win this one for him. Senior guard Jimmy Black called a meeting in his dorm room. "This is it. Everybody says Coach Smith is a great coach, but they say he chokes in the Final Four. I know he's tired of hearing it and I know I'm tired of hearing it. This is the year we're going to win the national championship for Coach Smith."

Houston? You would think the Cougars got in on a forged pass or, more likely, climbed over the fence like a street urchin slipping into the circus. They didn't even win their own Southwest Conference. If they thought about winning the national championship for somebody particular, other than themselves, it might be a stripper on Bourbon Street.

The two teams play like the personalities they project. Carolina is a well-oiled machine, meshing from this defense to that defense, pass, pass, pass the ball until some player gets a high percentage shot. And should the Tarheels find themselves with a lead approaching the halftime or game gun, they will shift into Smith's famed Four Corners stall, holding the ball, forcing the trailing team into fouling and then building the lead on free throws. Against Virginia in the ACC tournament, Carolina did not attempt a shot for the last 13 minutes of the game. Fans booed. Teevee brass turned pale.

Carolina's key word is "execute." With the Cougars, it's "shoot, baby."

Oh, for those who think Guy Lewis' game plan is written on a match cover, he once had a stall game all of his own.

"I quit it," he twanged recently. "The Houston newspaper-men got to criticizing us and the fans got to booing, so I decided the hell with that."

As for his lads' hully-gully style, Lewis defends it rather self-consciously. "We take good shots, we just take them quickly without passing the ball back and forth 30 times," said Guy. "If it's one pass and you get the shot you want, why the hell pass it around? You increase the chance of throwing it away. If that's undisciplined play, then I advocate it."

Still, the figures back up the left-right approach of the cops and robbers. Houston will trade shots with anybody, figuring its shooters are more accurate. Carolina just wants to take the easy shots and keep the other team from getting the easy shots. Houston opponents average 74 points; North Carolina's opposition manages but 55.

Lewis uses several reserves to keep his gung-ho attack refueled with fresh legs. The Cougars may run blindly like thieves, darting into alleys, leaping fences, bounding through open doors, but they do it at full tilt. If you try to keep up, the Cougars will run your tongue out.

And certainly it would not behoove the robbers to change at this late stage. They must not, if they can prevent it, let North Carolina dictate the pace of the game to a slow, deliberate tempo. The Cougars should study the parable of the back-woods rube who wandered away from his habitat and saw a locomotive for the very first time, chugging through the woods. He didn't know what it was, but it scared the bejabbers out of him and he fled ahead of the train with much desperate thresh-ing of legs. Eventually the train caught him and the cowcatcher tossed him off to one side. A witness rushed up.

"Man, are you crazy? Why did you keep running down the track?"

"Well, I knew if I couldn't outrun that booger on clear ground," said the hick, "I wouldn't have no chance in the brush." The Cougars best take to the brush and stay there.

UNLIKELY CHAMPS

APRIL 2, 1985

LEXINGTON, KENTUCKY—Oh, well, as the coaches are fond of saying, anything can happen on any given Monday night. The sun can rise in the west, lava can flow back up Vesuvius' slopes, a monkey can sqeeze toothpaste back into a tube. And an unranked fraternity of polite, gentle students can pull off the biggest upset in NCAA basketball championship history, over a mob of bruisers who could walk through Central Park in drag.

Of course, they will call it a Cinderella yarn, this 66–64 Villanova shocker over the powerful Georgetowns. This will register higher on the collegiate seismographs, even, than North Carolina State's upending of Houston two springs ago. That team also was unranked going into the NCAA playoffs. That team also had lost 10 games during the regular season, as had Villanova. But the bookmaker's yardstick says this was even more stunning. Those Carolinians were 7-point underdogs to the Cougars, while Rollie Massimino's Wildcats were rated 9 1/2, even 10 points down. A turtle on a freeway would get better odds.

Also, remember the Houston team was considered just another fine outfit before *it* lost. The Hoyas were billed the greatest ensemble of talent ever recruited. And remember, they had the eighth wonder of the buckets world, Patrick Ewing, in the middle.

The basketball scientists will explain how this upset was fashioned. It seemed to the casual witness Ewing played as hard as he could, with two Wildcats draped around his massive neck and another in his lap. But everything Villanova threw in the air came down in the net. Whoever heard of a team hitting 78.6 percent of its efforts? How about a saliva test here?

141

Massimino hoped for a 50 percent effort, but he undersold his sharpshooters. Some shots by Ed Pinckney and Harold Pressley seemed to be desperation heaves arched high over the awesome bounds of Ewing, like maybe they were shooting when they really didn't *want* to—a man forced to walk a high wire against his will. But the balls somehow found the net like prairie dogs after a gunshot.

And that unerring aim was even better at the free-throw line in the late minutes, when the muscular Hoyas grew a mite panicky when these soft souls from Philadelphia refused to fold. With 2:30 left and Villanova holding a trembly 1-point lead, the Wildcats sank six freebies in a row, and eight of the last 10. And, of course, their 22 free points (compared to Georgetown's 6!) was backbreaking to the losing effort.

The contrast was startling to the mad rooters jammed into Rupp arena and countless millions hawking the toob. Ewing and his fierce mates, glowering and menacing. "Proud warriors," coach John Thompson likes to call them. No. 1 in the land, of course, victors over Villanova twice already this season. Angry and bullying.

Ewing, normally a undemonstrative sort, once motioned from his high defensive post, as Muhammad Ali would beckon to an outclassed opponent, daring guard Gary McLain to come within range of his tentacles. Against these defending champs were the soft-spoken, articulate Villanova lads, happy, friendly, *grateful*, even.

Consider the two centers. Ewing, you know from song and story. The next superpro. Ed Pinckney is almost delicate in comparison. Slender, even frail, on a 6–9 frame. He doesn't glower, he looks anxious. He misses a shot, he stamps his foot like a chaperone at the prom. When he is fouled, he claps his hands up and down, like a child, not sideways as us machos teach. When Ewing guarded him under the basket and placed a restaining arm, Pinckney would slap it away with his hand, like a high school sophomore on the first date.

His voice is soft, and his grammar would not be out of place at a Harvard tea.

"Oh, we'll wear that glass slipper if you want us to, but we don't consider ourselves a Cinderella," he said earlier, a lamb going to the ax.

Yet this quick milquetoast gave a valiant effort against Ewing.

Once in the frantic late going, Pinckney lowered his shoulder and plunged into Ewing's midsection like a fullback, knocked the giant backward, raised up and made the shot. It gave Villanova a 57–54 lead, and Georgetown was good as gone at that point. That play, as much as any, told the strange ending to the NCAA story. O. Henry couldn't have improved on it.

International
Circus

QUICK TKO

JULY 28, 1976

MONTREAL, CANADA—The opening whistle was still a shrill echo in the Montreal Forum when a Yugoslavian citizen named Mr. Zoran Slavnic bounced once and fired the first shot of the Olympic basketball championship. He missed, and then the tide turned.

The United States' ugly ducklings, youngest and most slandered roundball congregation in Olympic history, began to dance Swan Lake. They might have done more damage to Yugoslavia with a B-29 bomb load, but it's doubtful. The Yugos are like the man with a terminal hangover: they may get better, but they'll never get well.

This was a U.S. team without a 7-foot center, of all things, and when you go to the Olympics without a giant post, you get caught at the junior prom with a busted zipper. This was a roster without several collegiate headliners who chose not to compete for flag, motherhood and apple pie. This was a squad loaded with four players from North Carolina, whose coach Dean Smith, not too coincidentally, happened to be the coach of the U.S. Olympic team. Nepotism was shouted from the highest steeples, especially by other coaches whose stars were bypassed.

This was a group inspected by veteran pro coach Red Auerbach and pronounced, "This is supposed to be an American team? Smith certainly has his work cut out for him."

Auerbach wasn't the only lecturer. Arizona State's Scott Lloyd testified, "These guys are in for a terrible shock when they play some of these international teams."

This also was the bunch that knocked immediate fire from their finals opponents. After Mr. Slavnic missed his opening aim, a Mr. Adrian Dantley, once of Notre Dame, assumed personal command of the hill. Four explosive goals in a row. Phil Ford, a mere undergraduate flea at North Carolina, twice swiped the ball from Yugo's Slavnic and slipped it to Dantley like a kid passing notes in arithmetic class. Ford was to steal three more Yugo possessions during the evening, with Mitch Kupchak and Dantley also charged with burglary.

Dantley gathered 30 points and a nasty cut over the eye in the 95–74 swamping, threw in a dozen of the Americans' first 18 points. By that time it was 18–6 and the Olympic gold medals were clearly headed back to the United States where they had been held captive since Howard Johnson had three flavors. Except, of course, for that 1972 misfire when Russia claimed a disputed victory.

Obviously, that was the only flaw in the Americans' unbroken march through seven Montreal foes. The Yanks, although they would never admit it, wished desperately to reclaim the title personally from the Russians. But the Ivans were squashed by Yugoslavia in the semi-finals.

"This may have cost us 10 million viewers," said ABC telecaster Curt Gowdy before the game. "All those people out there were waiting for revenge on Russia."

This was before Gowdy attacked such pronunciations as Georgijevski, Dalipagic and Kicanovic, and was carried off on an army cot with his tongue in traction.

Despite these misplaced syllables, the Yugos play an Americanized version of basketball. Mirko Novosel, the honest, likeable Yugo coach, has spent three months in the United States each of the last three years, visiting five states and studying basketball techniques. So when the two teams got together Tuesday night, they played unilingual techniques, and the Yugos were no talent match.

Before the finals, Novosel admitted his team had about a 30 percent chance at beating the Yanks, although it had won over Russia six straight times since the 1972 Olympics.

Why does his team have such success against Russia, and yet lost badly twice to the USA in these Olympics, once by 19 points and once by 21?

"The Americans are the best in rudiments," he said simply.

Smith said all the right things. He thought the Yugos played well, with poise and enthusiasm. He gave credit to his assistant coaches, and Scott May and Kupchak and Ford and so on. Earlier in the Olympic stay, Smith admitted that the scorn some had expressed for the make-up of this team, might provide an extra prod for the Americans. And in the last stages of the game, this was apparent in the players' actions. Quinn Buckner could scarce contain himself. He and guard Dragan Kicanovic waged a bit of spite scene, baiting each other with taunts and actions.

Then, as the clock ran out, the Americans' pledge of teamwork at the expense of fancy individual play became forgotten. Buckner and Ford did a little Harlem Globetrotting, dribbling twice through the tired Yugos for stylish layup buckets. It was a short span of joyous showboating, and even the losers could hardly blame them for that.

KATE THE GREAT

JULY 22, 1976

MONTREAL, CANADA—Her father was a weatherbeaten whaler, you see, straining his back and his hard gray eyes against angry nature off the rockbound coasts of Maine. There always was an old harpoon or two laying around the backyard. One day little Kathy waddled over, picked up the funny stick and flang it into Vermont. Of such background, Olympic javelin champions are formed.

At least, that was one of the wild yarns Kathy Schmidt used to strap on journalistic ferrets who wished to probe her id.

"Oh, that story came from a fit of boredom," Kate The Great said with an amused shrug. "I got so tired of people all asking me the same question over and over; how does a women get started throwing a javelin? I couldn't stand it any longer. A photographer friend and I dreamed up this whaler story. He even researched the name of a Maine high school I supposedly attended. I got a lotta mileage out of that story."

Kate The Great, actually the 22-year-old daughter of a California insurance company president, appeared the most relaxed citizen in the Olympic Village as she lounged in a basement room, wrapped in a warmup suit and her hair bound by a trademark red bandana. But she's not relaxed at all, even though she can find humor in all of this officious Olympic tangle.

"I got a bleeding ulcer. I had to lay off gin and tonic. I switched to beer and wine, but I haven't even had a beer in three days."

Kathy supposedly is America's best bet for a gold medal in women's track and field, an Olympic division expected to be dominated by East German women. Kathy won the bronze medal in Munich four years ago, behind winner Ruth Fuchs of East Germany who recently set a new world mark of 226 feet, 10 inches. Kathy's career best is 218–3.

"Oh, I don't think it will take more than 213 to win here. I don't think Fuchs will approach her record. Besides, East Germans don't do anything outside of East Germany. You notice that?" She rolled her eyes suggestively. "Funny thing, you look in the record books and you noticed the records are always set in Liepzig."

Kate has seen her East German rival only once in the 10,000-jock Olympic Village. "I went up to her in the cafeteria and said I'm Kathy Schmidt, congratulations on your record. As soon as she heard Kathy Schmidt, she turned her head away."

In a capsule she described as "boring," Kathy ran through her athletic history: she was playing softball when she was 13 and her coach noticed she had the quickest, strongest arm around. There was nothing else on the playground to throw except a football and a javelin. The coach handed her the javelin.

"Oh, my technique is terrible," she said with an honest laugh. "Some people who have seen me throw say I can go 260 feet if I threw correctly. I just have a quick arm. And I'm the biggest of the international javelin throwers, tallest and heaviest. You see these 5–9 gals throw and here comes ole 6–1 Schmidt waltzing down there."

Kate is not a raving beauty, (strong teeth, tilted nose, 173 well-distributed pounds), but her sense of humor and self-depreciation make her beautiful.

"Look, I don't feel throwing a spear is a significant thing and I don't know if that's good or bad. So what if I throw the javelin? Big deal. But if I'm a world record holder or Olympic champion, that's something."

But she has a bellyful of this Olympic falderah. "I'll be serious with you. This is the first time I've thought of quitting. All this training camp garbage, all this formality, all these politics, all this etiquette, all these procedures, just to throw a spear. We have 12 ladies to a room. Twelve sharing one bathroom. I need time and I need space. I'd been better off if I could have stayed in Los Angeles until time for me to throw. The true test here may not be who makes the best throw, but who will survive."

Kathy said she had the greatest time of her young life in Munich, when no one knew who she was nor expected any great deeds.

In Montreal, Kate said it took all her energy just going to

meals and doing all the formalities. "I haven't even been out of camp and that's not like me." Finals in her event come Saturday.

"Then I hope to get in some heavy beer drinking," she said.

Someone mentioned the proximity of men and women athletes in the Village and asked if she thought there was any hanky-panky going on.

"What do you mean?" she said. The poor guy tried to explain.

"Well, I certainly hope so," said Kate The Great. "If you're cool about it, nobody gets caught and nobody gets in trouble."

That conversational trend naturally gravitated into the sex tests the women athletes must now take, after some Czech women performed suspiciously like men several years ago. The test involves scraping membrane from the mouth for microscope examination.

"Some little man, not really a doctor, not somebody you'd trust your life to, gives you a little card certifying you are a lady," Kathy said with irony.

"The test is degrading, as you can imagine, but it's necessary," she said. "But you know, when they start talking about it, it makes you stop and think, even if you are Miss America. I can see it all now, going home from the Olympics and saying, hi, mom, hi, dad, I'm your son." Kate The Great laughed heartily as she strode off to her cramped room. Her charmed audience voted unanimously she should again fling the harpoon into Vermont.

FIDEL'S PRIDE

JULY 30, 1976

MONTREAL, CANADA—The greatest unbearded hero in Cuba, a brown television tower named Teo Stevenson, may indeed be rusty and unworked and susceptible to a burrowing onslaught from inside his long deltoids. This was one brave summation of American boxfight managers going into the Olympics. A strong young citizen like Big John Tate, for example, could dig a tunnel under the Stevenson tower and pound him on the belly button until all them rice and beans couldn't stand it anymore.

It's possible, they said, much as Alf Landon's campaign managers sat around hotel rooms, smoked cigars and speculated on which cabinet office they should accept.

The Americans ignored the Cuban's steely attitude and his arms that enable him to tie shoestrings without bending his knees. Why, this man won the upright marble shooting title of Havana before he had cut a stalk of sugar cane.

His stance can only be described as classic upright. His left hand sticks out like a lunar landing gear and is about as sensitive. He looks as if he learned boxing from an old James J. Corbett manual. Teo is close shaven and his hairdo can only be described as a kinky burr. He is two Harry Belafontes.

And what he did to America's colorful heavyweight hopeful, Big John Tate, the garbage trucker from Knoxville, was a quick lesson in standup boxing, the style that is so deadly against the European campaigners in this Olympics. They are a sturdy, awkward bunch unable to bend without creaking; in truth, most would have difficulty reaching the Texas Golden Gloves finals. Tate is a cut above this Teutonic quality, as he demonstrated in winning his first two bouts against a Pole and a West German.

But Stevenson, who won the 1972 Olympics with a decisive pounding over the THEN American hope, Duane Bobick, has a bit of fluid motion in him despite his 6-5 height, plus those long curb feelers he keeps out in front.

Tate had a bothersome cut over his eye, from the butt of a Polish head in his first bout, and the assumption was that Stevenson would tap on that target with a left jab until Big John's sinuses collapsed. But it didn't take that long.

Oh, Teo stuck a few jabs in there, while Big John crouched on the perimeter and peered for a non-existent tunnel. Then less than halfway through the first round, Stevenson shot a straight right, no farther in flight than his own chin. It landed with a sound not uncommon to a croquet ground on the left side of Big John's face. Not on the chin, you understand, but somewhere in the vicinity of the cheek bone.

Tate stumbled backward across the ring as if pulled by invisible wire, his eyes suddenly coated with gauze. His back hit the corner ropes, the first friendly touch he had felt, and he slid down them gratefully, as a man falling from Pike's Peak finds a stray bush in his grasp. The referee counted as a regulatory gesture, but the big sleepy-eyed Tate was off somewhere in the infinite, counting clouds.

Thus, for the second straight Olympics, the lean, 210-pound Stevenson who would seemingly break apart with a Marciano hook to the rib cage, has destroyed the American dream.

Stevenson then continued to destroy another American illusion, the dream of the ghetto, the ambition of reaching a pro boxfight plateau garnished with large coarse banknotes, fast cars, leggy starlets and an entourage to frizzle his hair and clip his toenails. In fact, he sat there calmly after the fight, pulled a comb from somewhere in his warmup jacket and roughed up his short hair above his clean, unmarked face, something Big John had neglected to do, and said all that capitalistic luxury is for the buzzards.

For the hundredth time in the last Olympic weeks, he said he wanted no part of the $1,000,000 he has been offered to box Muhammad Ali or George Foreman (a television commentator here) or even Slapsy Maxie Rosenbloom, from wherever he is.

"I am not a piece of merchandise," he said through an interpreter. "I am happy being what I am." Teo lists his occupation as "student."

Earlier he had told American reporters, "I have no stomach for it. It is no need to talk about what I might do against Ali or Frazier or Foreman. I will never fight them. I will always be an amateur." What is one million dollars more or less? With so many people in the world starving, it's a shame a clown like Antonio Inoki gets six million for that fight.

"I like to be an athlete. A pro boxer is not an athlete any more."

Three Cuban boxers won by knockouts in the Olympic quarterfinals; how did he account for that?

"Boxing in Cuba is supported by the Revolution. Anyone has access to being a boxer."

Then came the zinger from leftfield. What if Fidel Castro asks you to fight Ali or somebody for national pride and prestige?

"I'm sure Mr. Castro knows exactly what goes on in professional boxing. If they ask me to fight in world competition, I do, but not professional. He would never ask that. Everybody in Cuba is in favor of abolishing pro boxing."

Stevenson excused himself politely. He wanted to get down to Olympic Stadium and watch a Cuban colleague, Senor Alberto Juantorena, run the feathers off everybody in the 400-meter finals. He won by about the same margin as Stevenson.

Teo now says he has a 12-year program, to win three consecutive Olympic gold medals, ending in 1980 in Moscow. It hardly seems long enough. But then he can't be a student forever, or can he?

GOLD NEEDLES

Themistocles, being asked whether he would rather be Achilles or Homer, said, "Which would you *rather be—a conqueror in the Olympic Games, or the crier that proclaims who are the conquerors?"*
—Plutarch.

Well, sir, Mr. Themistocles seems to be saying that he had rather be the gent who wins the Olympic 1500 meters, than the guys who report it. Us slobs in the pressbox, in other words. In behalf of that large and untidy fraternity, I wish to announce that Mr. Themistocles is full of prunes or olives or string beans or whatever they had for supper in Athens in them days.

Of course, Mr. Themistocles lived way back there before the Louisiana Purchase and Plymouth Rock, when the Olympics were as pure as driven snow. The classic motto of the Olympics was *Citius, Altius, Fortius,* which is rumored to mean Swifter, Higher, Stronger. And that was all there was to it. A bunch of young Greeks got together in a nearby pasture, stripped to their underpants and decided who could outrun and outjump. This was considered a much safer outlet for their patriotic energies than transfixing one another with spears and things, and had the whole-hearted approval of their rulers and Blue Cross.

Now, of course, it is a new ball game. To win an Olympic event, especially in some countries Over There, is to become a national hero, with a free home, free car, a cellar full of yams, the damsel of your choice and a pension forever. To lose is to spit on the flag.

Leave us consider the recent Olympics at Montreal. Start with the Russian Pentathlon contestant, Boris Onischenko. In the fencing competition, the judges discovered old Boris was operating with a rigged epee. He could press a spot on his sword handle and the electronic impulse would register "hit" whether or not the sword point made contact with the opponent. Russian pentathlon supervisors first argued that their hero had shorted out, but when the device was fully exposed and Boris was caught redhanded, so to speak, the Ruskies growled, dragged Boris behind some bushes where he was heard to grunt heavily several times, and hauled him on a plane back to the homeland. Us pressboxers, or criers as Mr. Themistocles calls us, have not heard hide nor hair of him since.

Then there was the great blood caper. Lasse Viren of Finland won the 5,000 and 10,000-meter gold medals and some of his beaten opponents snorted accusations. "He's got that extra blood in him," said Ron Dixon of New Zealand.

Viren and other European distance runners were suspected of getting extra strength from extra blood. A pint of the runner's blood is removed a few weeks before the race and the runner continues to train so that his body replenishes the lost blood. Then right before the big event, the same blood is injected back into his system and now he has an extra pint and supposedly, extra stamina. Raises the hemoglobin or some dang thing.

Swimmers, skaters and cyclists also have been accused of blooding up, or whatever you call it. Under Olympic medical rules, it is not illegal. Only unethical.

Of course, there was the fierce conversation about the East German women athletes, the suspicion that they were fed male hormones and various other drugs too sophisticated for the current Olympic testing. American women athletes look at the likes of Ruth Fuchs, Kornelia Ender, Hammelore Ankle, Evelin Schlaak and curled their shapely Yankee lips. Laboratory robots, they said scornfully, fingering the beads around their necks where medals would hopefully hang.

The weightlifters, shotputters, hammer throwers, forget it. Most admitted taking steriods which, combined with certain exercises, supposedly gave them more strength. Olympic rules forbid such. It takes a certain time for drying out, that is, working the steriod traces out of the system. Two, three weeks.

Olympic athletes were subject to spot medical checks in the Olympic Village. Gossips said, for that reason, the East Germans refused to live in the Village. They had their own quarters in a nearby isolated town. After the competition three weightlifters were relieved of their Olympic medals because they flunked the post-event drug tests. Valentine Khristov and

Blagoi Blagojev of Bulgaria lost a gold and a bronze medal; Zbignieiv Karzmarek of Poland also lost a gold.

But now, Mr. Themistocles, we got the real topper. Some West German scientists have admitted they experimented with pumping air into their Olympic swimmers, to improve their buoyancy. They used syringe pumps and forced as much as a half gallon of compressed air into the swimmer's large intestine. How? Don't be silly, dear. They didn't use an ear.

Only volunteers were used, after they were assured it would not injure their health. One swimmer, Walter Kusch, said it didn't help in his specialty—the breaststroke. "My feet often stuck out of the water," he said. Another Olympic contestant, Peter Nocke, described the experiments as "unpleasant." Perhaps he is fortunate at that. They could have used a roman candle.

Anyways, the West German experiments were abandoned after a short while and were not, officials vow, used in the Olympics. But the whole bit demonstrates what lengths, or depths, Olympic competition has reached. Any day now, they may change the Olympic motto to Citius, Altius, Fortius, Seichius. Swifter, Higher, Stronger, Sicker. Quite honestly, Themistocles ole kid, I'd rather stay a crier.

THE NEXT BULLET

FEBRUARY 6, 1984

The first time I ever saw Bob Hayes, he wobbled like a flat tire.

This was at the Drake Relays in the early '60s. Hayes, to this memory, was a freshman at Florida A&M and already being acclaimed "world's fastest human."

There is a special magic in that particular billing. It's usually bestowed on the 100-meter champ, either the reigning Olympic champ or a new record-holder. The title was born in the 1920s, which was a great era for nicknames. Manassa Mauler. Galloping Ghost. Sultan of Swat. Wild Bull of the Pampas. The Four Horsemen. World's Fastest Human.

Charley Paddock, the Olympic 100-meter champ of 1920, was first to wear the title. Then it passed on to Eddie Tolan and Jesse Owens and finally on to Hayes, even though his Olympic glory was yet to come.

Anyways, the "world's fastest human" was on display in Des Moines and after I watched him for the first 50 yards, this Vaunted Expert shook his head and said no way. Not that I knew championship sprinting technique from gooseliver on rye, but clearly this kid didn't have it. I had been told that world-class sprinters were smooth machines, running like a Rolls Royce with no apparent strain.

Hayes wobbled and swerved and jerked. He ran with elbows pumping across his thick body like he was trying to force his way through a crowd at a supermart sale. His shoulders rolled and his head bobbed furiously. *Every*thing moved, and not necessarily in sync. Bob didn't *flow* like a graceful speed machine. He looked more like a man trying to outrun a bull on plowed ground. To hell with form, just get me to that blasted fence.

Of course, the main thing you noticed about Hayes was what happened when he finished. Judges would stare at their watches and then hold them to their starboard ear and shake. Hayes went over to the Tokyo Olympics and ran a 9.9 in a prelim, a world record were it not for a tailwind. He won the finals in 10 flat, equaling the world mark.

But it was in the 400-meter relay that Bob made unbelievers out of the track mob. He ran anchor on the U.S. team and took the baton in sixth place, four yards behind the leader, Jocelyn Delecour, an excellent sprinter from France. They still say no one ever ran 100 meters any faster than Bob Hayes that day. In that short straightaway, he exploded past the interims, caught Delecour and won the race by three yards.

Even though he had a running start, his numbers were stunning. Rut Walters, the assistant U.S. track coach, kept staring at his watch. "I know this is ridiculous," he said weakly, "but I timed Hayes in 8.6 seconds."

"Of course, it's ridiculous," said Bob Giegengack, the head coach, "but it had to be true for Hayes to win so big, from so far behind."

But now it is two decades later and Bob Hayes was standing in Reunion Arena, looking at a lithe young man and saying, "He's the best amateur athlete I've ever seen, physically, mentally, confidently."

His subject was Carl Lewis, the New Jersey flyer by way of Houston, who had just lost a 60-yard dash to Ron Brown in the Times Herald Invitational and was singularly unbothered. He had a faulty start, he shrugged, and besides, what difference does it make?

"Winning has nothing to do with it," he said. "I am the No. 1 athlete in the world and have been for a number of years, but it doesn't mean I am perfect. I was able to train only four times for this, so I am pleased with my performance."

There was a marked contrast between this confident youngster and the memory of Bob Hayes at Des Moines. Hayes was a rough runner; good heavens, there is no telling his clockings if he hadn't wasted so much motion!

Lewis is silky. He is not muscled and compact like most sprinters. He doesn't have the prominent backporch that marks so many outstanding black sprinters. He is tall and whippy, more like a half-miler or a hurdler or a jumper which, of course, he is also. The long jump is probably his best event and any day now, when he hits it *just right*, he will sail 30 feet. Bob Beamon's world record of 29–2½, set in the thin air of Mexico City in 1968, was considered beyond reach until they build a pit in Tibet, but Lewis has crept within four inches already.

Where Bobby Hayes exuded power, Lewis flows. In his prelim heat Saturday night, he had his field beaten after 30 yards and he shifted into the smoothest overdrive you ever saw. Like the old Texas sprinter, Bobby Morrow, you could set a highball glass full of Jack Daniels on his head and he wouldn't spill a drop over 100 meters.

Lewis will shoot for four golds in this upcoming Olympics. At least, he'll try for a U.S. spot in four events—long jump, 100 and 200 meters, and the sprint relay. Jesse Owens pulled it off in 1936. Harrison Dillard also won four, but he split them between two Olympiads—winning the 100 meters and running on the sprint relay in 1948. And then taking the high hurdles and another sprint relay gold four years later. You win a sack of Olympic golds in swimming or ice skating but modern track is a different story. Lewis may very well have the motor for it.

THE VICIOUS CIRCLE

FEBRUARY 8, 1984

We would probably understand it better if it were not for the blasted metric system. This new conversion pattern has thrown civilization, as we know it in The Colonies, out of kilter. I mean, if yards and feet and inches were good enough for George Washington and Ronald Reagan, they are certainly good enough for The Great Unwashed.

Why, it says right here in your basic U.S. Constitution, "No Electioneering Within 100 Feet of the Polls." Any day now, we will see new signs posted: "No Electioneering Within 30.5 Meters of the Polls," and the jails will be full before nightfall. How is anyone, off the top of this head, going to interpolate that?

I, for one, say the metric system is a communistic trick and if that be treason, hang this old gray head.

On the other hand, perhaps meters and kilometers are thrown into the biathlon competition only to confuse us further, like a false clue in a detective novel. To my way of thinking, the biathlon is perplexing enough without adding any phony footprints or mysterious whispers on the telephone.

You will hear considerably about the biathlon in days to come because it is a Winter Olympic event, and the ABC network must fill two weeks with *some*thing from Sarajevo besides a couple on the rink whirring like a top to "The Blue Danube." The Winter Olympics schedule is loaded with competition rather foreign to those of us in the tropical zone, but some events we can understand because the winner is the guy who gets to the bottom of the hill first and upright.

The luge seems rather complicated at first, but when you accept that it is like falling on your Flexible Flyer, upside down and backward, and shooting down the bobsled run, it is comparatively simple.

The biathlon is more complex because it involves skiing

161

around in a circle and shooting a rifle, with a scoring system that would cause IBM to blow a gasket. One of the ABC thousands will explain it all to you, maybe even Jim McKay, in the special reverent tones he uses for Winter Olympics and Dunkirk and state funerals. But in the meantime, perhaps you should have a running start.

The contestants are called biathletes, which is easy enough to accept, and maybe we should stop right there. The biathletes wear skis on their feet and a rifle, caliber up to 8 millimeter, slung across their backs.

It is a competition which began among Finnish soliders during WWII, although it wasn't considered much of a sport at the time. The Finns would ski awhile and then stop and shoot at something which, more than likely, would shoot back.

Now if they had left it at *that*, we would have the most speculator event in the Winter Olympiad. Personally I have always felt that lion hunting could be better classified as a "sport" if the hunter was forced to stay afoot and was limited to one cartridge.

(Dan Jenkins, the renowned social critic, used to say he would enjoy baseball a lot more if the base runner, once he reached first, had to fight the first baseman to stay there.)

Anyways, the biathletes compete one at a time, which doesn't exactly heighten suspense. He leaves the starting area and skis through undulating countryside in a 5 kilometer circle marked by *red* signs. What we're talking about here is three miles. When he completes the loop, he falls on his belly in the snow, unlimbers his musket and fires five shots at three paper targets 50 meters away. The bullseye is four centimeters, about the size of a golf ball. An outer ring is three times that. Miss the bullseye but hit inside the outer ring, the penalty is one minute. Miss the outer ring, the penalty is two minutes.

Then the guy jumps up and skis a 3.75 circle, this time following *green* markers. Now he must shoot five times at a set of bigger targets, this time the size of a grapefruit.

In the next stage, if his lungs haven't burst, he goes on another two-mile circle, marked by *blue* flags and shoots again from a prone stance. One more three-mile hike, following *violet* signs, and more standing shooting. Then it all winds up with a glorious 2.5 kilometer loop, identified by *orange* markers, to a finish line inside the biathlon stadium.

In the interest of simplicity, my explanation has been cut to the basics. There are other details that *could* be added. Such as the rifles must have no more than a 1 kg trigger pressure. And all ammo must be carried by the biathlete from the start, although he may not arrive or leave from the firing area with a round in the firearm. Shortcuts are also frowned on.

The winner is the chap with the lowest total of time, including all the penalty minutes caused by missing the bullseye because of sweat in the eyes and a 180 pulse beat and a short pause to curse the Finnish soldiers.

To add to the fun, there is also a "sprint" biathlon, in which the marksmen fire at breakable targets and actually have to ski their penalty laps. There are also relay races if they can round up enough people who haven't died of strokes or got lost in the forest or shot themselves in the feet. Oh, yes. The biathlon was added to the Winter Olympic program in 1960 and the first one was won by a Swede named Klas Lestander. I bet you didn't know that.

KNIGHT'S GAMBOL

AUGUST 1, 1984

LOS ANGELES, CALIFORNIA—Aw, come off it, Bobby Knight. Drop the disguise. Belay the balderdash. Sheath the sword.

You are not Horatio at the bridge, nor Davy Crockett at the Alamo. Mr. Knight, you are going to live and do well and be prosperous and heroic. Lo, it is written.

You are not walking through the valley of the shadow of death. You will win the Olympic basketball gold medal from here to Halifax, so quit biting your fingernails and pacing the floor.

To hear the U.S. coach rant, you would think this is Thermopoli with the original cast. *My god, the enemy is in the next block! Hide the children!*

The U.S. basketball team is in dire danger of defeat, Knight would have you *and* the players believe. He has got himself psyched on the subject and he has attempted to transmit that fear to the 12 all-stars on his squad.

When anyone dares mention that the U.S. is a prohibitive Olympic favorite, Knight pins the poor fool with his fierce glare.

"On any given day, anybody is capable of winning," says Knight, quoting from Aristotle or Landry. You would think the man has been smitten with a terrible vision.

His listeners roll their eyes and glance toward the heavens. They are not alien to the record books. They are boringly aware the U.S. superthumps have won 72 games in Olympic competition and have lost only one—the highly suspect Russian upset in the 1972 Games. Furthermore, they are convinced this current group is the most talented squad ever, even surpassing the 1960 immortals of Oscar Robertson, Jerry Lucas, Jerry West, Walt Bellamy, and Terry Dischinger.

Now, when somebody mentions the threats of Brazil, Yugoslavia, Italy, it is with half-hearted interest. Knight senses this sentiment and responds with the scream of a sergeant in the trenches.

"Canada ... Brazil ..." he says, waving an arm furiously. "Since 1970, basketball has undergone a tremendous growth explosion. We can look around and see a number of countries that can be competitive on individual team basis. I don't think any country is close to fielding the *number* of good teams that we can—perhaps we'll never reach that kind of parity—but on a one-on-one situation, national team against national team, I think there are a lot of teams that can be very competitive with us."

Sorry, Col. Knight. If any of these teams finish within 15 points of you, then somebody better check its water bucket. Brazil? Heck, they lost their first game of this round-robin competition to Australia, hardly known for its bounce.

Someone points to the tremendous height and Americanization of the West Germany team. This squad looks like a national forest. Three guys seven feet or better, including Uwe Blab, the ungainly national who does his collegiate toil for Knight at Indiana. Another skyscraper is Christian Welp, who is still learning the game at Washington, and 6–10 Detlef Schrempf, a decent forward who also represents Washington when he's on campus. And there is another seven-footer named Klaus Zander who best illustrates the theory that height doth not make godliness. Monday, in a losing cause against Italy, poor Zander lost the ball three times on one play.

Blab informed Knight that the USA team should beat everybody by 20 points. The coach laughed but not very much.

Knight professes much respect for Italy, a team composed mostly of professionals.

Knight was asked if he would like to have Meneghin on his USA team.

"Actually, I had rather have Kareem Jabbar. He's older and more experienced," Knight said drily. The speaker is not exactly a stranger to sarcasm, especially around the press.

Signor Meneghin, it would seem, is a more practical man than the American coach. He philosophized in halting English after his team's defeat of the West German antennas.

"I hope to repeat our second place finish in Moscow," he said, referring to the 1980 Olympics when the Italians were run-nerup to Yugoslavia, "I'm realistic. We know American basket-ball is stronger than Italy. Every country takes the USA as amazing. But that doesn't mean we go on the court all ready to lose. We think they are stronger but I don't think they scare anybody."

Knight, of course, is playing a rather juvenile mental game. The boot camp manner in which he trained his team, as bully-ing and profane as a Parris Island drill instructor, is so deadly serious it is almost a parody. In the Yanks' opening tromp of China, when Leon Wood slipped a behind-the-back pass to Waymon Tisdale, who zonked in a backward dunk, Knight did not allow himself a change of expression. He must have wished very much to laugh out loud.

"I think this is the best basketball team I have ever seen," said Canadian coach Jack Donohue after watching his team lose to the United States by 21 points. "Bobby makes them play de-fense. Most international teams do not play good defense."

Against China, a mere 49-point victory, Knight actually got a bit playful with his starting lineup. He had his monster middle-man, Patrick Ewing, on the bench. He sent forth a mixed bag of Tisdale, Jordan, Sam Perkins, Vern Fleming and Alvin Robert-son. It could have been Fee, Fi, Fo, Fum and Bubba with ap-proximately the same result. The only suspense about Olympic basketball is if the belligerent Knight will pull some temper trick that starts World War III.

Diamond Cutters

THE PERFECT MATCH

OCTOBER 12, 1978

LOS ANGELES, CALIFORNIA—This, of course, is the way a World Series game should be orchestrated. This would be the lyrics Babe Ruth would write. Well, maybe not Babe Ruth, but certainly Walter Johnson or Christy Mathewson or Sandy Koufax. This is the way the season is supposed to climax, the plot Abner Doubleday had in mind, or Major Cartwright or Abe Lincoln, whoever invented this business.

A World Series game ideally comes down to the last out of the last inning, one run difference and the winning runs on base and baseball's most feared clutch hitter in the box. Ideally, I suppose, the opposing pitcher would be some grizzled veteran, a wad of 'baccy bulging from his jaw, his shoes run over and his glove worn to the thinness of a handkerchief.

Instead, this pitcher looks like he should be working on his bike in the driveway. He still buys razorblades on approval. Bobby Welch won't be 22 until next month and he's been in professional baseball a year and some change.

Ordinarily, a youngster of this tender pedigree would take one look at Reggie Jackson and run behind his mama's skirts. Reggie Jackson eats young pitchers for brunch and older ones, too, during World Series time. This is the slugger's fourth Series and, going into the second game of the current event, his batting average was a magnificent .373. He had hit at least one home run in his last three Series games. Already on this balmy night in the hugging smog of Chavez Ravine, Jackson had knocked in all three of the Yankee runs.

What is Tommy Lasorda, a child abuser, to punish this stringy urchin in such a fashion? Let the Dodger manager send Welch to bed without his supper, but don't send him to face Reggie Jackson. Hell, they won't find his bones for days.

Lasorda already had his prime relief pitcher on the mound

and for three innings, Terry Forster had guarded the narrow 4–3 Dodger lead as if it were Sara Farrah-Faucet's backdoor key. Forster is not your basic grizzled veteran but he has been to the barn and back a couple times and he glares and stares and in the opening game of the Series, when he relieved briefly, he threw fast balls in the strike zone 17 times out of his 23 pitches. He has combat ribbons to match Audie Murphy.

But when Bucky Dent led off the Yankees' last inning with a single and, one out later, Paul Blair walked, Lasorda judged it time to make his second pitching change of the night. Thurman Munson was the New York batter in the circle, a righthand hitter. Forster is a lefthand pitcher, an arrangement Munson seems most compatible with. After a conference on the mound, the Dodger skipper motioned to the bullpen where young Welch was standing on the warmup mound, staring out at the drama that awaited him.

When he got his summons, Welch ran from the bullpen to the infield, as if he couldn't wait to get shellshocked. Perhaps a slow walk, through all that noise and tension, would have been more than young nerves could bear.

Twenty-one years old, are you kidding, Lasorda? Don't send the kid up in a crate like that.

"Look, I don't ever think about the ages of Manny Mota or Lopes or Bobby Welch," said Lasorda, lumping the kid in with a couple oldtimers. "I don't go by years, I go by ability."

"Tommy gave me the ball and told me to throw strikes," said Welch. "This was no time to walk anybody."

Welch's first pitch was his specialty—a high fast ball. Munson swung like a lion had poked his head in his pup tent. He hit air. The next pitch, Munson lined crisp and hard to right field, to the waiting glove of Reggie Smith.

Two outs, ninth inning, tying and winning runs on base. Reggie Jackson walking to the left side of the plate. Reggie Jackson takes fast balls from young righthand pitchers and puts cream and sugar on them. It hardly seemed fair.

Well, of course, youth and innocence triumphed as Voltaire and Horatio Alger Jr. and Burt L. Standish have long ago decreed. Jackson's first swing was beautiful. The night was bruised. The ball wasn't.

"I threw nothing but fast balls," said Welch. "Two kinds, high and higher."

The second fastball came right at Jackson's head. The slugger dropped unceremoniously in the dirt. Was it a "challenge" by this tall, calm brunet youth, a message to Jackson that he wasn't facing a quaking kid?

Another fastball, another fearful Jackson swing and a foul back in the stands. The Dodger crowd was now on its feet and the din was frightful. A standing ovation for a foul tip?

Another pitch, another foul, and now the crowd became strangely quiet. Perhaps the Los Angeles faithful sensed that Jackson was taking a toll of the youngster, fouling off his pitches until he found the one special flavor he wanted to send deep into right field.

In a war of nerves, surely Jackson would triumph.

Another highball inside. Ball two. Reggie stepped from the box, removed his cap and mopped his brow on his sleeve. Another foul. And now, another high pitch out of the strike zone. Full count.

Reggie backed from the box again, mopping again, perhaps milking the moment, teasing the kid. Babe Ruth would have done the same. Television producers loved it.

The climactic fast ball came, Jackson's swing caused 12-foot waves off Malibu. The slugger jerked his head as he spat some word into the night. He stalked to the Yankee dugout, every third step marked by another jerk of his head, another oath. He slipped the bat until his left hand gripped the trademark and he flung it into the dugout with all the anger in all the world.

"He's a major leaguer, I'm a major leaguer," Jackson said later. "He won this battle, give him credit. I did the best I could and I got beat." Baseball should bronze such moments.

TAKE STAND

APRIL 9, 1980

The way some of us heard it during midnight vespers, Gene Autry had already retired from the movies, sheathed his six-gun and unstrung his gittar and was leaning back counting his coupons when his faithful horse Champion bought it. Ole Champ finally went west, as Zane Grey and Max Brand would have put it so poetically.

A ranchhand brought Autry the sad news. Gene paused in his coupon counting to sigh regretfully, which led the cowpoke to make a suggestion.

"I know how much he meant to you. Why don't you have him stuffed and mounted by a taxidermist?" said the guy. "When Trigger died, Roy Rogers had *him* stuffed."

"Well, you know, that's something to think about," Gene said reflectively. He mulled.

"What would it cost to have Champion stuffed and mounted?" he finally asked.

"Oh, I imagine around $1,500," said the waddy. Autry rubbed his chin.

"And how much would it cost to bury him?" he asked.

"A couple hundred bucks."

Autry picked up his coupons, licked his thumb and returned to his counting.

"Bury the son of a bitch!" he said.

There have been those critics who faulted Autry's theatrical talent, others who likened his prairie tenor to the mournful twang of a bobwire fence when struck by a D-flat tumbleweed. But no one has ever questioned his ability to collect and preserve huge bales of greenbacks.

Gene might have been making $300 a week, but he was saving $298 and putting it in real estate, in ranch acreage, in radio and television stations, in old films suitable only to cut up into banjo picks or, lo, the fabulous new market called late-night movies for tee-vee. His judgment in scenarios may have been ragged, but with finances, he hit bullseyes. Verily, he sacked it.

When Autry entered the world of baseball as purchaser of the California Angels, he was greeted with tremendous respect by the jock establishment. Not for his vast baseball knowledge, for he has yet to understand the infield fly rule, but for his credit rating. There is nothing baseball men hold in awe more than cash money and The Cowboy, as they call him, had enough to fill a barn and maybe two.

For that reason, because Gene Autry has more millions than Bim Gump, he easily captured the headlines the other day with his reaction to baseball's labor troubles.

Let's close up shop for a year, said The Cowboy. Let's declare a one-year moratorium on baseball and see how the players like them apples.

He got the attention, much like a deacon who snored loudly in church, but Gene was immediately forgiven because he has a fat hip. Autry's suggestion was interesting enough, but was neither original nor practical.

As a matter of fact, I remember hearing Paul Richards offer the same idea—what was it, four years ago? Paul didn't get the headlines, of course, because he had retreated to the fringe of baseball by then, as a White Sox consultant or somesuch. And Paul ain't quite in Autry's financial bracket, although Richards has made and saved enough loot in his time to buy Waxahachie or maybe Uruguay.

Anyways, when Paul made his declaration during a World Series gabfest, it was received and filed away with other rather revolutionary Richards suggestions over the years.

What Richards proposed was to shut down baseball for a year to teach the players to appreciate it. His premise was that after a year of make-do, player demands would shrink considerably, both individually and collectively. Ostensibly, this was also the Autry theme.

Even before that, it seems to this memory that Carroll Rosenbloom made the same irate proposition when NFL players struck at beginning of the 1974 season. Lock the gates for a year, said Rosenbloom, that'll teach the ingrates.

Of course, Rosenbloom's temper was speaking; he really didn't mean it. Paul Richards *knew* the Lords of Baseball would never try any tactic so drastic and, incidentally, so costly to themselves. And Gene Autry probably was speaking out of resentment more than practicality.

After all, it was Autry himself, along with George Steinbrenner and Brad Corbett, who made the biggest splashes in the
free agent pool, strewing those million dollar contracts like rose
petals at a wedding. It was Autry and Steinbrenner and Corbett
who nurtured the monkey that baseball ownership is now trying to remove from its back.

But those occasional expressions from wealthy owners are
significant in this respect: The owners, for the most part, realize they are much better equipped to weather a costly strike
than the players. Even a year's embargo. Now that the owners
have padded themselves with strike insurance, it seems even
more likely that they are girding for a lengthy drought.

The owners' old motto has been, "Let 'em stay out until their
wives send 'em back!" Meaning that after a month or so of bills
stacking up and no income, the ladies of the household grow a
mite fretful. They get nervous seeing their husbands stretched
out on the couch watching soap operas when they ought to be
somewhere sweating and getting calluses on their hands.

Al Oliver spoke rather frankly in the Rangers' training camp
when the strike subject arose. "I might vote for a strike now,"
said Al, "but after the bills start coming in, I might vote no." Of
course, when Al is out of work for a week, he loses about $6,000
in gross revenue.

For that reason, the players best prepare for a long vacation
if they walk out on May 23. In the two previous negotiations,
the bosses have been the yielders and *still* it has cost them more
and more money to preserve the players. This time, the owners
may be determined not to stuff and mount them.

BONEHEAD ACHES

AUGUST 14, 1985

In the eerie aura that often hangs out in baseball basements, tanglefeet abound. It is not always clear whether the principals are attempting to perform basic maneuvers of the game, or whether they are trying to dislodge chewing gum from their shoe soles. Take Arlington Stadium the other night, when Mr. Duane Walker attempted to occupy first base and found it sold out.

Mr. Walker is a recent recruit in the Rangers' cause, an amiable chap who hits the ball crisply and with a bit more frequency than his new teammates. But confusion attacked him on the basepaths during Baltimore's visit, leaving him with a very red face and somewhat lighter in the wallet.

The outfielder singled to lead off the Rangers' second inning; this, as Arlington loyalists realize, constitutes a major uprising. Then on a hit-and-run play, Steve Buechele followed with a liner to right-center.

Walker didn't see the ball but looked as he ran, as he is supposed to, at the third-base coach. Art Howe was pointing at the ball, then being chased by outfielder Lee Lacy, but obviously Walker misinterpreted the act, thinking perhaps Howe was posing for a Pontiac hood ornament or maybe was frozen in shock that the ball had been caught. So Walker wheeled and ran back to first, only to find it occupied by young Mr. Buechele, understandably elated over what he presumed to be his 11th single of the season.

Like a mouse in a maze, the befuddled Walker spun again toward second, only to see, to his dismay, Lacy's outfield peg approaching the bag. So he stopped stockstill and sincerely wished for a spade with which to dig a hole to China. As it so happened, the peg skipped past the waiting glove, and Walker conceivably could have rectified his mistake had he kept running. It was for this fallacy that manager Bobby Valentine assessed a fine, supporting the ancient baseball adage that if one is to be embarrassed, it is economically feasible to be embarrassed at full speed.

The bungles of summer are not necessarily limited to cellar dwellers. A fortnight ago, the scholarly Yankees were guilty of ineptitude that would bring cringes from a sandlotter. With Bobby Meacham on second, Dale Berra on first, Rickey Henderson struck a humpback liner that rolled to the centerfield wall. Meacham paused to make sure the ball fell safe and then began his sprint to third. Berra had not hesitated; he put his head down and chugged like a commuter chasing the 8:14.

Meacham also slipped while approaching third, cutting down more distance between the two runners, so when they neared home base, Meacham and Berra were practically like car and trailer.

Chicago catcher Carlton Fisk accepted the outfield relay and nimbly enough, tagged each in turn. Double-play tag-out by the catcher! Billy Martin, the Yankees' resident professor, watched the scene much as one stares at a train wreck before breaking into words that would shock the Royal Navy.

"I've never seen that in grammar school, much less the major leagues," said Martin, still ashen after the game. Berra is most fortunate Martin was not armed at the moment.

One remembers, with a nostalgic twinge, similar acts of the old New York Mets. Example: Richie Ashburn was trying gallantly to survive in center field, and the shortstop was an enthusiastic Latin named Elio Chacon. Ashburn, with his speed, specialized in racing up on short flies and, of course, when center fielder yells, "I got it!" he is granted right-of-way on all such efforts. Chacon was not versed in this particular custom. He, too, considered every fly ball his personal property and frequently collided with Ashburn, causing considerable consternation on the latter's part, as well as large, bleeding knots. Someone remembered that Chacon did not understand English nor the frantic waves.

Ashburn took the shortstop aside and with painstaking gestures, got his point across. Richie also learned the words *"Yo la tengo"* which means "I got it!"

"Yo la tengo?" Ashburn tested.

"Si, si!" said Chicon.

The next afternoon, Ashburn sprinted in for a short fly, yelling, *"Yo la tengo! Yo la Tengo!"* Chicon pulled up, waved for Richie to procede. Ashburn reached up to make the soft catch—and was knocked down by Frank Thomas, the Mets' onrushing and English-speaking left fielder.

SOFT TOUCH?

MARCH 5, 1986

Say you were standing on the corner with a tin cup, and Peter Ueberroth came by and dropped a frogskin on you. The first thing you'd do is hold it up to the light. If Peter volunteered to fix your speeding ticket, you'd narrow your eyes and say no thanks, you'd pay the fine. Let Mr. Ueberroth offer to help a blue-haired lady across the street, she'd swat him with her satchel and yell for a cop.

For some weird reason, everything the baseball commissioner does seems suspect.

First psychiatrist: "Good morning."

Second psychiatrist (to himself): "Wonder what he meant by that?"

The baseball commissioner has this smoothie reputation, you see, gained from his autocratic, yet masterful handling of the 1984 Olympiad. Whoever heard of a municipal promotion showing a $200 million *profit?* Montreal will be paying for the 1976 Olympics until the cows come home. Lake Placid? Somebody ought to go to jail for *that* fiasco. New Orleans took a thorough bath on the World's Fair. So after young Mr. Ueberroth's well-publicized triumph at Los Angeles he could have written his own ticket. President of General Motors. Chairman of AT&T. A cabinet post. Name it.

That he chose the baseball office aroused immediate suspicion from the skeptics. This guy is bigger than baseball, so what does he *really* want? What's he up to? He's looking over baseball's shoulder at *something*, but what is it?

Bill Veeck, I think it was, once suggested that the commissioner's office, with all of its built-in attention and publicity and name identification, was an ideal stepping stone to the White House. Is *this* what Sneaky Pete has in mind? Time out while we all check our wallets.

And so it was the other day when the commissioner announced his drug verdicts, involving 21 players. His volunteer monitors, with aroused fervor, rushed to accuse Ueberroth of

(a) being too harsh, or (b) being too gentle. They read all sorts of ulterior motives into the commissioner's act.

Dick Young, baseball's devoted conscience, suggested Ueberroth showed all the grit of a duckbilled platypus, that he should have strung the culprits from the yardarm. Other pressbox pundits thought the commissioner overstepped his bounds, that he was punishing men for admissions they made under promise of court immunity. And that his timing, right at the start of training camp, was a grandstand act, swiping baseball attention poised to be awarded to the annual spring rites.

Sorry, but the view from this remote outpost contains no such criticism. The commissioner, it says here, did about as good as he could with the materials at hand.

The high sheriff wanted to do *something* to attract attention to the drug practices, to set some sort of precedent, to warn other players.

Newscasts and headlines yelled *Suspension! Commissioner suspends seven super-stars!* Of course, he did not. He issued what criminal law calls suspended sentences, meaning as long as you meet certain behavior requirements, you don't go to the joint. He gave the players that choice, which means he did not exactly deprive them of their livelihood.

He fined seven of them 10 percent of their checks, sure, but those fines are in the form of donations to drug programs and, in all probability, are tax write-offs. No big deal.

So they must contribute a certain number of hours of community work. Most players do some of that anyway, speaking to kids and what-not. So they step up that activity for a year, so what?

The "suspension" penalties sounded much worse than they were. *But* they gained attention. They caused players and public to sit up and take notice, which was Ueberroth's exact intent.

On the other hand, those probably were the stiffest penalties the commissioner could *legally* impose. Out-and-out suspensions, based on admissions gained under immunity, for acts committed years ago, might have overstepped baseball law. The whole kaboodle could have wound up in the Supreme Court, and the commissioner surely did not need that possibility.

So Ueberroth made himself a smoke bomb, chose his time

and place, and created a lot of commotion and attention without much damage. About the only thing the commissioner was guilty of was intelligence. Of course, there are those in baseball who consider that a crime.

Ring-A-Dings

THE WINNER

MAY 27, 1977

Just the other night, a band of rogues broke into my palace, bound the master hand and hoof, propped his eyes open with swizzle sticks and forced him to watch some fiendish banality on the toob called *Suzy Says* or *Suzy Batseyes* or *Suzy Namedrops*.

Whatever the name of the interview show, it was a wronger. It should have been *The National Throw-up Hour*. I'll tell you how bad it was: Muhammad Ali stood out like a new Rolls on a used pickup lot.

As a matter of true confession, this victim added a new degree of respect for Ali. Not just because he was the sole substance of this particular production; Attila The Hun or Maurice Tillet The French Angel could have won *this* charm contest. No, Ali won this decision because the interview was so inane, the questions so fawningly saccharine, that he had the good native gumption to treat the whole bit as comedy. He seemed embarrassed by the absurdity of the moment.

The interviewer was this society gossip columnist called Suzy Knickerbocker, which is not her right name and you certainly can't blame her for *that*. This sort of show is done best, if at all, under an alias with a fast car waiting outside. She did a lot of billing and also cooing, accompanied by great sweeping whips of dark eyelashes, and asked such questions as: "You are probably the most famous man in the world. Don't you have an urge to do something outside of boxing? Wouldn't you like to be President of the United States?"

Ali stared at the interviewer in—to his almighty credit—disbelief, as though Joe Frazier had answered the first bell, moved to the center of the ring, squared off and dropped his trunks. Then showing great recuperative powers, he finally said, "What you trying to do, get me shot?"

Ali has also won more and more respect among the barnums

and baileys and streetcorner hustlers and bunco artists for the beautiful hoakum he has sold for the past couple years.

Of course, the champ has always been full of it as a Christmas turkey, even back when he was throwing his wildeyed seizures at weighing-in ceremonies with Sonny Liston. He was selling and business was good and so was the product.

But the last few years, now that Ali has lost much of his cobra quickness and his arthritic hands sting with every solid punch, the man has peddled cotton candy for Schraft's bonbons and gotten away with more than the Brinks robbers. You do not blame Ali for this any more than you blame Elvis Prestone for cutting a gold one. If the suckers wish to shell $20 to watch a plump boxer gesture to an Oriental sand crab on teevee yet, power to him. What did you do to the man who started Pet Rocks? Stone him? Ali can gross $3 million for a pingpong match against a duckbilled platypus but that hardly makes him an ax-murderer. Only a thief.

Now that the curtain is about to drop, Ali finds himself stricken with frequent attacks of honesty. (Back in the old days, this could have been fatal but fortunately medical science has developed a cure.)

John Marshall, who produced Ali's screen biography *The Greatest*, made a recent Texas swing and told of an incident when Ali was stopped on Madison Avenue by a man and his young daughter. The guy asked for an autograph for his daughter. Ali squatted and asked the child if she *really* knew who he was.

"Yes," she said, "You're the one who always says he's the greatest."

Ali was quiet for a moment, then he told the girl he would send her an autographed picture if she would do one thing: if she would take it to school and tell all her friends Muhammad Ali gave it to her. "But tell them I'm really not the greatest. I just say I'm the greatest to promote my fights."

Probably publicity puff but what the heck, it's better than seeing the man eat a live rooster.

And then in Miami recently, Ali made a strange (for him) confession to an old friend on the Miami *News*.

"I never thought I was the greatest. I just said I was. A long time ago I saw Gorgeous George promote a wrestling match.

He promised blood and guts. He promised to kill his opponent. He said anything to sell tickets. I saw an opportunity to do the same thing. It worked. They started coming in with their ten and twenty dollar bills to see the "braggin' nigger."

"How would I know who the greatest fighter was? How can you compare fighters from different times? I was probably the best of my time but how do I know what would have happened if I fought Louis, Dempsey or Jack Johnson? I've looked at some old boxing films and some of those guys were tremendous. Look at Sugar Ray. He was incredible."

But, back to that horrible interview. The mushy woman namedropped a stroll on a Long Island estate once with Jack Dempsey. "I asked him to slug me on the chin, just a light slug, so I could always say I was hit by Jack Dempsey. He did. Now you give me a little tap right here." She pointed to the left of her sweet chin. "So I can say I was hit by the great Ali."

Ali stared at her again and saw the lady was serious. You could see him thinking. He should have given her the old right—to hell with arthritic pains—that got Cleveland Williams. Instead he gave her a gentlemanly buss on the cheek. He blew it.

SUGAR INC.

About one score years ago, I had occasion to board an aircraft in Atlanta for an upcountry flight to Augusta, Georgia, where I hoped to write inspirational prose about adult men chasing a little white ball. A rugged good-looking brunet chap in his late 20s got on the same plane, sat in steerage with the rest of us goats and joked easily with stewardi.

His features were disturbingly familiar. A football player from past acquaintance? No, he wasn't tall enough. A golfer en route to the Masters? Nope, not smoothie enough. But a jock of some sort, certainly. Fortunately, the flight allowed only one hour to stew over the elusive memory. It wasn't until the drive to the motel and a chance glance at a poster in a storefront, that the identification clicked.

The poster: *Willie Pastrano, Leading lightheavyweight contender, Vs. George Kartalian, 10 rounds, Such-and-Such Arena, Thursday night.*

The mystery passenger was Pastrano, of course, flying from his Miami home to the Augusta fight site, where promoters hoped to lure customers already in town for the Masters golf tournament. What threw the thought processes offtrack was that the boxer was traveling *alone*. This surely offends the Marquis of Queensberry, wherever he may be.

Pastrano was not yet a champion—that was three years away—and his cornerman and handler would probably arrive later in the week. But just the idea of a headline fighter all by his lonesome, out in the public exposed to common germs and such, was just a bit surprising.

The memory was rehashed just this week when I read somewhere that Sugar Ray Leonard's entourage for this Montreal fight tonight numbered 28 people and that he objected strongly to his party being called an "entourage."

Presumably young Leonard has access to a dictionary and has noticed that the word means "attendants, as of a person of rank." He says the accompanists are just friends, along for the ride. He did not wish them to be considered employees because some nosey fed might ask whatever happened to his withholding taxes and social security payments and other embarrassing questions. But one would assume that all he would have to do is snap his pretty fingers and some friends would run fetch him a cheeseburger medium well. This, you would think, would make them attendants. So *entourage* it stays, Shug.

For some reason, it has ever seemed necessary to cloak a boxer with a smothering layer of bodies. He is babied beyond imagination. *Here, let me lace those shoes for you, champ. Here, let me turn that page.*

Maybe some graybeards remember when Leonard's model, Sugar Ray Robinson, made his festive tour of Europe some 30 years ago. The callused citizens along Jacobs Beach were incensed to note that Sugar Ray's entourage included his *barber*, for goodness sakes. Who does he think he is, Zsa Zsa Gabor? It's accepted to have a couple trainers along and a business manager and a gofer or two. But the inclusion of a barber indicated that Sugar Ray Robinson's mind wasn't on the boxing business.

The sages nodded wisely when Robinson, barber and all, made bouts in Paris and Zurich and Antwerp and Berlin and then stopped off in London on his way home to fight a local chap named Randy Turpin and lose the middleweight title. In that day, it was as shocking as Muhammad Ali losing to Leon Spinks. The Jacobs Beachers said the entourage done him in.

Far before Robinson's day, however, the practice was there. When Jack Dempsey made his memorable trip to Shelby, Montana, to box Tommy Gibbons in 1923, he had a train car full. Jack Kearns, the manager, Jerry The Greek Luvadis, the rubdown guy, four or five more, including Mike Trant, a Chicago cop whose assignment, other than bodyguarding, was to hold a parasol over Dempsey's head between rounds to shunt that July 4 sun.

Dempsey's crowd of hangers-on so inspired one pressrow poet of the day that when he observed the champion making his way to the ring for one title defense, he began his story with a couplet:

Hail, the conquering hero comes
Surrounded by a bunch of bums.

Of course, most hangers-on are financed under the vague

term of "expenses" charged to the fight promoter. You may be sure it doesn't come out of the fighter's purse.

Once Robinson was booked to box Pedro Gonzales in Baltimore and Sugar Ray's manager, George Gainsford, prudently made a trip there before the fight to see how advance ticket sale was going. He found there wasn't enough in the till to pay expenses for the entourage. So Robinson didn't show up for the fight.

When Spinks lost his brief title to Ali in New Orleans a couple years ago, the local promoters were screaming because the Spinks party occupied 20 rooms at a local hotel, all charged to promoter's "expenses." And Spinks' corner during the Superdome fight became so crowded and confused with different people yelling instructions and arguing with each other, that George Benton left the ring in disgust after the fifth round. Benton is the knowledgable trainer from Philadelphia who was hired especially to prepare Spinks for his title defense against Ali.

Of course, Ali was always surrounded by a mob of lackeys. Bundini Brown was forever around, presumably to wipe off Ali's face with a towel and serve faithfully and loudly in the Amen Corner. Herbert Muhammad was usually in the background, preparing to rake the one-third cut taken by the Black Muslims. There were two or three trainers, in addition to Angelo Dundee, but Ali paid them no mind. He had Pat Patterson as "chief of security" and his personal masseur, Luis Sarria, and his cook, Lana Shabazz, and a sort of camp paymaster, Gene Kilroy, although Ali himself painstakingly studied and signed every check.

After all, John L. Sullivan set the pattern before the turn of the century when he made a "triumphant tour of Europe." He had a lady friend on the side, a show girl, who was quite devoted. She accompanied Sullivan on the entire trip, disguised as a young boy in uniform to fool the hotel dicks. Sugar Ray may have carried his own barber, but the Great John L. had his very own and very dear bellhop.

THE TIGER AS LAMB

NOVEMBER 26, 1980

NEW ORLEANS, LOUISIANA—This welterweight title fight already had its mysterious elements from the day it was made. But now it may go down in history with flying saucers, Jimmy Hoffa and the Bermuda Triangle.

The boxfight populace may never ever fathom the stunning finish at the Superdome Tuesday night when the legendary tough guy quit. When Roberto Duran, the bantam brute from the Panama gutters, turned to the referee and said, "No mas, no mas. No more box."

Sugar Ray Leonard, the man closest to the plot, didn't even grasp the action there in the eighth round when Duran backed away, spoke to referee Octavio Meyron, gave a futile wave of a glove and started walking to his corner. The Mexican referee also was shocked into paralysis. And Leonard ran up to Duran's side and pasted him with a right hook to the belly and a left to the back of the champ's shaggy mane. Duran didn't even turn around.

The referee recovered quickly from his trance and dragged Leonard away and it was only then that the new champ realized that his ferocious opponent, supposedly the baddest boxer in captivity or out, had quit like a kid on the schoolground. And this was a signal for the craziest scene of all. Roger Leonard, Sugar Ray's brother, leaped in the ring and squared off against Duran. And if Roberto was so dead set against fighting Sugar Ray anymore, he looked as if he would still like to punch someone else in the family.

In the pressrows, frantic newsmen leaped to their chairs and shouted questions. Old Freddie Brown, a gnarled boxing relic who worked Duran's corner, yelled at a reporter.

"He didn't say nuttin," Brown spat. "He just quit!"

While cops climbed over each other to get in the ring, while somebody separated Duran and Roger Leonard, pandemonium became the theme. One photographer was thrown bodily from the ring. A policeman somehow got a choke hold on Jose Sulaiman, the Mexican president of the World Boxing Council. Ray Arcel, another of the ancients who worked Duran's corner, entered his frail 82-year-old body in a shoving match with a television cameraman.

"Cramps! Cramps! Duran had muscle cramps!" the cry passed around the pressrows.

Guys looked at each other in wild disbelief. A fighter getting cramps in a championship fight? Tony Dorsett gets cramps. Roberto Duran doesn't get cramps. If a bicep muscle had the audacity to cramp on him, he would simply bite it out and spit it on the canvas.

"His shoulder! He dislocated his shoulder!"

This shouted explanation touched memories. It was in 1964 when Sonny Liston, another of those doubletough characters, quit in a heavyweight championship fight in Miami. Said he hurt his shoulder, an excuse hardly anyone believed, not even young Cassius Clay who became champion by default.

Oldertimers harked back to 1946 when Marcel Cerdan quit in a title match with Jake LaMotta, saying his shoulder muscle was torn or somesuch. Still, it didn't make this any more believable. Another surprise was that you didn't hear the speculation that his drinking water was poisoned.

The popular theory of the layman immediately was this fiasco set up a third match between the two—a rubber bout that would drag even more millions out of a gullible public.

From the cynics came another guess: That Duran's hatred of America and its citizens simply led him to a disdainful act, a thumbing of nose at the grandiose pomposity of a championship fight. *To hell with you gringos. I got my eight million of your republican dollars and you can take your show and jam it.* The rather ridiculous act of the Louisiana State Athletic Commission in "holding up Duran's purse until a further physical examination" was a toothless yelp. What purse? Duran got his money up front. It's already in a Panama bank.

Roberto seemed singularly undisturbed in the midst of all the doubts. He met the shouting press afterward in his warmup suit and baseball cap and he seemed in the best of spirits and health. He was not at all the surly angry Duran of yore. It was almost as if he were saying: mission accomplished. The gringo dollar will keep me fat and happy for the rest of my days.

Stomach cramps had hit him in the fifth round, he said through an interpreter, and they started getting worse and worse and he got weaker and weaker. The skeptics instantly thought, oh ho, this is something new. Creeping cramps. What happened to the oldfashion cramp that struck like a seizure? He thought the fight was even at the time. Leonard had never hurt him. And he still thought he was a better man than Sugar Ray Leonard.

"A thousand times!" he said. He waved cheerily when he left, further mystifying his audience. He didn't even ask for a rematch. He's through with boxing, he said with noticeable unconcern.

Of course, the fight was *not* even at that point. Leonard was ahead on all three judges' cards. This was a different Leonard than the dogged punch-trader who lost to Duran six months ago in Montreal. This was a swiftly moving boxer, backpedaling, side to side, punching in flurries, dodging the bullish rushes of Duran. He even outmaneuvered the stronger Duran in the clinches.

In the seventh round, Leonard was boxing with so much confidence, he started his childish showoff stunts, dropping his hands and sticking his chin out tauntingly, as his idol, Muhammad Ali, used to do. He faked the bolo windups, and did the Ali shuffle. At the time, he seemed to be making a terrible mistake, for the old Duran could switch a fight pattern with one terrible punch. And he fought best when he was furious.

But there was another part of the mystery. Duran wasn't the fire-eyed angry man he has been before. In fact, he fought most of the eight rounds with a curious half-grin on his face. When Leonard occasionally would jar the black mop of hair with a stiff jab, Duran frequently showed his dimples.

And then the doubters could think back to other factors of the mystery. Why was the rematch made this quick? It normally would have been sometime next spring. Sugar Ray wanted to retire after the Montreal loss. What changed his mind? Why was the fierce Duran suddenly a grinning, pleasant chap? If he were setting up a rubber match, why wouldn't he take one on the jaw and lay down, not quit with almost a nonchalant unconcern.

"Maybe his arm went, maybe his stomach went, maybe his head went," said Arcel. "I wish I could tell you what happened. Maybe it was just frustration."

From Sulaiman, "We shouldn't believe there is a fix. Boxing is a beautiful sport. Dirty thoughts belong to dirty people. Duran has been too great for too many years. The word 'fix' is not in his vocabulary. After so many years, people just get tired, they want out.

"Sugar Ray made a fantastic fight. Duran mentioned he was overcome with cramps. I think there is more, but there must be some important reason. Something happened to him."

Leonard was angry that anyone would doubt the fight. "He quit of his own free will," said the new champ, missing the point entirely. Certainly nobody held a gun on Duran. That would have made the mystery much easier to solve.

QUIET EXIT

LAS VEGAS, NEVADA—For the greatest fighter in the whole wide world, by his own admission, it was a strange exit.

He sat there on his corner stool, gazing fixedly at a spot on the canvas in front of him, oblivious to the turmoil around him. Angelo Dundee, who has worked Muhammad Ali's corner through three different championship terms, was gesturing wildly and pushing at Bundini Brown, Ali's foremost hanger-on.

Referee Richard Green cocked his head to listen to Dundee's shouts. Then he nodded rapidly several times, strode quickly to Larry Holmes' corner.

"He's stopping the fight!" came a cry from press row. And indeed the referee raised Holmes' hand high over his head, just a few ticks before the bell rang for the 11th round. And then, of course, the usual bedlam erupted in the ring, when every photographer in the world and maybe a few from Mars, plus cops and ushers and shouting wellwishers climbed in the ring for their typical enactment of the Battle of the Alamo.

But if the audience was confused, both here on the parking lot of Caesar's Palace and on closed circuit theaters all over the land, even on teevee sets in Russia and China, Muhammad Ali, the former greatest, did not seem at all bewildered. Nor did he protest when the referee halted a weird, ineffective performance by the 38-year-old showman.

Ali appeared, well, just tired and resigned and dejected that his gaudy bid for a fourth heavyweight title had been extinguished with such a mild pop, like a wet firecracker. He would have liked, you know, to go out with a memorable bang if indeed he had to go out. Instead, it was as if Father Time had stepped on a dust ball on his way to work.

Ali was simply no factor. He was a big zero. Oh, he tried to provide comic relief but even those antics came across like a cheap wrestling match. The three judges had Holmes winning every round. Ali didn't throw enough punches to disturb a bedsheet.

After a lackluster sixth round was greeted by hearty boos, the referee actually warned Ali to join in the spirit of things, or he would stop the fight. At the start of the seventh round, Ali actually carried the action to Holmes, trying a few jabs and a couple righthand leads that landed harmlessly on Holmes' thick neck. Then the ex-champ went back to his pattern of bobbing, feinting, covering up, dropping his hands occasionally and daring Holmes to swing at his unprotected head so he could prove his reflexes were still sharp enough to evade the blows.

His strategy seemed obvious. He had studied Holmes' history of tiring in the late rounds. He knew Holmes had only gone a full 15 rounds once in his career. He wanted Holmes to grow arm weary so he might finish him off in the last few rounds. So he sacrificed the first 10 rounds on the judges' cards as part of the scheme.

The plot was foiled, however, by Ali's own lack of stamina. It became apparent that his middleage legs and arms and lungs weren't equal to the task and that his crash weight reduction of dropping 32 pounds in four months had subtracted from his strength.

It wasn't that Holmes hurt him especially, although Larry offered 100 swings for every one of Ali's. Many of Holmes' efforts missed or were caught on Ali's gloves and arms. Neither was it the expected heat, for somehow the weather forecasters erred and instead of a sweltering night, it was a rather pleasant desert evening with a slight breeze.

Holmes did raise a red welt under Ali's left eye as early as the fourth round and then, in the ninth, ripped two punishing uppercuts to Ali's head. Some thought a thumb must have caught Ali's eye because he quickly turned away and covered his head with his gloves and cowered against the ropes. Holmes took that occasion to punch heavily on Ali's unprotected rib cage.

"I wanted to stop it in the ninth round," said the referee. "But Angelo Dundee asked me to give him another round."

A ringside pressman near Ali's corner said the order to stop the fight came not from Dundee nor the referee, but from Herbert Muhammad, a leader of the Black Muslims, of which

Ali is the most famous member and No. 1 breadwinner. At the end of the ninth, Dundee looked toward Herbert Muhammad and he shook his head.

"Then, after the 10th round, Pat Patterson, Ali's bodyguard, was on the ring steps," said veteran ring author Barney Nagler. "Dundee said something to Pat and he shouted down to Herbert, who was sitting in the first row of the press section. Pat yelled, 'What do you want to do?' Herbert said, 'Stop it!' Then he turned to us and said, 'He's getting defenseless.' "

Dr. Don Romero, the Nevada boxing commission doctor, was standing on the ring apron watching Ali when the word was passed to Dundee to give up the ship.

Bundini Brown, Ali's gofer all these years, disagreed. He didn't want his mealticket stopped. Bundini argued and pulled at Dundee, who pushed him away and shouted his surrender to the referee. Indeed, Dundee and Brown shouted at each other several times during the fight.

"The doctor said Ali told him he wanted to continue," said referee Green. But Ali certainly didn't look it. With his theatrical history, you would expect him to rant and scream protests at the referee. But he sat there, sweat cascading down his creased stomach, staring at the floor as if he were sitting in a police station anteroom, waiting to be booked.

Actually, Ali didn't appear to be hit that hard and often, except for the two uppercuts. But in the 10th round, Holmes landed 17 solid jabs that bobbed Ali's head back. There was a later report that Ali suffered two cracked ribs, but it was denied by members of Ali's family.

Holmes thought he was lambasting the whey from his idol.

"I think I hurt him a few times," said the younger champ, although he didn't seem all that certain. "Most guys I fought, if I hit them as many times as I hit Ali, they wouldn't be able to stand up to it."

Ali worked more on Holmes psyche than on his body. He went back to his old circus tricks, faking hysterical anger before the fight, glaring at Holmes and mouthing insults. Holmes ignored him but the 25,000 in the live audience, including Frank Sinatra, Tom Jones, Sylvester Stallone, Andy Williams and other show biz folks, roared at his pantomimes.

In truth, Ali hadn't pulled these childish tactics since the days when he was taunting Ernie Terrell and poor Floyd Patterson.

He talked and gestured and mocked Holmes so much during the fight that you thought perhaps he was play-acting when he covered his face after those two ninth-round uppercuts. But this time he wasn't kidding. He had gone to the well too often.

"He is a great boxer, a great athlete and a great human being," said Holmes. It was almost as if he were reading the epitaph off a tombstone.

CRUEL SEE

MAY 25, 1984

The sorriest act I ever saw was Gaseous Cassius against Floyd Patterson. It was a shameful show of human degradation, more associated with a prisoner-of-war camp than under the guise of sport.

Gaseous was Muhammad Ali by that time and had declared himself a minister; some of us thought it a rare way for a preacher of *any faith* to behave, or a hangman or sadist or anything else that walked on two legs and wore clothes.

Patterson was a brooding, sensitive and insecure man who never was much of a fighter. He was the exact opposite of Ali, who was setting world records for arrogance. Of course, most of Ali's show was pure carnival, designed to woo headlines and build box-office. But this night, in Las Vegas in 1965, the champion went far beyond the bounds of decency.

It was a mismatch, of course, and to make it even more one-sided, Patterson's back went out on him in the first round. He became a stiff sitting duck, dragging his right leg behind him like a paralyzed man, unable to do more than paw feebly at Ali.

The champ tortured him. Ali would count for his partisan crowd as each punch landed. "Bam!" he would shout with a jab to the forehead. "Bam!" another jab. "Bam! Bam!" two jabs.

When Patterson was ripped by an uppercut or a long right and seemed on the verge of collapse, Ali would withdraw and dance around the staggering man, dropping hands to his side, sticking out his handsome jaw and yell "White man's nigger! Uncle Tom nigger!" for all ringside to hear. He would deliberately let Patterson recover and slash him again. It was a cat playing with a mortally wounded mouse and it was a miserable thing to watch. It made you want to get up and go walk in the woods or take a bath.

Gaseous Cassius on stage was a caricature, a harmless cartoon to be chuckled over when there was nothing better to watch. But what he did on this occasion—as well in a later bout with Ernie Terrell—was not humorous. It was a disservice, not just to a business that was making him millions, but to a fellow laborer.

The boxfight business deserves a disservice occasionally, but not the honest workmen therein. You wonder, you *really* wonder, what would have been the public reaction if Larry Holmes had taunted and degraded the helpless Ali in *their* championship match.

Memory of Ali's abasement returned recently when Ray Leonard did his return number. Leonard has always had a little Ali in him, perhaps more than a little, and it just doesn't fit.

In the middle rounds against the earnest journeyman, Kevin Howard, Leonard went into a taunting dance, hands dropped, chin out, the threat of the bolo punch, all the phrases of the classic showboat act. There had been no animosity, real or faked, between Leonard and Howard, no reason for this juvenile streetcorner prance. No reason except Leonard seems to have this streak in him, this desperate grab at smart-aleck theatrics that smacks of phoniness.

Remember his garish "retirement" announcement, first edition: black tie, testimonials, tearful speeches, television cameras. Then his comeback "to prove himself" or whatever excuse he used, that also was a bit saccharine, with all of his television appearances, his pleas to his "public," his gratitude for his "public's concern."

Ali, after his early cruel steak, got by with his sideshow because you knew it was an act and *he* knew you knew. But with Leonard, it doesn't play.

Like Leonard, there will be others to follow the Ali pattern, the jabbering, the peacock struts. It is like Gorgeous George, the renowned rassle thespian and all the grunters who followed his cues.

Just this week, NBC breathlessly announced that Wilbert "Vampire" Johnson would box John "The Beast" Mugabi for the junior welter title this very Sunday afternoon. "Vampire" dresses in a black satin cape, styled by Belo Lugosi, enters the ring in a coffin and drinks water that has been colored red. I mean, are you reading this?

The NBC publicity sheet gives no hint of what "The Beast" will do as a topper, but it will probably be something basic, like eat a live lamb.

One supposes Ali will be recognized as the innovator of heavy boxing drama. There were dabbles before. Max Baer was a bit of a clown in his day but Baer recognized the foundation of all humor. He made fun of himself, before he made fun of others.

Now and then, us old goats get nostalgic for the quiet work of champions like Joe Louis and Rocky Marciano, who pulled their shift, toweled off, shook hands all around and went down the street for a beer with the boys.

Louis was the most serious and stolid and hardest of workers; he treated opponents with respect and they loved him for it. Louis historians claimed their man showed expression only one time in the ring. That was when he was matched against Arturo Godoy, the South American who came out of his corner all crouched over and scrambling like a sand crab. Louis paused just for an instant and grinned.

"Man fightin' me sideways," he explained later.

APT TIMING

Joe Louis perhaps will be certified as the greatest heavy-weight fighter of all time, and he died on the rocks.

Larry Holmes probably will be filed in the Average Heavy-weight Champion class and he will have vaults full.

No matter how roughly Holmes treats young Gerry Cooney on June ll. No matter if he retires unbeaten at the end of his 33rd year, Larry still will rank along with Ezzard Charles, Joe Walcott, Max Schmeling, Max Baer and the like as rather ordinary champs who filled in until somebody like Louis or Muhammad Ali or Rocky Marciano came along. Oh, he will still get the call over such title-holders as Primo Carnera and Floyd Patterson and Leon Spinks and *that* ilk. But the historians won't invite him to the head table.

Some will say Larry Holmes had bad timing. That he was overshadowed, for much of his career, by Ali and Joe Frazier. And when he finally got his chance at the big gravy, he was already 28 and the cupboard was dang near bare of exciting opponents. And the boxing public was drained emotionally by Ali's desperate rantings from his middle-aged craze.

Even before Holmes beat a blubbery Ali two years ago he acknowledged his awkward situation.

"If Ali beats me, people will say I was no good at all, getting beat by an old man," Holmes said then. "And if I beat him, people say, so what, he beat an old man."

Now, Larry has other, more comfortable thoughts.

"I've heard that about me coming along at the wrong time," Holmes said the other day on his visit here. "Actually, it was the *right* time."

This conversation with the champ, at leisure in his hotel suite, was not about dealing with immortality, but with bankers. Holmes will collect $10 million for his part in the Las Vegas show next month.

So here he was, a middle school dropout, diamonds on two

fingers, enough gold dangling around his neck to anchor the *U.S.S. Forrestal,* custom-made boots on his feet, silk shirt straining at his biceps. Back home in Easton, Pennsylvania, he has a mansion with *nine* bathrooms, for goodness sakes, and a garage full of luxury automobiles and an indoor pool built like a boxing glove. And still a $10 million payday coming up.

Could he ever imagine such fortunes, back when he was hustling for a buck on the streets of Easton, washing cars, delivering packages?

"All I ever thought of, the most I could hope for, was to make a little money and buy my own home and maybe own a little business, so I wouldn't have to kill myself working all my life," Holmes said.

"That television show, about the guy who came around, knocked on the door and gave away $1 million. What was his name? Mr. Anthony or something? I used to pray, man, let that guy knock on *my* door."

Holmes paused to study some hotel chits a camp worker handed him to sign.

"No, I don't put Larry Holmes on these," he said to the guy. Well, said the guy, Holmes wouldn't have to pay for them. It was just to certify that they were legitimate expenses, presumably so the hotel could include them on the overall bill.

"No, I don't sign these," Holmes said. "They would show up later on Form 140." (Or maybe he said 240 or whatever. Something to do with taxes and expenses.)

He turned back to the conversation and grinned. "Naw, I never thought about making no million dollars or talking about taxes or tax money in escrow, or the way I'm set up now, in a corporation with 30 people on the payroll. I just wanted to live comfortable without killing myself with hard work."

Holmes wasn't eaten with ambition, even after he got in the boxfight business. After he dropped out of school, he was a pretty good sandlot and playground athlete and naturally gravitated to a community gym and boxing gloves. A short amateur career ended with Larry taking a job as a sparring partner. He worked seven years as a training target for both Ali and Frazier.

"I got $500 a week," he said. "First professional fight I had, I got $65.

"But then I got to thinking one day. Here was Ali, eight years older than me, and Frazier, six years older. These were guys on their way out. I was doing all right sparring against them, holding my own I thought.

"I started thinking, what's going to happen when they are gone. And all the b-a-a-d guys—Norton and Shavers and Lyle—they were going downhill and George Foreman had turned preacher. Who was there to take over?

"So really, I came along exactly at the right time."

Holmes' first big payday was a $75,000 bout with Shavers in 1978. Since then, he has had 12 biggies. And this $10 million date with Cooney will be the capper. All this, mind you, in less than four years.

And yet, when you speak of right timing and suitable skin pigmentation, you must award Cooney first prize. He hasn't boxed enough professional rounds to learn how to grunt, and yet he, too, will draw $10 million.

Louis worked long and hard and boxed everything that would stick its head out of a hole, and each of these two guys will draw a bigger check for one night than Louis did for his 73-fight career. It wasn't that Louis wasn't paid, commensurate with his era. He blew most of it on bad investments, such as gold and gin rummy and income taxes. Joe Louis never even had a boxing glove-shaped swimming pool in his life, poor guy.

NO MATCH

MAY 22, 1985

At the top of the show, as goldythroats are fond of saying, there was an unfortunate film clip. The tv folk, in a desperate attempt to pump juice into the production, decorated it with all sorts of window dressing. There was Gene Tunney shadowboxing with that jerky film speed they always use to make Charlie Chaplin shuffle down the street. I think I glimpsed Madcap Maxie Baer, for goodness sakes, lambasting poor Primo Carnera and being lambasted, in turn, by ancient James J. Braddock.

But the one significant clip, repeated several times, showed Rocky Marciano grossly frustrated in his attempt to knock the heavyweight belt from Jersey Joe Walcott.

On record, Walcott was 38 years at the time and there were whispers that was his *boxing* age, meaning he might be several years older. But he was supple as a buggy whip and his waist was lean and he had grace in every movement.

This scene was the 13th round and the indefatigable Walcott was flitting in and out of range, his jab just as crisp as in early rounds. And here was Marciano leaning forward, off-balance as usual, chin jutting like a dreadnought bearing down on a U-boat. Marciano's favorite stance was always that of a ski jumper just leaving the launch. His stubby flippers flailed like a furious turtle, but in this match, he was striking mostly air and forearms. Walcott was too elusive.

They were near the ropes when Joe ducked neatly to his left, under a sweeping Marciano hook and suddenly there was Rocky's right fist on his chin. Rocky might have been the only boxer ever to start a swing with one hand before the other glove landed, or so it seemed.

Walcott bent slowly to the floor, head down, as a Hindu on a prayer rug. His knees touched and then his brow and there he remained, like an upended slice of cantaloupe.

Marciano bounded to the nearest corner, but referee

Charley Daggert shouted and pointed to another. Marciano *ran* eagerly to that corner. *Ran!*

Mind you, this was the 13th round. Marciano had been fighting wasps with those heavy arms, lunging ahead constantly at that tormenting shadow. He was 29 years old, no youth anymore, and this was longer by three rounds than he had ever boxed in his life. Yet he had a knockout remaining in his right glove and the inestimable energy to *run* to the neutral corner. And if Walcott had managed to regain his verticality, Rocky would have decked him again and again and then looked around for the horse he rode in on.

The reason this flim clip is labeled "unfortunate" is that it furnished NBC viewers a degrading comparison to the incumbent heavyweight champeen, who came on next, live and breathing heavy. Larry Holmes was so spent during the late rounds with the raw youngster, Carl Williams, he couldn't have knocked anybody out or *run* to a corner if bloodhounds nipped his heels.

Holmes is 35 but, he insists, a "young 35." He has not been belabored much during his career. He has not, as they say on the plains, been rode hard and put away wet. He should not have had all this much trouble with Williams. Six or eight heavy blows to the pancreas, it seemed to me, and the lad would have sought a suitable place to repose. But Holmes was unable to mount any sort of sustained charge.

Holmes says he was undertrained for the bout. Trainer Eddie Futch said he *overtrained*. Physically now, Holmes reminds one of Sonny Liston, with muscles heavy and soggy, like you find Secretariat after he has been out to pasture for a decade. An old stud, solid and healthy and, well, *comfortable*. He doesn't look like a heavyweight champion.

Marciano, the guy in the film clip, now *he* looks like a heavyweight champion. And that's the guy Holmes wishes to compare his record with; he asks for the same niche in history. Forget it, Larry, please.

WAR HEROES

APRIL 16, 1985

LAS VEGAS, NEVADA—The greatest first round in the history of boxing. You can carve that on a mountain.

Old-timers may hedge. They will call back the wild opening of the Jack Dempsey-Luis Firpo slugfest back in the dark ages, when both men were up and down like yo-yos. But you'll never convince eyeball witnesses here that they saw anything but a classic. Marv Hagler's three-round explosion, and the berserk retaliation by Tommy Hearns, surely established a high (or a low) in savage brutality that will occupy a permanent page in ring records.

Historians will wear this film to shreds, still not believing the amount of frantic action before referee Richard Steele shook his head and stood in front of a tottering, dazed Hearns with a minute left in the third round. The tall challenger had just managed to weave to uncertain feet after the fight's only knockdown. But he obviously was in no condition to continue. Another round at this gait and nobody could have continued, including the stunned spectators.

The fight was misplaced. Instead of an outdoor arena on Caesars Palace tennis courts, it should have been held in a back alley or a jungle. This was a brawl, starting with Hagler's whirlwind attack at the opening bell. This was no pushing, shoving, mauling fracas, as so many rough-house rumbles tend to be. Instead, it was a furious display of crisp, hard punches by both men—Hagler instigating the pace and Hearns, seemingly, fighting for his life.

The bookkeepers said Hagler threw 173 punches in the three rounds, and Hearns pitched 166. Each landed about 55 percent, according to auditors, but that seems like a low count. You were not aware of that many misses, from the time when Hagler quickly stunned Hearns with a massive right hook while the rubberneckers were still gawking at the celebrities at ringside.

But the wallops never stopped coming and when the 15,000 customers finally snapped to the fact this was no impudent opening flurry, they were almost too shocked to make noise.

They were preparing for a careful 12-round experience. Hearns might attempt an early knockout before calming down to his boxing skills, but not Hagler. Hagler usually has been a cautious performer, working his way inside so he could bang away at the other guy's ribs. But here they were, ignoring any semblance of defense, whanging away with almost insane vigor.

Misses? It seemed every effort ended with a jolting, jarring thud, with first Hearns', then Hagler's head snapping back with terrible frequency.

Hagler came flying from his corner like a berserk wild animal, seeking to put the taller Hearns on a quick defensive, throw him off-balance with a suicidal attack and never let his longer reach and snappy jab keep Hagler at bay.

"I knew I had to fight like a challenger," said Hagler. The middleweight champ is leery of the quality of Nevada judging. He fought a previous draw with Vito Antuofermo here in Vegas, which was highly controversial. And in his 15-round decision over Roberto Duran here, the judging was much closer than he thought it should have been.

So this time, he wanted to leave no doubt. Hagler fought like it was a four-rounder and only one person would be left standing. He must have landed 70 punches, both lefts and rights, in that first round. And Hearns fought back, almost on equal terms. The tempo slackened somewhat in the following two rounds, but not much. Referee Steele said he had never seen so much action packed into three rounds.

In that final round, Steele summoned a doctor to the ring apron to study the forehead and eye cuts on Hagler's shaven head. But Dr. Donald Romero didn't even look at the cuts, which were flowing blood over both fighters. He merely asked Hagler if the wounds bothered him, Hagler shook his head, and the war was on again.

It was shortly after that southpaw Hagler caught Hearns with yet another sweeping right hook that sent the Detroit boxer reeling across the ring. Hagler almost ran to Hearns in his eagerness to follow up, and clouted his victim with another half-dozen shots before he collapsed on his back, stomach heaving and limbs akimbo.

It couldn't have possibly lasted much longer. Something had to give. On this night and in the history books forevermore, that something was Hearns. But in this wildest of pitched battles, even to survive was a victory of sorts.

SECOND
THOUGHT

After breath mercifully had been returned to press row, your Vaunted Expert here made a pronouncement. Tilting the metal chair, I motioned for the shell-like ear of Rick Talley, a familiar rogue from Los Angeles, and explained to him as follows:

"We just saw the greatest first round in the history of boxing!"

Oddly enough, the world did not pause in its revolutions. People around us did not suddenly hush and cup a palm to their sideburns, like the E.F. Hutton commercial. It was not an earth-shaking statement, mainly because throughout the press section, approximately 300 wretches were leaning toward neighbors and saying the same words.

Talley nodded enthusiastically. Because of surrounding noise, he understood me to say I would buy the first round in our regular social hour after work was done, and Talley seldom disagrees with such judgment.

However, it was apparent to all that Marvin Hagler and Thomas Hearns had just constructed a classic. Certainly, for fury and nonstop violence, none of us had seen its equal. At the bell, Hagler rushed across the ring and cleverly intercepted a big left hook with his shaven head. It affected him like a gnat in a cyclone. He then grimly belabored Mr. Hearns with every punch in the book and several that have yet to be invented. On a couple wild swings, he planted a glove in the Hearns groin, but there was no time or opportunity for the victim to complain. He was too busy clouting his tormentor in return.

Monday evening, Home Box Office ran the fight film for its subscribers, many of whom will claim us Vaunted Experts full of prunes. There were fascinating camera angles and wordy interviews, but somehow the lens did not portray the fight.

On film, it appeared an excellent match with a goodly number of punches thrown and caught, but no better than any number of others, such as the Thrilla in Manila, starring Frazier and Ali. The knockdown of Hearns was graphic and impressive, but it was a rather cold, detached copy. It was like a typewritten love letter, the *warmth* just wasn't there.

The film did not capture the *urgency* of the moment, the *constancy* of action. When you watch pictures of the fight, you see it as disjointed flurries—perhaps because the camera angles constantly are shifting.

The fight itself, to eyewitnesses, was a frantic continuity of movement, with no pause for breathing for fighter or spectator. The wildness of the scene was missing in the film.

In this report, it was suggested that first-round fighting between Jack Dempsey and Luis Firpo was a possible rival to the Hagler-Hearns beginning.

Apparently, there was wild, wild enthusiasm in *that* fight, also, because—unlike Hagler or Hearns—Dempsey generated interest whatever he did. Firpo was a handsome caveman from Argentina, a crude but strong brute who once hit Jess Willard so hard, Willard's right leg became paralyzed.

There were 88,000 jammed into the Polo Grounds September 14, 1923, and half that many turned away. At the bell, Dempsey ran across the ring and launched a wild right. Firpo uncharacteristically sidestepped and caught Dempsey on the button with a short left uppercut. Less than five seconds after the opening bell, and here was Dempsey on his knees.

The champ jumped up, grabbed Firpo by the nape with one hand and knocked him down with a right hook. The visitor struggled up at nine and Dempsey put him down again. This went on for several minutes. Finally, Firpo unleased a right-hand haymaker that traveled about four yards and landed on Dempsey's 5 o'clock shadow. Down went the champ.

Dempsey arose and floored Firpo for the *seventh* time, whereupon the Latin reeled to his feet and, using his right fist like a persimmon club, pounded Dempsey four times on the top of his noggin and knocked him through the ropes. Sportswriters shoved the groggy champion back in the ring. He lasted out the round and then KO'd Firpo in the second.

The crowd had gone insane the first time Dempsey went down. There was pushing, shoving, screaming. One ringsider promptly died with a heart attack. Babe Ruth climbed on a bench to see better, and Mickey Walker, the middleweight, pushed him off. Babe took a swing at Mickey. Maybe this Hagler-Hearns thing was the *second* best.

SECRET
WEAPONS

It has come to our idle attention that a British chap named
Frank Bruno has invented a secret punch, and it's about time.
We haven't had one of those in quite awhile and, frankly,
they've been missed.

Mr. Bruno says he will use this covert weapon to deposit Tim
Witherspoon on his Yankee cannister this week and relieve him
of the WBA heavyweight surcingle. Or maybe it is the WBC
belt, or the IOBA title, or the undisputed heavyweight ruler-
ship of North Dakota.

Anyways, the studious Mr. Bruno has dispatched several bul-
letins from his London laboratory, indicating his discovery is so
revolutionary he will shield it from public eye until Saturday
evening at Wembley Stadium. He has barred public and press
from his training quarters, establishing a protectorate reminis-
cent of Gen. Leslie Groves and his precious stacks of uranium
oxide and cadmium in a Chicago basement four decades past.

This action so infuriated the sensitive Mr. Witherspoon that
he straightway closed *his* gates also, presumably to work on
some devious invention of his own, like maybe a left jab thrown
from behind the back. At any rate, the two plotters are leaving
a certain portion of the boxing world completely in the dark as
what to expect from the encounter. Perhaps it's better this way.

The cauliflower crowd has not mulled over a real mystery
since, oh, since Kid Gavilan came up from Cuba after World
War II with something called a "bolo punch." Boxing publicists
worked up a fine froth over this maneuver learned, they explained breathlessly, in Gavilan's long hot days as a harvest
hand. A bolo is a large curved machete used extensively in the
cane fields and on certain street corners in Havana on Saturday
nights.

The "bolo punch" was a grand circular uppercut, much like

210

the delivery of a softball pitcher, and it normally did all the damage of a runaway library curtain. However, it was a showy gesture and audiences never failed to ooh and aah when Gavilan and his mimics unwound this action.

Even Muhammad Ali copied it as a part of his showtime routine, which included the Ali Shuffle and the Rope-a-dope, two carnival acts he had stolen from Charlie Chaplin and Ben Blue. The Ali troops obediently moaned in ecstasy when their man went into one of these theatrical gyrations, much as when your favorite rassler applies the Iron Claw or the Great Mongolian Spleen Clamp.

Every student's favorite secret weapon, of course, was the illustrious Cosmic Punch, developed by Prof. Lou Nova.

This was back in 1941 when Joe Louis was entertaining the populace with his famous Bum-of-the-Month series. He defended his title seven times that year. Prof. Nova was elected to one of these dubious honors and immediately retired to his laboratory where he was soon heard to exclaim, "Eureka!"

In an effort to figure some method to derail The Brown Bomber, Prof. Nova had chanced upon scientific data that the earth moves through space at the speed of 45,000 mph. Also, while speeding along its track, the earth rotates on its axis at a speed of 1000 mph.

Nova figured if he could get lined up exactly right, his punch would not only have his own physical strength behind it, but would gain additional velocity from cosmic forces of the earth movement. To break it down simply, he needed to be due east of Louis at the time he launched his Cosmic Punch.

You must admit the theory was easily more interesting than, say, trigonometry. Various shadetree physicists, bribed by fight publicists, scratched their beards and ventured that Mr. Nova indeed might have something there, and took their free tickets and sold them to the janitor.

However, the New York boxing commission refused to let Nova carry a compass into the ring, so he had to operate by dead reckoning. And every time the challenger stopped to calculate his true bearings, Louis would reach out and bop him on his scientific nose.

This eventually became so boring to the professor that he went to sleep in the sixth round, along with a goodly number of the spectators. And that was the end of the Cosmic Punch.

Perhaps this bloke, Frank Bruno, has unearthed it, like the mad scientists were forever doing to the poor buried or frozen or burnt body of Frankenstein's monster. It behooves us to hope so.

HISTORIC MEMORY

NOVEMBER 9, 1983

LAS VEGAS, NEVADA—The old-time boxing poets called it The Sweet Science. This is like confusing Charles Bronson with The Great Profile.

Oh, there may be a tad of science in boxing, like you use a teaspoon of sugar in a pot of chili. It's not enough to affect the flavor.

Some dramatists have likened boxing to a grace of sorts, but it generally is subtle as a falling boulder. Ernest Hemingway was a great devotee of boxing, but then he loved anything considered macho, like those silly fools trying to outrun wild bulls down the alleyways of Pamplona. Or waiting in a tree to put a .458 magnum slug in some poor elephant's skull. Real he-man stuff.

To most of us, boxing is about as beautiful as a train wreck. But that's all right. Pugilism was never meant to look like a bed of gladioli. You accept it for what it is. It is a basic ugly on the outside, primitive on the inside. And it is our most ancient game, other than the great sport of outrunning a hungry lion.

At the most, boxing is esthetically pleasing as a wart hog, even when it is clean and courageous. But when it is soiled and suspicious, it is double ugly. That's the way most of us remember Roberto Duran, the No Mas kid.

Whatever Duran has done before and whatever he does after, even to winning the middleweight title from Marvin Hagler here tomorrow evening, we will remember him most when he quit in the Sugar Ray Leonard rematch. When suddenly, as he was being outboxed and taunted in the eighth round in the Superdome, Duran turned away from Leonard, yelled "No mas!" at referee Octavio Meyron and walked to his corner. No more.

We will always remember the disgust on the weary, creased

213

faces of Freddie Brown and Ray Arcel, the stooped and ancient eagles who worked his corner. There was Brown, turning his back to the tumult in the ring, looking down at press row from where frantic questions were being shouted.

"He din't say nuttin," Brown spat the words. "He just quit!" It was unthinkable to the old second. The champion quitting? Stomach cramps? Are you kidding?

We will remember, also, the sight of Duran a half-hour later, in his warmup suit and baseball cap, flip and sneering. His entourage of a half-dozen Panamanians grouped around him like a protective fence. He was overcome with cramps, Duran said with a shrug, so what? He was still a better man than Leonard.

"A thousand times!" he said scornfully, waving his hand and stalking out with his escort, as unconcerned as if he had found a flat on his neighbor's car. Some of us, at the time, thought we saw a secret satisfaction in Duran's attitude. He had made no attempt to hide his disdain of Leonard, nor of this particular country and the habits and customs thereof. He and his Panamanian pals had swaggered through New Orleans streets, beards and soiled t-shirts, portable stereos screaming gourd music, harrassing waitresses, caricatures of classic bullies.

Now he had eight million gringo dollars in his pants and he had quit in the middle of a title fight and thumbed his nose at the suckers. At least, that is the way some of us read it. And maybe it is unfair and biased and prejudiced and all those things, but that is the way we will remember Duran and we can not help it.

We have all heard the stories of the remodeled Duran, the rededicated, the humble and hungry. Harry Markson, the old Madison Square Garden president, telephoned the other day. He had been enlisted by Promoter Bob Arum to help pump up this Hagler-Duran match.

"Duran has great motivation, great family concern," said Harry. "He wants to erase the one stain on his record, the New Orleans fight. He wasn't ready physically or emotionally for that fight. I think he regretted it five minutes later."

(Well, Harry, he sure didn't *seem* to regret anything when he swaggered away after the fight, laughing and exchanging Latin *mots* with his pals.)

Duran went back home to Panama and found himself no

longer the national hero. *"Cobarde!"* his countrymen yelled. Coward. *"Una gallina!"* Chicken. He found himself staying inside his walls, doors locked. "Traitor" read signs painted around his house.

So he came back. Don King promoted a couple of meaningless fights for the pudgy Duran and then walked away in disgust.

Duran started fighting as a middleweight. He knocked out Davey Moore in eight rounds. Bob Arum, King's rival vulture, smelled money. Hence, Duran vs. Hagler, here on Caesars Palace parking lot.

"A year ago, as an attraction Roberto Duran wasn't worth a plugged quarter," says Arum. "Now he's the biggest thing in boxing."

Arum, you understand, is speaking for himself, not for the rest of us. Except the magazine *Sports Elevated,* supreme authority on everything, which has seen this bout as one for the ages. "Duran is involved in a quest," the magazine sobbed recently. "Hagler is fighting to retain his title, but Duran is fighting for history."

To others of us, Duran doesn't have to fight for history. He's already made it.

CHRISTMAS CAROL

DECEMBER 25, 1985

Everyone's favorite Christmas story, of course, is the one set in Bethlehem with an all-star cast.

Taking place money, to me anyway, always has been the parable of Billy Miske, the prizefighter. I have passed it along before since stealing it from the late Red Smith, but not in a decade or so. Besides, Jim Murray, the West Coast author, once called upon the gods of hackdom and received special dispensation for columnists to repeat themselves every three years, especially during benevolent holiday periods. So, hence:

Billy Miske was a good, sturdy fighter who gave an honest dollar's worth. He had fought Jack Dempsey three times, the last for the heavyweight title and this was back when you could deck a guy and stand over him and slug him when he tried to get up, like on a parking lot, and this is what Dempsey did to Miske for three rounds.

Billy also fought Tommy Gibbons and Battling Levinsky and Jack Dillon and Harry Greb, who was first cousin to a buzz saw. Miske twice went 10 rounds with Greb to no-decisions.

When Billy was 25, he was felled by a terrible fever and doctors shook their heads and advised him to quit the ring. Billy didn't have a trade, but he had a family and bills to pay, and boxing was the only work he knew, so he kept at it.

Now he was 29 and his kidneys were shot; he was dying of Bright's disease, and he knew it and kept it to himself. He had one bout, early in January, and then for months he was too weak to go to the gymnasium. He stayed home with his wife and two children and tried to stretch his meager stash of funds. But now the calendar said Christmas was nearing and his wallet said no way.

One day in early November, Miske left his bed, dressed and

went slowly downtown in Minneapolis to see his friend and manager, Jack Reddy.

"Get me a fight," said Billy.

"You can't be serious," said Reddy.

"I mean it," Miske said sternly. "Get me a fight."

The manager knew of Miske's condition, of course, and he wouldn't listen to the proposition until Billy said, "Look, Jack, please listen. I'm broke. I can't afford to buy a single Christmas gift for my family. I haven't got long to be around, and I'd like to have my family around me, all happy, for just one more Christmas. It will be my last one. You got to get me a fight."

"I don't like to say this," said Reddy, "but if you went in the ring now, in your condition, you might easily get killed."

"What's the difference?" said Miske. "It's better than waiting for it in a rocking chair."

The manager squirmed. "Do one thing for me," he said. "Go to the gym and start working out and let's see if you can get into some kind of condition. Then we'll talk about it."

"That's out," said the fighter. "You know I can't work. I can't get in shape, but I've got to have one more fight."

Reddy finally gave in for his friend. He matched Billy with Bill Brennan for a bout in Omaha. Brennan also had fought Dempsey and had gone 12 rounds with him. He was past his prime, but he was still big and rough and dangerous. It was a good bill.

Miske didn't go near the gym. He stayed home, swallowed soup and aspirins, tried to conserve his strength until it was time to go to Omaha. Boxing commission doctors weren't as strict with their physical examinations then. They gave Billy a pass.

After the fight, the pale and spent Billy Miske picked up his $2,400 purse and went back to Minneapolis and blew the bundle on presents. It was the biggest and grandest Christmas the Miske family ever had. There was a feast and music and laughter and stacks of gifts and Mr. and Mrs. Miske and their two children were together and gloriously happy.

On December 26, Miske called Jack Reddy.

"Come take me to a hospital," he said calmly. "I'm dying."

Reddy carried him to a St. Paul hospital, and on New Year's Day of 1924, quietly and with dignity, he died.

The last fight on his record had been just six weeks before

and his friends couldn't believe it. Billy was weak and dying, and it would have been easy for him to take a quick plunge, grab the money and run, but he didn't. Billy Miske knocked out Bill Brennan in four rounds. You could look it up.

Personal Diary

MYSTERY
GUESTS

From a pressboxer's memorybook:

The sportswriter, in Dallas, picked up his phone. On the other end were a couple of pals in New York, calling from a luncheon table at P.J. Clarke's. One was connected with a sports documentary movie company. His outfit had just finished a highlight film on Cotton Bowl games.

A fledgling actor was flying to Dallas to record an intro and some voice commentary on the film, said ole pal. He was a football fan. In fact, the young actor had played a little college ball in Florida. And he was donating his time and talent to the Cotton Bowl project. He was doing it for expenses only, just for the exposure he might get from the film.

Could the sportswriter do ole pal a favor and fix the actor up with a date in Dallas? Some chick who would show him the sights?

"I'm not in the date business," protested the sportswriter. (I wasn't going to volunteer for social director for some young punk egotist I had never heard of.) "Tell him to go to Old Town. I hear there are some swinging single bars, or whatever you call them."

Later on, I learned that is exactly where Burt Reynolds went, and enjoyed himself quite successfully.

●

The sportswriter had been in his room high in the Hotel Americana in Houston, typing his prizefight column. It was after midnight when he finished, and he threw on a jacket and went downstairs to file his copy back to Dallas with Western Union.

There was one person on the elevator when the writer

220

boarded. It happened to be one of the boxers who had won a fight that night. He had knocked out Cleveland Williams, in fact.

"Helluva fight," said the typist. "That's probably the best you've ever looked."

The fighter seemed almost embarrassed. "Do you *really* think so?" he said softly. "That's awfully nice of you to say so." He looked at the writer's jacket. The collar was haphazardly up-turned.

"Here let me fix that," said the fighter. He turned down the collar and patted it gently in place. "There, now you look nice." He smiled and ducked his head and studied his shoes.

Just then the elevator stopped on the mezzanine floor, the doors opened and there was a crowd of fight followers packed outside. Instantly, the quiet, retiring fighter became another personality.

"Ah'm the greatest!" he yelled. "Ah'm Muhammad Ali and ah'm the greatest that ever lived!" The champ raised his arms above his head and marched out into the adoring masses.

●

The fuzzy-cheeked sportswriter was on the far outskirts of a table at the old Toots Shor's in New York, where some respected elders were gathered. One had just finished a book and the others were wishing him a successful market.

"Oh, it doesn't have a chance," said Bob Considine. "The only four-letter words in it are Babe and Ruth."

●

Some promotional brain came up with a gimmick for the Texas League, which was beginning to struggle a bit after a flush of postwar prosperity.

There would be a beauty contest to elect Miss Texas League. Each of the eight member cities would be represented by a local beauty and the troupe would be sent around to appear at each ballpark. The fans would vote at each park; the ballots would be tabulated. And the winner would make public appearances for the league for the next few months.

The girls would be presented in bathing suits, of course, and they were strictly chaperoned by a matron and an advertising guy who accompanied the beauties around the league.

After the tour was half completed, the ad guy confided:

"There may be prettier gals on the tour, but that Miss Houston will win it. She does the most with what she has. She's a bright one and, buddy, she knows what she wants."

The perky Miss Houston became Miss Texas League alrighty, and then stepped off to Hollywood and changed her name from Grandstaff to Grant and finally to Mrs. Bing Crosby.

•

The sportswriter-to-be was then a sailor on shore leave in Los Angeles, just before a wartime Christmas. A shipmate had been a Wabash College roommate of a chap named Steve Crane, who was then married to Lana Turner.

Crane had some Christmas shopping and errands to run one day, and he took the two sailors along. One stop was a barber shop above a haberdashery in Beverly Hills. Rothschild's was the name? Or something similar.

In the chair next to Crane was a husky, well-groomed guy, slick dark hair parted in the middle like Richard Barthelmess. Crane introduced the sailors to the guy, Bennie Something Or Other. He was robustly friendly. He had a son, he said, in the Air Force in England. If there was anything he could do for the sailors while they were on leave, anything at all, please let him know. He shook hands goodbye and repeated the offer.

Downstairs, in the car, Crane asked: "Do you know who that was?"

No. Bennie Something Or Other. Some nice middle-aged guy with a son in the Air Force.

"It was Bennie Siegel," said the host. "They call him Bugsy. Bugsy Siegel. Maybe you've heard of Murder Incorporated?"

═══════════════

ROYAL RITES

All the fancy doings in London these days seem a bit foreign to one who has some inkling of the workings of a cotton hoe. The elaborate falderal surrounding the royal wedding, no matter the *savoir faire* of the observer, could be rather awesome.

Dorothy Parker, the gifted lyricist, was scarcely a bumpkin. She knew the proper forks and could conjugate a little Latin if need be. Yet once in England when the American poet was presented to the Queen, she felt a certain crack in her sardonic poise.

"I felt like I was wearing a papoose on my back," said Miss Parker.

Most of the world, of course, will come no nearer to a royal wedding than the telly, or the rotogravure pages. To the best of my recollection, I have been in only one.

Well, perhaps it wouldn't qualify as a genuine regal production, but it certainly was a cut above the normal knot ceremony. What it was, was a ballpark wedding, and you may have a difficult time believing, but it was solemn as a Supreme Court photograph.

I have had considerable experience in the *other* kind of weddings. Once I stood up for an old pal, George Bernard Dolan, now an ink-stained columnist at the *Fort Worth Star-Telegram*. The presiding official was a justice of the peace named, I believe, Gus Brown, and he had only one leg.

"This marriage sure got off on the right foot," Dolan said as we left the porch. "It was the only one he had."

Anyways, back to the ballyard. One fine day in 1950, some members of the Fort Worth Cats were riding a baseball Pullman and speaking of their intentions to marry hometown sweethearts after the season.

"Heck, we ought to get married together," said one.

"Hey, why wait until after the season? Why don't we do it *during* the season?" said another.

"Why not get married at the ballpark—at home plate?"

"I will, if you will."

"Think of all the presents we'd get."

The four guys were shortstop Russ Rose, second baseman Joe Torpey, third baseman Don Hoak and pitcher John Rutherford. And they weren't kooks. They were fun-lovers but not hellraisers.

They went to John Reeves, then the president of the Fort Worth club, and told him of their wish. Reeves was a somber man. He knew there had been other home plate weddings and they had been sort of gags, like getting married under water or floating down in parachutes.

"We'll do it," he decided, "but only if it's done *right*. We don't want anybody laughing."

Well, sir, it was done right, and, if you can imagine, with dignity. Nobody laughed.

The brides came into town several days beforehand and they were introduced to the LaGrave Field crowd and Gwen Bragan, the manager's missus, and several matrons honored them at parties. (Do they still call 'em *showers?*)

There were four ceremonies, by four ministers. One couple was Catholic, so they did their church thing in the afternoon and repeated it that night at the park.

Reeves was one best man, Manager Bobby Bragan was another and player-coach Tommy Tatum was the third. This fledgling pressboxer, in a rented tux and borrowed black shoes, attended bridegroom Rutherford. Like so many Navy wretches, I had sworn a mighty oath never to own another pair of black shoes. So these I filched from an apartment mate, a teevee fop named Larry Morrell, and they were a full size too small. *That's* what I remember mostly.

Flowers were banked shoulder high around the infield. A huge carpet covered home plate. An electric organ was moved near the third base dugout.

I will never forget peeking from the home club locker room, where the menfolks were dressing, and seeing fans walk past in their Sunday best. Men in dark suits and white shirts, even though it was summertime, and ladies—if you can believe this—in flimsy tea frocks with big picture hats and *white gloves!* Must have been 10,000 there. At a minor league baseball park yet, before a Texas League game. And nobody scoffed.

Somebody sang *Oh Promise Me* on the ballpark p.a. and the Fort Worth squad, in spotless uniforms with bats in hand, lined in two rows from home base to the pitcher's mound. The lights dimmed and there were candelabras lit. There was such unbelievable silence, you could hear the frogs croak on the Trinity levee behind the left field fence.

Grooms and their group climbed from the first base dugout and took their places. And the gals came from the visiting dugout, all gowned and hatted and blushing like Mary Jane on the syrup bucket.

The vows were said and the facing players made an arch with their bats, guys like Dick Williams and Dee Fondy and Farmer Ray Moore and Chris Van Cuyk and Joe Landrum, all of whom later became major league names. We walked through the arch and then the bridegrooms changed into unies and ran on the field and, as I remember, lost to Tulsa with the new husbands making four errors. After the game, there was a reception under the stands for *every*body, with punch and cake and long tables covered with presents from the fans.

Now, three decades later, Rutherford is an orthopedic surgeon in Detroit. Russ Rose is a highway patrolman in Altadena, California. Torpey is a high school teacher in Pueblo. Hoak, who went on to fiery careers in Cincinnati, Pittsburgh and Philadelphia, died of a heart attack a dozen years ago while chasing a car thief. He was afoot and the thief was on wheels, but Don never was one much for odds.

LaGrave Field is a far cry from Buckingham Palace, but that was about as close to royal rites as a pressbox clod will ever get, and somehow, I don't think I would trade. Of course, that was years ago. Today, somebody would probably throw a beer bottle and yell play ball, you bums.

MEMORY
BOOKED

MARCH 1, 1978

The white drifts outside were miserably foreboding, so naturally it was memory time around the tables at the Joe Miller A.C. Among the snowbound, Long Gone Dupre had the rostrum.

As with most former jocks, the Dupre memory was graphically keen. (Byron Nelson can tell you about his second shot on the fourth hole during the third round of the 1939 PGA at Pomonok Country Club in Flushing, for goodness sakes.) Dupre was recalling his days with the Baltimore Colts and their benevolent owner, Carroll Rosenbloom. He remembered the exact spot on the bridge leading into Baltimore that winter night when the car radio informed that he had been traded to the neophyte Dallas Cowboys.

"Some of us had been to Philadelphia to play some of the Eagles a basketball game, the way you do in the off-season," said the Baylor halfback. "We were the prelim before a Philadelphia Warrior game. We collected our $100 apiece and drove back to Baltimore. There were six of us in a station wagon. Unitas, Ameche, Marchetti, Jim Parker, Big Daddy Lipscomb and me. Right in the middle of the bridge, the guy on the radio said I had been traded to Dallas. By the time we got off the bridge, I was crying. I called Carroll quick as I could get to a phone. He said I didn't have to go to Dallas, I could stay there and run our bowling alleys. But I finally decided I was near the end of my career after five seasons there, so I might as well go back to my home state and finish off."

Rosenbloom inspired a devotion from his players that still lasts. He encouraged his Baltimore players to go into business and he would join them as a partner, putting up the credit.

"Carroll joined Unitas and me in the bowling business. We built three lanes. Marchetti and Ameche bought a hamburger stand and Carroll backed them. We laughed at them. A hamburger stand! We had *three* fancy new bowling alleys. When I left for Texas, Carroll and Unitas bought me out. The bowling alleys later folded. Gino and Ameche now have restaurants all over the Atlantic seaboard. They're both millionaires."

That phase of the Dupre career yielded conversationally to earlier days.

"You were from Texas City, weren't you?" asked Smokey, a used typewriter man. (That is, for a typewriter man, he was *really* used.) "Who was your high school coach?"

Dupre grinned appreciatively and opened his mouth. Nothing came out.

"That's funny," said the man with the amazing memory. "I know his name. Uh, just a minute." He leaned back and looked at the ceiling in silence while other philosophical topics took over.

"Damn!" Dupre said a moment later. "Why'd you have to bring that up? Now I've *got* to think of it."

The others glanced at him, recognized his mental struggle, and offered assistance.

"Was it Knute?" asked Tom, the lawyer.

"How about Pop Warner?" said Barry, the real estate man.

"Bob Zuppke was about that time," said another guy.

"Shut up!" Dupre barked. "It's right here, it's . . ."

"Walter Camp?" Tom, the lawyer, said helpfully.

"He was like a father to me!" Long Gone cried. "I know his name well as my own."

"Maybe we should start with your name," said Smokey, the used typewriter man. "You want to give it to us?"

"He's now the principal of a high school in San Antonio," Long Gone's voice was quivering. "I can see his face. Give me a minute, *please!*" He gripped the arms of his chair and his knuckles turned white. His eyes became blunk like Little Orphan Annie's. Not blank. Blunk. His eyes were OO.

Joe Miller, the proprietor, stopped by and glanced curiously at Dupre. He waved a hand in front of ole memorybank. Not a tic.

"What's the matter with *him?*" Joe said. "He ain't had that much."

"He's trying to think of the name of his high school coach," said Tom, the lawyer.

"He was like a father to him," said Smokey the used typewriter man.

Dupre suddenly broke his trance and bolted from his seat.

"I got to get away from you guys!" he howled, making for the gentlemen's water closet. "I won't be back til I get it!"

He stayed for a half-hour. When he returned, he sank in his seat, a broken man.

"Homer. It's Homer Something," he said weakly. "Homer . . ."

"Grand slam?" asked a guy.

"Inside-the-park homer?" the real estate man said kindly.

"How many syllables?" said another.

"Run through the alphabet," suggested a guy. "Homer Adams. Barker, Cunningham, DuBary . . . "

"You guys wait!" yelled the stricken Dupre. "I'll think of it tonight! I'll call every damn one of you at four o'clock in the morning! It's driving me crazy. It's never happened to me before. I can remember anything! Homer . . . Homer what?" He clapped palms to both ears and tottered to the door.

There was no call at 4 a.m. Nothing the next day. Four days later, the door to the Miller A.C. was flung open violently. Long Gone burst through and his wild eyes swept the dimness, finally spotting his tormentors on end stools.

"SMITH! SMITH!" screamed the memory expert. "Homer SMITH!"

GOLDEN EGGS

When the local Golden Glovers started unreeling last evening, they were organized within an inch of their franchise.

There were a couple hundred volunteer workers from the All-Sports Association and the Jaycees, and hardly any of them ran into each other. The boxers' hands were all neatly wrapped in fresh gauze and the resin box was primly full and, presumably, everyone operated under his square name.

Why, this is a $20,000 production, and the showers were in working order and there were clean towels and 24 sets of gloves in good shape, some of them still resting in tissue, and my story to you is that it was not always thus.

Just the other day, a couple of us old goats were kicking around our early trials as Golden Gloves promoters back in the dim ages and we almost transmitted nervous breakdowns over the phone.

Oh, we don't go back to the actual *pioneer* days. The Golden Gloves began in 1926, brainchild of a genius named Arch Ward. By title, Arch was sports editor of the *Chicago Tribune,* but by nature he was a promoter. Football and baseball all-star games also were Ward innovations.

Anyways, Ward's blueprint awarded the GG franchise to a newspaper in each city, if so interested. For that reason, many of us ink-stained slobs were later forced into staging Gloves tournaments in our respective towns, an act as foreign to us as fingerpainting. Boxing we knew, but there is considerable difference in recognizing a left hook and arranging for ticket printing and making out government tax forms.

Dan Cook, a San Antonio pressboxer of some vintage, remembered that in his first GG tournament, the handlers ran out of handwrapping gauze halfway through the opening card. Cook broke a sweat and ran angrily in circles, yelling that some foul culprit was stealing the gauze. Subsequently, it was pointed out that he had bought one roll of gauze for each fighter, somehow neglecting to realize that most had two hands.

This personal experience started right after your hero had climbed out of his little sailor shirt and reported to a newspaper job on the *Temple* (Texas) *Daily Telegram.*

"Your first assignment," said the man behind the desk, "is to put on a Golden Gloves tournament. You got two weeks."

Had I been of average intelligence, of course, I would have sprinted to the local post office and reenlisted in the Navy. There had been no Golden Gloves thereabouts for years. Heck, there wasn't even a *ring* to be found, nor time to have one built even if funds were available, which they were not.

Somehow a veterans hospital was persuaded to donate use of its gym for a couple nights. A ramshackled old ring was discovered in somebody's barn. It didn't even have turnbuckles under the ring floor to unite and stabilize the posts and ropes. We used baling wire for this, as I remember. Incidentally, they were real hemp ropes, donated by a hardware store. We wrapped them in adhesive tape we had caged from Scott & White Hospital. The canvas was handscrubbed with brushes and detergent and still looked like original wagon covers from the Oklahoma land rush.

The local YMCA loaned four sets of old gloves. Kindly printers at the newspaper ran off cardboard tickets on a proof press.

Two days before the magic event, the production was set. A half-dozen chums were roped in as handlers. We would unfold and align the chairs, sell tickets, even double as ring announcers and referees and judges and cornermen. Then it suddenly struck your embryonic promoter. The grand & glorious Golden Gloves tournament, Central Texas region, had everything except boxers.

There was a six-man team entered from Allen Academy of Bryan, a talented and well-trained group under a coach named Angus Stocking.

There were several lads from Wichita Falls on the Allen team; names like Weldon Wyatt and Leonard Ludke come to memory, and Mitchell Dorsey and Deno Tufares, who called himself the Grinning Greek and later was elected to the state house of representatives. And there was a Galveston kid, a baby-faced flyweight named Freddie Morales who could have passed for a teddybear. But other than the Allen boys, there were maybe three, four entries.

We had expected nearby Fort Hood to furnish 30 or 40

boxers, but at the last moment, the military sent word that army boxers would not be allowed to enter a segregated tournament. (Black boxers, at the time, did not compete against whites in Texas, or other southern states.)

Panic set in. A desperation call was placed to an old Austin pal, Tom Attra, himself a former national Golden Gloves champ.

"I got to have some fighters!" cried your poised promoter. "Save me!"

"How many you need?" said Attra, bless his heart.

Somehow Tom combed the Austin gyms and the streets and the back alleys, probably, and scraped together maybe 20 guys who knew how to hold their hands. He promised them a hamburger apiece and a peanut patty, loaded up three or four old cars and delivered them up the interstate and somehow the magnificent event went on.

Afterward, an anonymous tipster blew the whistle. An Attra import, the guy who won the flyweight title, had fought under an alias. He had been beaten in another regional tournament and therefore was ineligible.

So when it came time to crate our regional champs to the state tournament in Fort Worth, we had to sub the runner-up in that division, Freddie Morales, the teddybear.

On the long, cramped trip to the Cowtown finals in my old convertible, little Freddie rode behind the one seat, couched in the canvas sling that held the top when it was down, brown eyes big as salad plates, the poor kid. I was actually afraid he would be seriously injured when he met a bigshot city boxer. I could envision carrying the sad word to his parents, perhaps facing tremendous lawsuits. That was yet another mistake by young Tex Rickard here. The teddybear won the state flyweight championship.

ABOVE AND BEYOND

APRIL 25, 1984

When it comes to gut checks, television doesn't count. We all have seen any number of heroic sports scenes on the toob, with enough derring-do to shame Audie Murphy or Clint Easterwood or even Doc Savage, The Man of Bronze.

The subject is maniacal effort, as if life and limb and mother's honor were at stake.

Who can forget the sight of Julie Moss at that Hawaiian Triathlon, crawling to the finish line, gasping, sobbing, out of muscular control, soiling her pants, hysterical with effort. *Silly* with effort, is what it was. She had lost ability to reason and dang near killed herself for a trophy that wouldn't hold as many jellybeans as a peanut butter jar. She went above and beyond, driven by some animal instinct that would not allow the white feather.

Another time, there was an idle flip of the dial to a Las Vegas ring, where Bruce Curry and Leroy Haley were meeting for the junior welter title or one of those hybrid champeenships that seem to be all over the place. It wasn't especially a classic billing, but halfway through the match, it dawned that these guys were dubbing the whey from each other.

They kept it up for the entire stretch, first one and then the other landing terrific shots. No misses. Good clean smacks, like a movie fight between Alan Ladd and Bob Steele. Each punch looked as if it would remove a man's noggin from its moorings. Just when it seemed that one fighter would collapse, he would reach back and fetch the other a fearful clout on the old button. For the full 10 rounds, or 12 or whatever it was. Over the last century or so, I must have seen a million of these old boxing bouts but never one with such staggering and continued effort.

But those scenes were on the telly and, as stated up front, they do not count.

There have been two eyewitness experiences of efforts beyond belief.

The last was on Long Island in June of 1978 when Affirmed and Alydar hooked up in the Belmont Stakes. They were the prized colts who staged a classic duel in the Triple Crown. Affirmed had won the Kentucky Derby by a length and a half. But Alydar was a fast-closing second, despite a wide trip and a bump in the stretch.

In the Preakness, it was Affirmed again by a half a length and again it appeared as if Alydar would have won in another rod.

Now it was the long Belmont where Alydar's closing rush was best suited, and where the generalship of veteran jock Jorge Velasquez would be an advantage over the fuzzcheek Steve Cauthen. The feud chased away all but three challengers. Forget them. They finished 13 lengths back.

Out of the gate, Affirmed went to the front but after a half-mile, Alydar was alongside, a half-length on the starboard flank. Then they ran a mile with no daylight. Rather, they *flew* a mile. The last six furlongs was the fastest the Belmont had *ever* been run.

It was unbelievable that two colts could lock together for that distance, both going absolutely all-out. At the head of the stretch, there wasn't a windowpane difference and they stayed that way to the wire, Cauthen and Velasquez flailing and rolling and hunching, the animals with wild eyes and sure, slashing hooves that *clawed* at the dirt. Never a yield, never an *inch!* Watching transfixed, I remember wondering insanely if a horse's heart had ever burst. Surely one would explode; it was beyond human concept that the battle could go on at such a mad pace for so long.

The other personal memory returned with the arrival of the World Championship of Tennis doings here this week. This was on another spring day in 1972, at Moody Coliseum, with Rod Laver and Ken Rosewall meeting in the WCT climax. They cut and they raced and they lobbed, and they smashed until there came a horrible suspicion that this could go on until next Thursday.

Laver had beaten Rosewall in three previous matches that year; he jumped to a 5–1 lead in the first set but had to scrap mightily before winning 6–4. His service cost him a 0–6 set and then he began to rally in the third set, although losing 3–6. Just as it seemed Laver had outlasted his fellow Aussie, here came Rosewall with some inner font of strength.

Well, they went five torturous sets and it was fitting that it closed out 7−6. These weren't kiddoes, understand. Laver was 33, a tough little pink pine knot with bowed legs and a seaman's roll. Rosewall was 38, also small, beetlebrowed, gaunt of cheek.

During that last set, it seemed impossible to keep up that savage pace. Each overhead smash was hit with a suicidal fury, the final effort of a maniac. You tried to read the thoughts. *Well, okay, I'll get everything I've got left, smash it this one time and then collapse and to hell with it.* But no collapse. The other guy did the same thing. Crimson spots appeared on Rosewall's cheekbones, like clown daubs on a chalky face. Laver looked like a sick rooster you had dunked in a horse trough. It was impossible, but it happened and happened and happened again, for 3 hours, 34 minutes. Affirmed's win at Belmont has been called the greatest race ever run; Rosewall's WCT victory, the greatest tennis match ever played and, should the debate ever arise, you could prove it by me.

LOST HORIZONS

JULY 16, 1984

It was one score and four years past when a local newspaper editor was stricken with a brain seizure. The Democratic convention, of which you will hear much more later, brings it to mind.

This daily blade had made preparation for coverage of the 1960 Democratic conclave in Los Angeles. Mr. Felix McKnight, the aforementioned editor, and his staff of political experts would observe the doings for Metroplex readers, who would wait breathless, or very near, for their reports. At the last moment, a bubble formed above Mr. McKnight's noble pate and a light bulb appeared. *Why not send Sherrod along to the convention and let him write his nonsense? Poor chap has never been exposed to a civilized and meaningful operation before, having spent all his time in Fun & Games.*

Actually, it wasn't exactly an original thought by McKnight, who was not above lifting an idea now and then when nobody was looking. Four years before, the *New York Herald Tribune* had dispatched the late Mr. Walter (Red) Smith to report on the political conventions. Mr. Smith was, by trade, a sports author but a rather rare one in that he had graduated from Notre Dame, wore a tie every day and knew Chaucer from Slapsy Maxie Rosenbloom. Anyways, Mr. Smith composed some intriguing essays from the political ringside. And the next time the conventions came around, other editors played copycat. They rounded up a few pressboxers, held them down and curried burrs from their manes and tied shoes on their feet and sent them west.

The late Mr. Jimmy Cannon was there, representing the Toy Dept. of the *New York Journal-American.* Also the late Mr. Jack Murphy of the *San Diego Union.* You will note how many of these guys are late. A sobering thought, if you are looking for one.

One lasting impression is that political conventions are long on noise and short on manners. Poor Joe Kuharich, at his lowest moment as Philadelphia Eagle coach, was never treated with such boos and catcalls as a political candidate draws from rival camps.

As for the noise, well, sir, maybe you remember a Cowboy game at New Orleans when Don Meredith tried for 17 minutes to get a play off, only to have customers drown out his signals each time. But that din was chickenfeed compared to convention reaction when, say, the John Kennedy demonstrators paraded the aisles, blowing their devilish air horns, waving their placards, doing the rhumba and standing on their heads and other such adult gyrations. The convention chairman, Florida Gov. Leroy Collins, grew extremely rosy of countenance as he tried to gavel order from the podium. I'm telling you, pal, a good umpire would have kicked half those guys out of the hall.

There was a mystery: A spacious, open platform protruded directly above the podium and apparently this was reserved for very great Americans indeed. There was Tony Curtis and his wife, Ms. Janet Leigh, whose dress fit like a freckle and was split up to her *pectineus,* on purpose, I think. And Mr. Frank Sinatra, chewing gum furiously. And Peter Lawford and Sammy Davis Jr.

The movie folk would stroll out on this platform, gaze curiously down at the great milling masses as the Roman emperors must have done. This was back in the days of The Rat Pack, as I believe they were called, and nobody was asked to explain why they occupied such a balcony of honor. You can bet Pete Rozelle would never get by with *that.*

There was one exciting moment when we thought we had a real event. Lyndon Johnson, who could see the nomination slipping away, challenged John Kennedy to a debate. They met in the Biltmore ballroom before Texas and Massachusetts delegations. Thousands of other gawkers tried to crash the gates. Good boxoffice.

Us pressbox bums were there early to nail down good vantage points.

"You cover it like you would a heavyweight championship fight," said the late Mr. Jimmy Cannon, with supreme confidence.

Had this been a fight, both licenses would have been suspended. Each candidate got up and said a large amount of nothing, although the younger man showed flashes of a sharp jab.

"Sen. Johnson has always had my support as a majority leader and he will continue to have," he said slyly. "I think we can work very well together."

That was about as close to a haymaker as it got. I have seen more action at a flower show. The lasting memory of *that* incident was Sen. Kennedy having the worst haircut yet invented. His thatch looked like a Kansas wheatfield, temporary mashed by a windstorm. Sen. Johnson was memorable only because he wore a tailormade shirt and had his jowls powdered.

But surely us sports neophytes grew wiser from the experience. Mainly this week's events remind one of the time the late Will Rogers (him, too) showed up at a Democratic convention and some somber editorial pundit said kindly, "Well, I imagine you are here to write your little humor pieces. If I see anything funny, I will let you know."

"Gee, thanks," said Rogers. "And if I see anything serious, I'll let *you* know."

THE
BREATHLESS
MOMENT

MARCH 26, 1986

There comes a time, as ole Papa Hemingway used to say, for the moment of truth. *Papa used to say a lot of things, especially when the red juice from the wineskin spilled onto his broad flat forehead and flowed into the deep crevices around his nose and down into his dark cavern of a mouth and Maria sat silently on a stone and the sun glinted off her golden hair, cropped as ripened wheat, and Pilar fussed about the cave, dropping dried cebolla and patatas into the stewpot and Enselmo smacked his toothless gums and thought of the tender and good and true ears of corn he had gnawed in his youth before the unprintable carceleros knocked out his teeth with their rifle butts.* Papa had a way with words, and with *vino*, too, come to think of it.

According to Mr. Hemingway, the Moment of Truth comes when time pauses and even the earth brakes on its axis and a man must get a grip on his nerves and declare himself.

Mr. Hemingway was a former sports writer, incidentally, and it would not surprise me one whit if he first experienced the Moment of Truth one blistering July afternoon in Toledo as he sat at ringside and prepared to watch Mr. Jack Dempsey flail the whey from Mr. Jess Willard.

Every sports writer worth his salt, and even a few unsalted ones, has one particular moment before one particular event when he must pause and have a serious talk with his goosepimples. When he must separate himself from a spectator, when he must wash the contagious excitement from his emotions, when he must jerk himself away from sheer pleasure of watching and get down to the business at hand.

Hey, buster, settle down, you're here to work. If you jump and yell and scream like the citizens around you, you might miss seeing the right uppercut or the key block or the look in the champion's eye. Excitement is for the paying stiff, not the working press.

Therefore, there are several instants that bring this predicament to pressrow, when the ink-stained wretch must fight his way off that emotional plateau and back down to the realistic earth of details and deadlines.

There is one pressbox school that believes the prologue to a heavyweight championship fight is that magic instant—the most dramatic moment in sports.

Another vote favors the Kentucky Derby post parade, when the gleaming colts prance out of the paddock chute onto Churchill Downs dirt, stepping daintily, bobbing their long noble necks as the band strikes up *My Old Kentucky Home* and 125,000 sentimentalists, overcome with julep encouragement, try to hit the high notes.

Others believe the most dramatic moment is when the announcer bawls, "Gentlemen . . . start your engines!" at the Indianapolis Speedway and immediately 33 furious whines cough and begin their throaty screams that will take over your eardrums for the next three hours.

The playing and singing of national anthems of the two countries involved in the World Cup final soccer match is another dandy, mainly because of the intense nationalism involved.

There is no tenseness involved, but for sheer spectator enjoyment, the opening parade of any Olympics will bring chill-bumps to a lard bucket. Television engineers may improve cameras a hundred times over, but they'll never be able to capture the pageantry of this particular ceremony. The very *absence* of suspense in this moment is its charm.

And then there is this Final Four basketball championship which has climbed—on *these* shores anyway—right up on the pedestal with the older, more established tinglers. There are purists who stamp this event as certainly the most dramatic moment in *college* athletics, and deserving of ranking in the unlimited category. Over the last decade, the Final Four has grown into that stature.

The World Series and the Superbowl, you can forget those. By Superbowl kickoff, there has been so much hoopla and celebration that the game seems anticlimactic. And the start of the World Series, there is always the thought of many days and nights of action ahead before the thing is settled.

Actually I first became aware of that heavyweight championship magic in Chicago a quarter-century past. Floyd Patterson, a mixture of man and milquetoast, was defending his title against Sonny Liston, more monster than man.

When the fighters stood in the middle of the ring, while the ref gave instructions, the magic moment suddenly asserted itself. Liston, a ferocious sight at best, fixed his malevolent glare on Patterson. The tension seemed to build and build with the intensity of that fierce frown, as if any second Liston would bend over and bite the champ's nose off and spit it in his eye. Patterson squirmed and looked down, as a puppy will escape your reproving stare. The air suddenly became almost too thick to breathe and it seemed as if the instructions would never, never end. On pressrow, you had to shake yourself into reality and prepare to be the Vaunted Observer, the cool, calm role all us bigshot journalists try to assume.

The later Muhammad Ali-Joe Frazier bouts had that same strange airless moment. But don't look for it when Tim Witherspoon fights Pinklon Thomas or whoever, for the world heavyweight championship of Idaho and Western Montana.

Likewise, at the Kentucky Derby, there is that stifling instant. Especially at your *first* one. This was in 1958 when the California stretch-runner, Silky Sullivan, was the focus. He was a glorious red animal, heavy in the forequarters like a quarterhorse; his trappings were red, his groomsmen wore red uniforms, his mane and tail were braided with red bows and he seemed almost to dance to the music of "My Old Kentucky Home," as if he knew he was the star of the show.

That was a hypnotic moment, also, that carried you away from concentration. Fortunately, there is 15 minutes or so separating the post parade from the start of the Derby itself. And there was opportunity to make your way back to level ground, in ample time to watch Silky Sullivan run 12th in a field of 14.

Come to think of it, that's about how Floyd Patterson finished, that night in Comiskey Park.

There is scientific proof of the electric moment at Indianapolis. When Neil Armstrong became the first man to walk on the moon, his low-key manner amazed observers of the Apollo

11 shoot. Throughout the flight and his historic step, he spoke like a man fighting off a yawn.

After the moon landing, a curious sports writer on the NASA scene happened to ask the chief flight surgeon, what was Armstrong's pulse at the time he stepped on the moon. The surgeon said for all of Armstrong's calm manner, his heart was thumping 156 times per minute, more than double his normal rate.

The sports writer thought that sounded dangerous.

"At one time, this was thought so," said Dr. Charles Berry. "But then someone put monitors on Indianapolis race drivers while they were on the grid, just before they started their engines. Some of the pulses went as high as 180."

However, also at the Indy 500, there is a calm-down interval from the Moment of Truth time, when the engines first roar and the crowd goes berserk, until the actual start. There are two comparatively slow pace laps before the flag drops. Why, sometimes you are dang near breathing normal when the race actually gets under way.

Now here is the Final Four, with its version of electric moments. To some of us, it is the best sports event we work all year. But maybe this is selfish reasoning. It is superbly run. It is condensed. Saturday afternoon, the four best college teams all jammed into 4,700 square feet of hardwood. Likewise, all attention, all the pressures of a long season, all is squeezed into one small package.

The event is unmatched for sheer noise, especially in the compact structures like Reunion Arena, and noise begats electricity. It is unequaled for follower fanaticism. These are not just basketball fans wandering in from the street. They have traveled hundreds of miles, spent hundreds of dollars for the blessed privilege of busting blood vessels in their throats.

And it matters not the records brought into this explosive little cell. Firstly, a team doesn't get this far on luck, freak games, on happenstance. Any team here is entirely capable of gobbling the whole enchilada. Memories dictate that. There was North Carolina State knocking off favored Houston in Albuquerque.

Most of all, there was Villanova almost unconsciously perfect in pulling perhaps the biggest upset in Final Four history. Georgetown, playing in the Lexington event last March, performed good enough to beat any college team anywhere, perhaps any *year*. But Villanova's miraculous sharpshooting (78.6 percent) was proof enough that the cow indeed can jump over the moon.

Villanova's triumph was compared, and rightly so, to the U.S. hockey team's upset of Russia in the Lake Placid Olympics. There was that much electricity, that much Moment of Truth. Remember that when you're trying to hear and breathe. Along pressrow, we'll try to forget so as to come to better grips with old debbil reality.

CAPTAIN HOOK

MAY 29, 1981

With a certain amount of vicarious doubt, I have just finished reading of the bullish power and fierce fight of the Gulf Coast cobia. And I wish to say at this time, you couldn't prove it by me.

The cobia is more widely recognized as the ling, and it is a great prize of coastal prowlers because of its combative nature on the end of a line and its attractiveness on the supper table. Tastes like catfish, says our deepwater professor Tom LePere, although here again, I must take somebody's word for same.

In looks, the ling is somewhere between catfish and shark, and it grows to 90 pounds in Gulf waters. The plump solid fish is curious about boats and baits and shadows and commotions, but it is most temperamental about accepting food. Once you hook one securely, this article said, then prepare for Star Wars. "Go to open water for a long, backache fight," warned the author.

Ling come north earlier than most Gulf gamefish and even now, they are congregating in good water around oil and gas rigs and buoys, and there will be 40 and 50-pounders soon showing in the catch reports.

However, it was on a blistering July day out of Port Aransas that we learned about ling. There was a redheaded ex-Marine named Jeff, about the size and shape of a tramp steamer, and a spindly pharmacist called Pills and, of course, your bluewater correspondent here, resplendent in sneakers, cutoffs, terrycloth blouse and ice bag from the night before.

The swarthy, rotund boat captain was a grade A thief named Capt. Eddie who protested his vessel was in need of an overhaul and he, of rest. After hearing our pleas, he consented to take us after kingfish for a pittance of $200 and change, a medium-sized family diamond and first lien on an East Dallas mansion.

Capt. Eddie was all heart and stomach, as we soon discovered. En route to shrimper waters, he and his sleepy son sniffed out our cache of freshly fried chicken from a bayshore diner and dived in uninvited and headfirst. As they polished off breakfast and a half-case of Bud, we deemed ourselves rather fortunate to have escaped injury from flying bones.

The sun was high and simmering, and several modest king and some small shark thumped around in the boat box. Capt. Eddie turned from his favorite hobby, which was castigating his teen-age son for being a worthless sleepyhead potsmoker who took too long with the ribbonfish.

" 'Bout out of bait," he called cheerfully. "Got to go in soon."

It was then that we solved one of his tricks. He was chumming off the stern (fertilizing the water with chopped bits of bait) using *whole* ribbonfish, instead of half-baits discarded on the deck from missed kingfish strikes. The quicker the bait vanished, the sooner he could be back ashore in his hammock and his worthless son could be hustling pot or whatever he did for a hobby.

We also found two packs of frozen ribbonfish stashed behind a battered pail.

"Well, how did that get there?" he said, eyes blunk as Lil Orphan Annie.

Shortly after, as the sleepyhead was gaffing one of Jeff's kingfish, Capt. Thief discarded all his malevolent lethargy.

"Ling!" he cried, much in the manner that Dad Joiner brought in the Daisy Bradford #3 in East Texas. "Ling!"

"Gimme that!" he jerked a rod from Pills' feeble grasp and flung the line off the starboard. Gone was the condescending charterboat captain, placating his customers. Instead, he became Captain Ahab. Here was a goldern ling! and he wasn't gonna let no city sucker goof it up.

The ling took the bait and screamed off to China or thereabouts. The captain reeled in his snapped line and rattled off a string of curses that soured mayonnaise in the galley.

"There'll be another one! There's always two! Look, there he is!" he yelled at me, standing transfixed by the starboard gunnel, line dangling. Below in crystal water, a bluish brown shape appeared and disappeared, appeared and disappeared. Saltwater pros can see *every*thing that happens under the surface. Neophytes see figments.

"Hit the water with your pole!" I stared at him. "Hit it!" I slapped the rod tip gently against the water. The fellow clearly had lost his mind.

"Harder, you fool, harder!" I threshed wildly. Humor him and perhaps Jeff, the ex-Marine, can get a headclamp on him and we can lash the poor man to a bunk.

The rod tip arched sharply and the line sang for just an instant. The rod straightened.

"You lost him! You Dallas fool! You lost a ling! Best damn fish in the Gulf and you lost him!"

Rod tip bent again and again, the brief rasp.

"Wait! Steady, maybe he'll take it!" The captain peered over the side. "Get ready for the fight of your life!" There came the usual dry throat and wet hands, salty perspiration stinging the eyes, but nothing happened.

"He's gone," the captain announced in disgust. "Reel the damn thing in."

"*Some*thing's on here," I said timidly.

"Naw, if it was the ling, you'd be over the side. Reel it."

Reel, reel. The bluish brown body rode meekly to the surface; only a gentle waving of the tail denoted any life at all. Capt. Eddie stared at it, then at me, and was still staring as his son gaffed and lifted 20 pounds of ling routinely to the deck. The fearsome fighter of the Gulf had met its master and had realized it immediately. A fish after Roberto Duran's own liver. The captain said not another word as I flipped a cig to sardonic lips, scraped a match with my thumbnail, steely eyes squinting into the noon sun, and ordered him to make port.

STAR TREK

JUNE 4, 1984

Well, here it is exactly one week later and the telephone hasn't rung. Surely there has been a breakdown in communications.

It was Tuesday last that several of us, shall we say, *seasoned* pressboxers became Movie Stars or very near. From various pressboxes about the land we were summoned to Atlanta to star in a baseball movie called *The Slugger's Wife*.

Maybe *star* isn't the correct verb. Actually we were type-cast. We were assigned roles of sportswriters following the exploits of an Atlanta Brave slugger Darryl Palmer, played by a rather plain chap named Michael O'Keefe, as he was closing in on Roger Maris' home run record. As near as we could tell, this was the primary background of the drama, although it also dealt with rock-and-roll singers and occasional rolls in the old hay.

However, the writer Neil Simon must be aware of the strict moral code endorsed by The Froth Estate, so he did not include us in the romantic scenes. This came as a marked disappointment to some of our more daring members such as Furman Bisher, the distinguished Atlanta author and part-time *amoureaux* who has been known to carry a hand mirror in his pants pocket.

Anyways, even if we were withheld from the heavy breathing, we felt assured we would be accorded large important roles. It was the general hunch that we would be used in a big dramatic scene, like maybe a press interview after a record homer with hero Palmer or maybe the Atlanta manager Burly de Vito, played by a placid veteran named Martin Ritt who put his hands in his back uniform pockets just like real-life managers.

Surely we would have speaking roles. Mr. Bob Verdi, a rather foxy thespian from the *Chicago Tribune*, thought he should be the reporter at the press conference to stand and deliver our favorite question of such events:

"What was going through your mind when you were circling the bases?"

Privately I had written my own opening soliloquy: "What happened?" It's really not the number of words you have, but how you say them.

Both interior and exterior scenes were being filmed at the Braves Stadium and we were on the set by eight ayem, ready for makeup. Instead, we were shunted aside while a small army of technicians milled. As any of us movie folk can tell you, there is a large amount of milling done, at union scale. One chap kept peddling a bicycle by our group, yelling over his shoulder, "Check with Caleb!" For two hours this was the most interesting conversation we heard.

Finally some pleasant assistant broke the news. There would be no speaking lines. Instead, he stationed small groups of us by the dugout, and by the coaching box, and by the bat rack and on-deck circle and explained that this would be a scene in which hero Darryl Palmer gets beaned in batting practice. In batting practice?

Anyways, all clusters of pressboxers would be chatting with this ballplayer, or that, and when the star got beaned, we were to rush to the batting cage.

"Look aghast, please!" said a young fellow with a bullhorn. "Be perfectly natural and do not look into the camera or into the sun." This may sound easy to *you*.

Your budding thespian here was stationed with Mr. John Mooney, a 300-pound ham from the *Salt Lake City Tribune* and Mr. Hal Block of the AP and Mr. Jim Smith of *Newsday* at one corner of the dugout. A friendly lad in a Braves uniform was assigned as our interview target. He turned out to be one Andre Pattillo, who spend a couple seasons in the Atlanta farm system and is now employed as a counselor with the Educational Opportunity Center.

Bisher and Verdi managed a spot much nearer the camera, of course, but still were outmaneuvered by Phil Pepe and Murray Chass, who are from New York and experienced in pushing. Bob Roesler of New Orleans and Dick Fenlon of Columbus were assigned strolling roles, which promptly went to their heads.

Of course we had 413 walk-throughs and long waits in between during which Mooney practiced looking aghast until he had it down pat. He also shot a critical eye at the situation and estimated our group was 732 feet from the camera with Pepe and Chass edging in front and blotting out the lens.

Then there came the action! The batting practice pitcher faked a throw, Mr. Michael O'Keefe winced and fell poleaxed (on a couple air mattresses the prop man had placed in the cage). We all rushed to the batting cage. Verdi and Bisher practically sprinted, figuring early arrivals would be prominent on camera.

From the rear of the crowd, I remembered my soliloquy and offered it as an added attraction. After all, I could be spotted by some bigshot director and made into another Cary Grant or Lash LaRue.

"What happened?" I said, not unlike Charles Bronson.

"Stuck it in his *bleeping* ear!" growled Mike Downey, a coarse chap from the *Detroit Free Press*. Method actor.

Apparently the cameras and microphones did not capture this impromptu act because no one has called with any sort of career proposition. Dear Diary: What's to become of me?

JET SET

Hard by the sparkling blue of the Mediterranean with snowy yachts rolling in bay waters, the angry bugs climb the weathered cobblestone streets, whine down the gentle slopes into hairpin turns, pausing to cough protest over downshift of gears.

Along the roads and intersections, tanned young men with wavy black hair, shirts agape to the bellybutton, lift high the *vino* goatskin while their girls swirl skirts around long, gorgeous legs and show perfect teeth to the sun. During sudden silences between arguments from furious pistons, a concertina is heard. On the balcony, Papa Hemingway and Lady Ashley, he in white linen and a planter's straw, she in pink organdy fluttering in the sea breeze and a picture hat. They watch the race silently, occasionally raising champagne crystal to Frederico as he buzzes past La Rascasse restaurant and the Grand Casino of Monaco.

They also were joined in April, on a villa roof 8,000 feet high in South Africa, the clean gray towers of Johannesburg standing across the Rand, when Derek almost bought it, his Renault Turbo clawing the wall and miraculously flipping a somersault to land again on its fat tires. "A *valeur!*" Camille said, waving her sigaretta in its long golden holder. There was the aroma of strong *kaffee* in the mountain crispness and the tantalizing waft of javelina roasting over an open pit.

Again in Dijon-Prenois, land of mustard and wine, Valerie was impassive behind her giant sunshades when the right front blew and Jean-Paul rolled the Lotus. "*C'est destin,*" said Jacques, dropping his scarf over her brave shoulders. The smell of honeysuckle and thyme came to the terrace where they sat, overlooking workers sweeping metal from the dread *Courbe de Pouas* turn, oblivious of hurtling machines behind them. The waiter, Rene, brought more of the rosy red *zinfandel*.

In Austria, they could talk, the growl of the Brabhams absorbed by the Alps *magnifique,* and Niki suggested they meet in Dallas in July. Remember that amusing Texan last winter at Nice, Billy Joe Something, the one who kept drinking *chianti* out of his bloody winklepickers? It might be great fun. Dallas is between Palm Beach and Palm Springs.

So here we are in Dallas, all except Rolfo who is laid up in Vienna with *der gout.* The gala has certainly been varied. First there was the Grand Prix polo, and then the Grand Prix golf. This was quite festive, even though Billy Joe Something neglected to tell us that Dallas was situated on the equator.

The calendar also includes a Grand Prix art exhibit and a Grand Prix ballet, performed, to most everyone's great surprise, without boots. A Norwegian Viking band is being fetched to render Grand Prix tunes, and certainly fun-loving Olaf will get a bit of a boost from *that,* providing he can be persuaded to remove himself from his hotel bathtub filled with ice.

One of the local poets, a Mr. Ray Wiley Hubbard, has been engaged for Grand Prix recitation. Two artists named Star Mitchell and George West will offer Grand Prix tunes, if we can believe the program, on something called a dulcimer and fiddle. One doesn't recall seeing these chaps at Hockenheim or Silverstone, although they may have performed in one of the lesser tents.

Of course, there is a Grand Prix barbecue and they tell us, late on Sunday afternoon, there will be a Texas shootout using real bullets. The other night, Tyrone, after too much of the native drink *Coors,* threatened to send for his custom Wemberly and join in. You know Tyrone when he's bloody smashed.

The course itself, well, what does one say. It has a sort of native charm and certainly is in bully shape. It is mostly on the flats, as we say in Belgium at Zolder, and twists through an old fairgrounds, as it were. It is spiffy new, but it has some local traditions, they say.

The start-finish line is snugged against some sort of livestock barns, one is told, where such celebrities as Prince Domino are quartered during carnival. As Nigel and Keke and the rest pass under the first walkbridge, they can glance to their right and through a hedgerow, there is a broken view of the sturdy Missouri-Pacific tracks and one is sure, if *those* rails could talk, they could tell many a tale.

To the left is the historic old Cotton Bowl, a stone relic where folk groups sometime gather and sing peasant songs and smoke grass sacrifices. Even now, as the Alfa Romeos whiz by, colorful natives may be seen high on the structure lip, stripped to the waist, frying eggs on the concrete.

At the second turn, there is a hallowed spot where a heroic bovine named Elsie Borden was once stood during fairtime. And less than a kilo farther is a rock structure called a Music Hall, where such artists as Herbie Kaye and his lovely Dorothy Lamour once entertained the commoners. You remember her from Zanzibar. Had a thing going with Carlos, eh?

Later, as the driver whips into the backstretch, he can look over vast parking lots to his right, where once stood the picturesque ghetto. And over the perfume of gasoline fumes and scorched rubber, if the west wind is just right, one can catch the pungent whiff—just the whiff, mind you––of Fletcher's Corny Dogs, a prized delicacy of the area.

There are other frills, valiantly glamorous, but many have melted together like Carlotta's mascara. It's not Monte Carlo, darling, but what is?

WAR AT SEA

NOVEMBER 19, 1986

It has just struck home with a soggy thump that we are sitting up here on our big fat placid latitude, fretting about such trivia as college jocks being on the old tenderloin, when down below, they got a war going on.

Most of us, I sense, consider America's Cup a remote event, belonging to the Four Hundred and their assorted chefs and valets and sun-streaked blondes. What these chaps spend on one vessel, designing, building, equipping, testing, transporting, guarding, *competing* would buy a sizable South American government.

The Great Unwashed tends to see it as expansive fun in the sun, when Reggie and Phillip and Sir Gordon gather in a spasm of *savoir vivre*, go for a brisk sail during the day and loll the evenings in shoes with no socks, one hand draped languidly on a lanyard, the other clasping something tall and icy with cherries in it, exchanging chitchat with leggy *femmes fatales* wearing lowcut bodices and shades after dark

Admittedly, there was a surge of curiosity when first I learned this America's Cup would be staged near Perth on the southwest tip of Australia. Fremantle is the port and I have a vague recollection of docking there once on government business, and some of us stout lads boarding a primitive train for a brief trek to Perth.

We were armed to the teeth, of course, lest hostile natives try to boil us in shark oil or worse, and were a trifle disappointed to find that Perth looked rather like a small Chicago. We holstered our weapons, bought a sewing kit and a lemon squash at a native Woolworth's and beat it back to safety. Those were thrilling days.

At any rate, I managed to shelve America's Cup, adopting the theory proposed by a colleague, Bernie Lincicome of the *Chicago Tribune,* who recently reviewed the activities and announced that boats ought to do one of two things. Get us from here to there until a bridge can be built, or bring back the catch of the day. But then the fireworks started Down Under.

There were clues of mischief in the *last* America's Cup, something about the Aussies perfecting a secret keel on their craft, guarding its design against underwater spies with a trained patrol of great white sharks and things. Then they seized the Cup for the first time ever and made off to the reefs with shouts of coarse laughter.

Then last week, two Australian yachts named *South Australia* and *Steak 'n Kidney, rammed* each other, by gum, like the *African Queen* and *Old Ironsides* and them. Put a hole in one hull, ripped the other bow, knocked a crewman overboard and he had to be fished out and his sternum squoze. There were shouts of rage and clenched fists and protests lodged with governors.

This week, the *Kookaburra III* and *Australia IV* smacked each other on purpose and enraged charges and countercharges were thrust at arbitrators, over right-of-way and whatnot. Nights are no longer filled with the good life; they are rent with rants and oaths and a great outbreak of illwill. Yesterday, the *Kookaburra II* (now don't get these mixed up) and *Australia IV* engaged in "a fierce tacking duel on the windward leg" and something dire must have happened for both scudded across the line flying protest flags.

Mind you, all these boats are under the Australian flag, just to determine which shall represent that country. And this is only the second round of competition; they race dang near all winter, an endless series of round-robins. Or in light of current developments, until the armistice.

Heaven knows what to expect in the finals, when the U.S.A. champ takes on the home blokes. We have every reason to expect gunnels lined with cannon and crewmen clenching cutlasses in their teeth. I best dig out the trenchcoat and binoculars and get Qantas on the horn. Keelhaul the supercargo and batten the mizzenmast! This thing may need bozo coverage after all.

CUP RUNNETH OVER

FEBRUARY 6, 1987

At this particular time, I wish to take to the podium and agree with Mr. Robert Louis Stevenson when he wrote:

The world is so full of a number of things; I'm sure we should all be as happy as kings.

To begin, the world is mostly full of water and I, for one, am completely overjoyed about that. The demon researchers in our company's hallowed reference halls report that 71 percent of Earth's surface is covered by salt water, and if this is not cause for happiness, I hope to kiss a mule.

If there were more land mass, then there would be more humans thereon, speaking in strange tongues and holding out hands for foreign aid. Then we should have to erect more foreign embassies, to dole that foreign aid and to provide windows as targets for rock chunkers when the foreign aid does not contain the right flavored bon bons. No, our world is so full of brine that we should all be happy for its deliverance.

Likewise we should be happy that we Yanks have regained control of that water. I speak of the America's Cup, details of which, in the last fortnight, have beat us about the eyes and ears with more intensity and scope than the Rev. Jim Bakker or Col. Oliver North.

America's Cup is now all over but the shouting, of which there seems to be considerable, and the substitution of Mr. Dennis Conner's likeness on the U.S. dollar bill now that he has replaced Mr. George Washington as the daddy of our land.

The world is also full of good old Yankee grit and technology and good old filthy Yankee lucre that enabled us to build a sailboat to whip through the Indian Ocean at the speed of a dog sled, and let us be thankful for that.

I mean, there are some who would deem the yacht race as not that much of an international feather for our velvet berets.

After all, this wasn't an individual match, such as Greg Norman against our Jack Nicklaus on the links.

This was competition of money and scientific resources and computers and money and the brainpower of NASA and Grumman and AT&T and Budweiser. We're matching the richest nation on the globe, 260 million souls, master of the seas and skies and gravity and the moon, we're pitting all that against 17 million game chaps, living upside down and trying to scratch a living from a desert and a great variety of lizards.

Heck, we're *supposed* to win America's Cup. We won it 132 years, so what makes it so great that we had to win it *back* from poor Australia? That's like re-winning the Mississippi River from Napoleon.

At the Superbowl scene, a colleague confessed he was mesmerized by America's Cup on television. He stayed up til all hours watching. So I had to witness his enchantment.

I found out in an hour. If you've seen one hour of America's Cup, you've seen 100. Oh, I watched much more than that, thinking maybe one boat, out of sheer frustration, would ram the other or somebody would fall overboard. No such intrigue. Same ocean. Same sails. Same gradual pace. Same on-board cameras focused on same folks with white lips doing the same things, turning a crank, winding a line, staring at the horizon.

There were tv mikes also on board and occasionally a word would come through. There seemed to be plenty conversation, just barely beyond mike range. Once I heard someone say rather clearly, "Twenty-two, I think." Another time, I heard, "This is all right."

ESPN cameras never wearied of beer parties on the dock, no closer to the race itself than the canoe pages in your Sears catalog.

However, the world is so full of Yank ingenuity that made the *Stars & Stripes* so superior we got the blamed thing over mercifully in four straight races and certainly we all should be appropriately happy for that.

ON DUTY

JUNE 12, 1987

Seven days from now, Ensign David Robinson will report to a submarine base in Georgia, a fate that is creating great disturbance among those who would make the world safe for democracy and celebrated jocks.

Ensign Robinson will begin two years of naval service instead of running up and down a hardwood floor in his underwear for $5,400 per day American. Despite his address, Ensign Robinson will not do submarine duty. At 7–1 in altitude, he would have trouble getting through the hatch unless he folds up like a Barlow pocketknife. To you landlubbers, of course, hatch is Navy for door. Floor is deck, ceiling is overhead, john is head, candy is pogey bait and tattoos are mandatory.

It is that cursed height that arouses protesters. Fortunately, that handicap did not disturb Robinson's basketball participation at Annapolis. But now that taxpayers spent $140,000 educating the lad, the size is discovered to be a horrible affliction.

What a disgrace, cry the reformists, that this young man should be forced into military servitude when he could be of such great benefit to so many people, including NBA fans, his mama and daddy and banker. Why, he could serve his country much better as an image than an awkward ensign butting his forehead on submarine hatches.

Well, unless the Navy has slipped in efficiency, it probably can find enough chores to occupy Ensign Robinson outside of a submarine or a jet cockpit. The Navy has great antidotes for idle hands. I recall the ancient enlisted man's creed: *If it moves, salute it. If it doesn't move, paint it. If it's painted, chip it.*

Oh, there was plenty to do on the bounding main, alrighty, even for officers. After all, other than depleting the coffee supply in the wardroom and researching Harold Robbins paperbacks, someone of authority had to stand around in the shade and watch enlisted men chip paint.

I can refer you to another handicapped sailor. Roger Staubach was discovered, *after* he was enrolled at the Naval Academy, to be partially colorblind, strictly a no-no for our sea warriors.

Some hospital corpsman fouled Roger's eye tests but, what the heck, said the admirals, what's done is done. And as long as the young fellow is in the Academy, he might as well go ahead and play football.

In fact, NFL gossips once whispered the reason the Cowboys drafted Staubach while he was still in the Academy was that they thought they could get him out of the service *early* because of his colorblindness. But us patriots just can't believe Gil Brandt and his trenchcoats would be so devious for personal gain. Can we?

I think it fortunate for the Capt. America legend that the Cowboys could not manage his early discharge. Somehow, it just wouldn't fit.

Anyways, the Navy found a niche for Staubach whereby his colorblindness would not cause us to lose any warships. And he did four years, just like the kid down the block.

Last season, a rather pliable Navy Secretary named John Lehman allowed Ensign Napoleon McCallum to be stationed within driving distance of the Los Angeles Raiders, for whom he worked out daily and returned for kicks on weekends. A new Secretary, James Webb, cancelled all such concessions for jocks or anybody else. However, Ensign Robinson will be discharged after only two years, which is indeed a favor, even for a person of average height.

If you'll pardon a personal harkback, I remember a college roommate back yonder in the dark ages who was 6–8 in height, a giant in those days. His name was Willie Florence and he managed to sleep in a normal bed and keep his brow away from door sills and throw the discus a respectable distance.

Willie also, along with thousands of Texas youths, got himself mobilized by the National Guard when it became apparent there was going to be some unpleasantness in Europe. He found himself in the 36th Division Infantry, an assignment he did not relish. He wished to request a transfer to some less heroic duty, like maybe a filing clerk in some safe basement.

It was his height, he explained to the supply sergeant, that didn't agree with the infantry. At 6–8, he was not compatible with trench warfare.

"Why I can just hear them now," said Willie, "the very first day, some German will yell, 'Shoot that dummkopf off that barrel!' "

The sergeant laughed heartily and handed him an M-1.

BOMB SIGHT

AUGUST 7, 1985

Oddly enough, ferric oxide were the first words to come to mind. Ferric oxide. Iron rust. The barren Hiroshima countryside, its view filtered through plexiglas, seemed smothered in iron rust.

Frankly, I remembered the formula as *ferris* oxide, but then I had never been much of a chemistry student. I always had trouble remembering whether there were two parts hydrogen, or two parts oxygen in a chaser. But now, for some unexplicable reason, the words ferris oxide popped into my mind and nested there, to be dislodged Tuesday when stories marked the 40th anniversary of the first atomic bomb drop. The memory struggled back through cobwebs of long tenure. I can't remember where I parked the car today, but some of *those* impressions are indelible.

This was a matter of a few days after the bomb had leveled some place called Hiroshima. (At the time, we pronounced it HEE-roe-sheema, and we didn't know it from Copenhagen). I can't remember the exact day of our Hiroshima visit; my old Navy flight log is hazy about details and besides, we weren't supposed to be there in the first place.

We were on an aimless mission, some admiral's son, en route to Japan immediately after the surrender, never made it, and several carrier search patrols were dispatched to seek any sign of seaplane wreckage or a rubber dinghy on beaches of Ryukyu Islands, off the tail of Japan. There were two of us in the TBM torpedo bomber, the pilot and young buster here in the belly.

The pilot came on the intercom. "You wanta go over to the main island and see where that big bomb hit the other day?" he asked. "The area is off-limits but we might sneak a quick look." The pilot was a harum-scarum lieutenant from South Dakota, Bill Majerus, and he cared little for regulations even though he was executive officer of the torpedo squadron.

Why not? Really, the curiosity was not that acute. So somebody dropped a couple of science fiction eggs and the war suddenly was over. Bombs are bombs, some are bigger than others, so what. So let's get home and see if we can find some ham and redeye gravy and grits.

The turret gunner had remained aboard ship that day, so I crawled up in his bubble for a better view. Majerus swooped down to, oh, maybe 400 feet, so that any view was fleeting and scrambled. The dominant impression was of ferric oxide, not the deep color of iron rust, but a faded shade. Not a pastel hue, pleasant to the eye. This was a harsh color, harsh and pale at the same time. As far as you could see in that hasty moment, everything wore that same dead, depressing blanket.

Not that there was a lot to see. The scene sweeping past the turret was mostly flat desolation and there seemed amazingly little rubble. It hadn't been cleaned up yet; there had not been time. But perhaps most of the rock and wood, along with many of the inhabitants, had simply disintegrated or melted and left this pale red ash.

There would be an occasional wall standing, maybe one in an area of what would be five city blocks. No wrecked building, merely a bare stone wall, forlorn and useless. Unbelievably, there were trees! There was an occasional tree, or the skeleton thereof, stripped of any sign of foliage, a scarecrow of a tree, pale red like its background.

There seemed to be a strange odor, permeating even the turret of a rushing aircraft, a sort of musty smell, like of old houses, dark and shuttered against the outside, furniture squatting under sheets. But that could have been a young imagination, and probably was.

We were aware of no living creature or plant. Probably there were scattered work crews, or maybe the whole area was isolated because of the danger of fallout, if indeed we knew about fallout at that time. But we saw nothing but a vast, flat wasteland covered with this pale red dust. The pilot made only two quick runs and then got the hell out of there. There was perhaps 15 minutes of silence as the plane pointed back toward the task force somewhere over the horizon.

Majerus broke it. "Well, that was something, wasn't it?" his voice came into the earphones.

Indeed it was, but we did not know exactly what and somehow the curiosity was not overwhelming. Just days previously, at the time "Little Boy" was dropped on Hiroshima, our air group was staying at a bleak airstrip on Saipan. When a carrier makes port or anchors offshore, its planes fly off beforehand and set up at the nearest airstrip. This is so, in event of submarine or air attack, the motionless carrier is not caught with its planes on deck, unable to launch same.

For several days, we had watched these huge B-29s take off from Tinian, a sister island perhaps four miles west. We were awed by the size of these huge silver cigars, because ours was a world of short chunky carrier planes. The morning of August 7, we gunners were called to a Quonset hut for an unusual briefing by the air group intelligence officer, a young and rather nervous chap. He said he didn't know a lot, didn't have many details, but the previous day, a B-29 from neighboring Tinian had dropped something called an "atom bomb" on Japan, and the devastation was so vast that surely Japan would be surrendering within a matter of days.

"A whole city was leveled, the way we understand it," said the briefing officer. "Hundreds of thousands of people killed." Well, we knew something about bombs. The TBM bay would hold a 2,000-pound torpedo or a 2,000-pound bomb, and it could raise considerable ruckus. But an entire city with just one bomb?

The first question was how big was this rascal? "As I understand, it's about the size of a walnut," said the young officer. "It has something to do with atoms expanding, some sort of chain reaction."

We stared at him. (As we later learned, the first atom bombs were big as a small barn.) The walnut was beyond belief, except at that time so were many other subjects. So nobody worried much about it, nor talked much about it when the *U.S.S.* Santee recalled her planes and wallowed north toward the defeated land.

Somebody had done run in a Buck Rogers war on us, and if it got things over in a hurry, well, bully for them. And if you could look up the remnants of that group and ask about the walnut that turned Hiroshima into a pale red desert 40 years ago, I think you'd find they thought it came in mighty handy.

PARALLEL BARS

JULY 15, 1987

Just recently, Irate Reader took umbrage at certain deep, philosophical studies in this space, referring to Al Campanis and Jesse Jackson and such. Irate Reader issued the considerate invitation for your obt. svt. to keep his beak out of politics, leaving that field to more learned colleagues. Irate Reader suggested I stick to subjects within my assigned scope, such as the three-point field goal and the mindboggling formulas involved in working Tony Dorsett and Herschel Walker into the same backfield.

"I find your opinions on sports topics less offensive," Irate Reader wrote with kindly restraint.

Point well taken. Those of us wretches sentenced to pressbox servitude certainly should realize our limitations and be content to serve our threescore and 10 describing Fun & Games to an innocent populace. However, sometimes we forget and overstep our prescribed bounds and for this, we tug forelocks and beg understanding.

For example, during these Investigative Committee sessions now and forevermore on the toob, it is difficult for us lowly wretches to stay on the perimeter. Especially when we sense a relationship to our arena.

After all, even if we are clothed in sackcloth and helmet, we have certain inalienable rights. When Mr. Thomas Jefferson penned the Declaration, he did not write, "We the people, with the exception of those oafs in the pressbox . . ."

Try as we might, we can not help drawing mischievous parallels between this Iran-contra mess and the unholy tangle of SMU's football program.

Both had covert operations and middlemen and profiteers and liars and fall guys. Both had secret funds floating around, unidentified and unaccounted, and bag men and executives in high office. There is arrogance and immunities and accusations and stupidity and blame juggled like a ticking package.

You have heard Col. Oliver North, he of the earnest fore-head, described as a "loose cannon," and if the phrase struck a familiar note, it may have been because that was the term used by Gov. Bill Clements to describe fellow SMU plotter, Sher-wood Blount.

However, those comparisons are best left to more agile minds, and it is doubtless disrespectful to notice commonages.

But aha! Finally, the esteemed lawmakers have acknowl-edged us bourgeois. They have dealt with us. They have admit-ted, probably with great personal embarrassment, that The World of Perspiring Arts is not without its weight.

There is little doubt these hearings are tailored for television, just as most events in our own little pressbox world. Were it not for the cameras and the preening and self-service thereon, the thing would have been over days ago. This is not unlike sports events being altered for television.

Then Tuesday came the capper. When us peasants stood straight and tall. When cats looked at kings.

Situation: A dispute over whether a certain slideshow should be exhibited before the panel, a presentation Col. North used to lasso potential donors for the contra cause. Chairman In-ouye painstakingly explained that the slides could not be shown because the room would have to be darkened and that would violate the security bonds. Also, television lights would make it impossible to darken the room enough for slides to be seen. So he had made arrangements for the slides to be shown at 7:30 that evening.

Oh, gracious, no, shouted several of our august representa-tives, that would conflict with the Baseball All-Star Game tele-cast. And they were serious! And by gollies, after an hour's hassle, it was decided to bypass the showing of this evidence. Somewhere up there in the clouds, Mr. Abner Doubleday must have winked at Mr. Jefferson and giggled like a schoolboy. Let's have a little more respect, if you please.

Index